REGULAR MARVELS

a handbook for animateurs, practitioners
and development workers
in dance, mime, music and literature

François Matarasso

with contributions from
Sibyl Burgess, Mark Homer,
Richard Ings and Jac Wilkinson

LEARNING
RESOURCES
CENTRE

The Community Dance & Mime Foundation
1994

REGULAR MARVELS
First published 1994 by
The Community Dance & Mime Foundation
13-15 Belvoir Street, Leicester LE1 6SL
Company no. 2415458   Charity no. 328392

The publishers and authors make no representation, express or implied, with regard to the accuracy of the information contained in this book and cannot accept any legal responsibility for any errors or omissions that may occur.

This publication has been made possible by the generous financial assistance of the Arts Council and the Foundation for Sport and the Arts.

ISBN 1-898409-01-3
A catalogue record for this book is available from the British Library.

Written and edited by François Matarasso, with contributions from Sibyl Burgess, Mark Homer, Richard Ings and Jac Wilkinson, who assert their right to be identified as the authors of this work in accordance with the Copyright, Designs and Patents Act 1988. Based on an original idea by Penny Greenland and Anthony Peppiatt.

Design	David Everitt and François Matarasso
Illustrations	Julie Rose Bills (0604 863947)
Production	Eco Consulting, Melton Mowbray (0664 68316)
Printing	Enviroprint & Design, which aims to provide a print service which, through the careful choice of materials and processes, is as environmentally friendly as possible. (0642 363373)
Paper	Paperback, (Birmingham 021 643 7336; Sheffield 0742 664416; London 081 980 2233)

Printed on NAPM approved recycled 80gsm SylvanCoat (45B/45C)

REGULAR MARVELS

PREFACE

Community-based arts work is undoubtedly exciting, challenging and rewarding. It can also be extremely hard work requiring, as it does, a complex mix of skills and knowledge. When you are starting out you will want to know how to develop your work, where to start and how to decide which direction to go in.

Regular Marvels aims to answer all your questions, giving you confidence, support and ideas, as well as making your work more enjoyable. Although the book is aimed primarily at those who are new to the field, it provides plenty of back up and reference material for more experienced practitioners. Some parts of the book may appear at first glance to be addressed to people employed as animateurs or development workers, but in most cases they are equally applicable to free-lance practitioners.

Management committee members, employers and funders of community-based arts workers will also find much of interest, particularly in the chapters on setting up, management and planning. It is important to note, too, that practitioners throughout the UK and beyond will find much here to help them, even though *Regular Marvels* focuses largely on practice in England.

The scope of *Regular Marvels* is even wider than this. It brings together four artforms: dance, mime, music and litera-ture. Although each artform is different in its own right, the philosophy underpinning community-based arts work and the way in which it is undertaken is often the same. For this reason the Community Dance & Mime Foundation (CDMF) approached artform specialists, organisations and funders from all disciplines to explore the idea of a combined publica-tion. The idea was received with great enthusiasm, especially as it was recognised that a joint publication would further raise the profile of this growing area of arts activity.

The result is a comprehensive and unique publication which, we hope, will be welcomed and used by many people. To cover such a broad range of practitioners and to incorporate four artforms has been a difficult task. Whilst we have endeav-oured to be as thorough as possible, it is quite possible that something may have slipped through the net. If you notice any errors, or omissions, or you have any ideas for additions, please let CDMF know for any future edition.

I was delighted that François Matarasso took up the challenge of writing this book, and that he has been able to produce what we believe to be an accessible, lively and useful publication. Many practitioners will benefit from his wide range of experience in the field, and his skilled approach to developing the arts.

Thanks are also due to the organisations who invested in this publication and therefore made it possible. Generous funding was granted by the Foundation for Sport & the Arts, as well as the literature and music departments of the Arts Council. Past and present Arts Council officers have willingly offered their support to the book: Gary McKeone, Andrew Pinnock, Jo Shapcott, and Jeanette Siddall. *Regular Marvels* has also given CDMF the opportunity of collaborating for the first time with its sister organisations: Mime Action Group, the National Association for Literature Development and Sound Sense. These organisations have endorsed and supported the book and given generously in time and expertise.

Finally, a word to you, the practitioner. It is often difficult to step back from your work, recognise your many achievements and see the extraordinary impact it is having on the shape of art and society, shifting perceptions, shaping policy and enhancing the lives of so many individuals. I hope that *Regular Marvels* will support you in your work: use the book to illustrate the range of community-based arts work and to take pride in what you are doing.

Lucy Perman
Chief Officer, CDMF

INTRODUCTION

In 1986 Penny Greenland and Anthony Peppiatt produced *A Handbook for Dance and Mime Animateurs*, a pioneering work which quickly became indispensable to many people working in the field. It was at once a reference book, a source of advice and a sign of the growing strength of the animateur movement. The original handbook has long been unobtainable and, in any case, the environment in which animateurs operate has changed greatly in the past eight years. They now have a wide range of titles, roles and duties while the model itself has been taken up by other artforms including music and literature. Hence the need for a new publication which could support today's generation of animateurs, practitioners and development workers. The Community Dance & Mime Foundation, itself an organisation set up since the original handbook, took up the challenge, and this book is the result.

The scale of the task quickly became clear: anyone developing community-based arts projects is involved in such wide-ranging tasks that the information they might require is vast. A book trying to cover it all would be several inches thick, and finding what you wanted would be like searching for a leaf in a wood. Instead we have concentrated on dealing clearly with the main areas of concern to arts development workers, indicating where further details can be found if necessary. The book has been designed like a large-scale road map: it shows you where everything is and how to get there, but you may need a local street map to find your way through the back-streets. The references in the left- and right-hand margins, as well as others in the text itself, refer to sources of more detailed advice or information.

Some references point to other parts of the book (eg **5.9 Working in schools** refers to chapter 5, section 9), while others refer to books listed in chapter **14 ☛ Further reading.** Occasionally the margin notes simply draw attention to particular points or give brief examples.

Chapter 1 brings together some of the underlying issues - the theoretical principles which inform community-based arts work - and describes how the different artforms have developed their practice in this area. It concludes with a look at the changing social and political landscape in which animateurs operate. Chapter 2 looks first at the logistics of setting up a new post, before moving onto the concerns of anyone taking on a new arts development job. If you are new to the work, you will probably want to start here. The next two chapters look in detail at the management and administration of community-based arts work, addressing the needs of people working within organisations and those working on their own. They contain a lot of factual information and, whilst they are designed to be read through from start to finish, you may find yourself dipping in to look for answers to specific problems.

Chapter 5, Programming, is the heart of the book. It describes in detail the process of setting up and running community-based arts projects. Chapter 6 examines fundraising for those projects at some length. Chapter 7 deals with the training and personal development of practitioners and arts development workers. Chapter 8 summarises the basic principles of equal opportunities, though reference is made to these issues throughout the book in various contexts.

Chapter 9 introduces the four specialist organisations supporting workers in the fields of community dance, literature, mime and music. Chapters 10, 11, 12, 13, written by Richard Ings, Mark Homer, Jac Wilkinson and Sibyl Burgess respectively, focus on some recent work in the field with the aim of putting the preceding theory into a real-life context. They describe very wide-ranging examples of community-based projects with the aim of providing a snapshot of each area of work. The projects described have not been selected because they are inherently better than others - there isn't space to cover a fiftieth of the good projects run in recent years - but simply to illustrate the range and imagination of contemporary work in the field. Whatever your own artform, it will be worthwhile reading about all these projects since each contains ideas which could be explored further or differently.

Having explained what the book does, it is as well to explain what it does not do. Because it seemed necessary to build on good foundations, a lot of what follows may already be familiar. If so, we hope you will understand that it may be helpful to a less-experienced reader. Given the range of jobs in the field, there will certainly be sections that are not relevant to you, and again we ask your tolerance for this. It is also essential to understand that the book is not prescriptive. It presents ideas and approaches which have a track record, and which have been shown to work, but there are others, equally valid and equally workable. There is no single right approach because communities, artists and people are all different. Finally, and most importantly, the book is not infallible. It contains information, advice and ideas on which you can draw, but you need to test them against your own experience and, where appropriate, take further advice before making your own decisions.

No book of this sort can come to fruition without the help and support of many people. I owe a large debt to the many people with whom I have worked over the past fourteen years, not only artists and practitioners, but the participants in projects, administrators and others. More immediately, the project has benefited from the invaluable support and experience of Lucy Perman and her colleagues at the Community Dance & Mime Foundation. Many other people have generously given their time to discuss the project and particularly to read and advise on various parts of the text: Diane Bailey, Rod Bailey, Richard Blanco, Neil Blunt, Sibyl Burgess, Nikki Crane, David Everitt, Esther Davis, Kevin Ford, Rachel Grover, Julie Holdway, Mark Homer, Pat Hughes, Richard Ings, Emma Jackson, Linda Jasper, Charlotte Jones, Sharon Kivity, Terry McGinty, Gary McKeone, Ross Moore, Keyna Paul, Andrew Pinnock, Mhora Samuel, Bisakha Sarker, Jeanette Siddall, Mala Sikka, Biant Singh, Marion Stonier, Monica Stoppleman, Julie Tait, Dave Price, Debbie Read, Marcus Weisen and Jac Wilkinson. My thanks go to them all: the book is much the better for their contributions.

François Matarasso
January 1994

BACKGROUND

1.1 COHERENT AND WORKABLE

The nature of art ◆ The function of art in society ◆ Presenting the case

1.2 BASIC PRINCIPLES

Everyone should have equal access to the arts on their own terms ◆ Different identities and cultures deserve equal respect ◆ Working relationships should be equal ◆ The process and the product are equally valuable ◆ Every artform is flexible, multi-faceted and open to re-interpretation ◆ The constituency should be involved at all levels of the decision-making process which informs the work

1.3 PRINCIPLES INTO PRACTICE

Community dance ◆ Community literature ◆ Community mime ◆ Community music

1.4 A CHANGING AGENDA

Changes to the arts funding system ◆ Contracts, grants and service level agreements ◆ Local government reorganisation ◆ Changes to education ◆ Changes within the charitable sector ◆ Changes in the National Health Service and Social Services

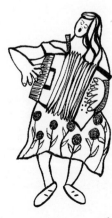

1 BACKGROUND

Summary

This chapter brings together a range of background material. The first section seeks to outline a coherent and workable theoretical underpinning for community-based arts work, which the second section translates into a number of basic principles. Section 3 gives a brief account of the development of community arts in general and of community dance, literature, mime and music in particular. The chapter concludes with a review of some of the changes which have affected the environment in which practitioners and arts development workers operate.

1.1 COHERENT AND WORKABLE

Everyone has the right freely to participate in the cultural life of the community, to enjoy the arts and to share in scientific advancement and its benefits.

Article 27, The Universal Declaration of Human Rights

Although, given the infinite range of human personality and culture, it would be impossible to get general agreement on a definition of art, arts development workers must be able to explain the nature and purpose of their work. This is essential for two reasons: if you don't know clearly what you are doing and why, you can't know whether you are achieving your aim or wasting your time. Secondly, if you can't explain your work and your reasoning to someone else you will find it hard to persuade funders and others to support your work. Because these questions are so important, this section seeks to outline a coherent and and workable vision of art and its role in society. It is certainly not the only way of defining art or of analysing its social function.

The nature of art

Art may be defined as a means through which we can examine our experience of ourselves, the world around us and the relationship between the two, and share the results with other people in a form which gives free rein to our intellectual, physical, emotional and spiritual qualities. This definition characterises art by *purpose* rather than *type*, the distinguishing system favoured by the arts establishment. It makes no distinction between painting and ceramics, fiction and non-fiction, baroque and reggae or any of the other categories commonly used to define what is art - and worthy of public funding - and what isn't. Instead it places art's function of communication at the heart of its nature, so that any human activity which seeks to express individual or collective experience creatively may be termed art.

This does not imply the abandonment of critical judgement. There is, and will always be, good and bad art. Bad art is the result of an artist abandoning faith to a true articulation of their perceived experience. Reasons may vary - a desire to please, to express only what is expected or accepted, to imitate other work and many others. But even good art can have different value because different artists' intentions and skills vary enormously. A poem about living in hospital produced by someone with mental health problems is, in its nature, the same as T.S. Eliot's *The Waste Land*, but in scale, range and ambition there is no comparison. They are both works of art but with different intentions and produced by artists with different gifts.

The function of art in society
Art is an ever-changing mixture of the intellectual and the emotional, the physical and the spiritual, and it makes a virtue of subjectivity. It offers a unique means by which we can explore ourselves and our position in the wider world, and a way to exchange with other people about what we see and feel and think and sense. Art is a way of opening dialogue within and between individuals and communities. That dialogue may be obviously intellectual, using words, or it may be the invisible dialogue of the musician and audience, or the physical dialogue between dancers, or a shifting mixture of all those and more. The key point is that it is dialogue.

If this analysis of the nature and function of art can be accepted, then the extract from the Universal Declaration of Human Rights which opens this section begins to make sense in the context. Art is a system through which a society analyses, debates and develops its experiences and aspirations, so access to it is critical. Any individual or group in society which is denied access to that debate is marginalised, their experiences denied and their voice unheard. And then, whether by lack of care or by deliberate policy, they can be disadvantaged and oppressed.

In Britain today, access to the range of the arts and to the debate which they enable is very uneven. On the one hand there are numerous economic, social, physical and cultural barriers to the established arts; and on the other the cultures and artistic activity which people support in their own communities are relegated to the margins or unrecognised by the arts establishment. That establishment represents a social minority which manages the funding system and much of the subsidised arts world according to an exclusive and arcane set of value judgements, which largely prevent the majority from being actively, rather than simply passively, involved in the recognised arts. Whether or not this supports, or is a by-product of, the effective exclusion from power of most people is a moot point, but exclusion from the dominant culture and exclusion from power go hand in hand.

The situation of disabled people is a case in point. Disabled people have, until recently, been largely excluded from active participation both in the arts and in society as a whole. It could be argued that their artistic exclusion is a cornerstone of their social exclusion because it makes it so difficult for people to share their experiences with other disabled people or with the rest of society, which remains largely ignorant of their needs, interests and gifts. As long as disabled people - individually or in groups - are unable to use the arts to examine and question their experiences, to dream up new and different ways of living and relating to others and to share their visions and creativity with non-disabled people, their unequal treatment by society can continue.

However, the recent growth of the disability arts movement provides a forceful demonstration of how getting access to the means of cultural expression naturally provokes political and social change. Through various routes significant numbers of disabled people have become active in the arts and created platforms for their work - Graeae, CandoCo, New Breed and Second Stage, Disability Arts Magazine, Tragic But Brave, and many more. They have established support structures like the National Disability Arts Forum, and begun to debate the nature of a disability culture. They have also forged links with disabled people working in the political and social arenas. And they have begun to make an impact. Not only is the arts establishment starting to address the needs and interests of disabled people, and the broadcast media changing their approach to disability, but the attitudes and ideas of thousands of non-disabled people are evolving as they begin to meet disabled people through the arts. It is the beginning of a process whose fundamental importance to the development of an equitable society is evident.

What is true in relation to disabled people is true of other groups, of distinct cultural communities and of individual people. Women, older people, ethnic communities, homeless people, single parents, people with HIV and aids - the list of

John Carey's analysis of literary attitudes to the 'masses' in the period between 1880 and 1939 provides a startling insight into some of the intellectual prejudices which have marked the development of British culture in the 20th century. Although concerned principally with figures like D. H. Lawrence, H. G. Wells, Wyndham Lewis and Arnold Bennett, the underlying arguments are relevant to anyone working in the arts today. **14.1** ☛ *The Intellectuals and the Masses*

14.7 ☛ *Equal Rights for Disabled People* and *The Creatures That Time Forgot.*

people who should have better access to our common culture is long. Active participation in the arts and culture is the cornerstone of our development as individuals and members of society. That is why art matters. That is why it has a revolutionary agenda. And that is why working to help every single person to gain the skills and confidence to articulate their unique vision on their own terms in the great cultural dialogue is so important.

Presenting the case

You may or may not agree with the analysis presented above, or subscribe to all the conclusions drawn. But whatever your own views and beliefs, if you are working to support and develop community-based arts projects, you will share with others in the field an appreciation of the value of creativity. However, you can't assume that other people, and particularly those who fund or manage your work, necessarily understand or share your views.

Arts practitioners sometimes complain that to set the closure of a day nursery against that of an arts centre is unfair. But it is not only fair - with insufficient resources to meet our combined social needs and desires, priorities must be made - it is also the reality of decision-making for most local authority councillors. You might argue against a decision to cut spending on music in schools in order to keep the cost of school meals low, but you cannot question the fact that choices have to be made. Since local authorities have only discretionary powers to support the arts, these budgets will always be targeted by councillors hoping to avoid cutting services which they see as more essential. You have to be able to present cogent arguments - in their terms - as to why community-based arts work has a legitimate call on scarce public resources. The following reasons are drawn from the analysis of the nature and social function of art set out above. Depending on your own views you may add to these arguments or find others; they are not meant to be complete and not all are persuasive in every situation.

'Expenditure on discretionary services is under scrutiny. Those services which have explicit objectives and can demonstrate what they are achieving will be better placed to justify themselves' **14.1** ☞ *Local Authorities, Entertainment and the Arts*, The Audit Commission

A significant list of possible aims for local authority arts funding is included in **14.1** ☞ *Local Authorities, Entertainment and the Arts*

Public funds should be spent on community-based arts activities because:

- The Universal Declaration of Human Rights, to which Britain is a signatory, defines participation in the cultural life of the community as a basic human right.

- Control of their own cultural identities strengthens the ability of individuals and groups to participate equitably in the local community and the democratic process.

- Millions of people do not have access to the existing provision for economic, physical, social or cultural reasons.

- Spending on the arts is determined by criteria which unfairly disadvantage certain artforms, ways of working and cultures.

- Terms of access to the arts should not be determined by any single sector of society to the disadvantage of any other.

- Investing in the cultural vitality of local communities improves the quality of life of those who live there.

- They are the constantly-renewed base of the arts in general, and so contribute to an important and successful sector of the economy.

- Broadening the range of people involved in the arts challenges existing aesthetic values and enriches the arts and culture generally.

- The huge response to community-based arts activities proves that people want them.

- The work which results is fun, exciting, unpredictable, infectious, positive, awkward, imaginative, challenging and human.

1.2 BASIC PRINCIPLES

The ideas touched on in the last section translate into some basic principles which to some extent inform the practice of most people engaged in community-based arts work:

Everyone should have equal access to the arts on their own terms

The point about promoting community-based arts work is - for whatever motive - to make access to the arts more equal in every sense. Since not all sections of the community are disadvantaged in these terms, most animateurs and practitioners prioritise those whose access is restricted. The centrality of this aim places equal opportunities principles at the foundation of good community-based arts work. Good equal opportunities

60% of people from households with an annual income of over £25,000 attend the theatre; the figure for households with an annual income of under £5,000 is 22%.

14.1 ☞ *Local Authorities, Entertainment and the Arts*

7

practice in the main areas of your work - programming, man-agement, marketing and employment - is less difficult than it might at first appear, because it is the same as doing the job well. Consequently, although there is a section which looks at equal opportunities principles and training in more detail, the issues are discussed throughout the book in relation to particu-lar areas of work. Thinking about equal opportunities is not a matter of drafting a policy while you get on with the work: it's why you do the work and the thinking must permeate it like salt in sea water.

Different identities and cultures deserve equal respect

Britain is a complex, multi-cultural society whose citizens have many different, and sometimes overlapping, concepts of iden-tity, commonly expressed through culture. Identity can be both a source of pride and confidence, and of mistrust and conflict. Whatever your own background or culture, you must meet the identities and cultures of the people with whom you work with equal respect. Identity is a personal statement, so avoid making assumptions: you might think of an individual as dis-abled or unemployed only to find that they don't think of themselves in those terms at all. Finally, if you offer respect for other cultures and identities, you are entitled to expect it for yours in return.

Working relationships should be equal

Everyone involved in a community-based arts project has dif-ferent things to offer, and their contribution and involvement should be valued equally. No community is a creativity-free zone: there is at least as much artistic activity and ability already going on as you can bring in. The artist, animateur or performance company is not there to donate something to pas-sive recipients. Instead the process must reflect a group of peo-ple working co-operatively, sharing their various skills, per-ceptions and experiences. Central to that is the principle that control must be shared between all the participants. This doesn't imply that as an artist you reduce yourself to a blank: you have skills, experience and imagination which you are placing in the joint control of those involved in the project, yourself included. They are there to learn from you, as you from them.

The process and the product are equally valuable

The process - ie how the work is done, what happens in the workshops - is seen by many practitioners and development workers as being paramount. This view is advanced against the conventional idea that the product of creative work - the book, the performance, the piece of music - is essential, and how you get there doesn't matter very much. A third, more holistic approach places equal value on process and product, indeed blurs the distinction between them, as some of the best community-based arts work blurs the distinction between performer and audience. In this analysis creating a product is seen as an essential part of the process because that is fundamentally what art is about. No dancer trains for the sake of the technique, no musician learns only scales: people learn skills and develop their creativity in order to express themselves in some outward form, and to remove that part of the process is to distort it completely.

What needs rethinking is the concept of product. Of course, it may be a finished poem, the performance of a new piece of music, or a show in the local town hall, but it can mean much subtler things. A single gesture, a hand shape, a verbal image, a chord sequence, a rhythm held, a facial expression - there is no end to the things that can constitute real, tangible artistic product. Because these things are often small, they may pass unnoticed by the casual observer of a workshop. Because they can be hard to explain to someone outside the group, or someone with little or no experience of the work, there is a temptation to stress the process. But the product - the thing that each of us is trying to work towards - is what gives purpose to the learning process and its importance must not be underestimated.

**Every artform is flexible, multi-faceted and
open to re-interpretation**
No-one who is protective of, or dogmatic about, their artform will be happy or effective in community situations. The process of opening your work to people who haven't had access to it before, will quite properly result in it being challenged and changed. People with different social or cultural backgrounds, people with different physical attributes, people with different beliefs will produce different art work. A classical dance culture is the product of a time, a place and a society: it is a rich tradition which many people will delight in learning about. But it is not an absolute. Although people's responses to it will not necessarily be those of a dance worker, they are not less valid and their different expression through the tradition will add to its richness. The job of a good arts worker working in the community is to give access to their artform, with no strings attached. Only if people take it, work on it and mould it to their own experiences and needs will you know that you have succeeded. The excitement for you lies in

discovering the previously unimagined possibilities inherent within your artform.

The constituency should be involved at all levels of the decision-making process which informs the work

3.3 Democratic or accountable? If your commitment to promoting equal access to the arts and to creating equal working relationships is real, it must extend into the decision-making process that governs your work. Unless people have an input into that process they remain dependent consumers of what you offer, however sensitive your programming. You can involve the people you work with by building democratic structures or by working towards accountability, or sometimes both. Although the first route is probably the more common approach in community arts, it has weaknesses and may in any case be closed to sole or free-lance workers, or those working within large organisations like local authorities. Making your work accountable through formal consultation and reporting procedures is a realistic alternative.

1.3   PRINCIPLES INTO PRACTICE

The contemporary community arts world has its immediate roots in a number of initiatives developed by artists in the late '60s and early '70s. They had the common aim of taking art out of galleries, theatres and colleges and making it relevant to people whose relationship with the arts, if it existed at all, was that of the consumer. Many had a visual arts training, though they often learnt to apply their skills to a wide range of work, but a simultaneous impulse in theatre saw the development of small-scale touring companies, producing work in new venues like pubs and community centres. The rationale behind the movement varied widely: some people would have agreed with the ideas described above, but the agendas of others were more immediately political, or more directly concerned with aesthetics.

The work had a significant impact on the arts establishment, securing funding first through the Arts Council and then, after devolution of community arts, through the Regional Arts Associations (RAAs). By 1980 there were locally-based community arts projects and theatre companies throughout Britain. The 1980s saw the community arts sector, in the face of **6.2 Funding From the** considerable pressures, maintain and develop its position, with **Public Sector -** new projects being established and a growing professionalism, **Regional Arts Boards.** earned, some might argue, at the price of radicalism.

But, even in the late '70s, it was apparent that community arts was stronger in some art forms and some regions than others. Perhaps because of the motivation or background of the first arts workers, there had been an emphasis on forms which were obviously able to carry a clear message. Part of the original intention was to help people acquire the skills to be articulate in an age of sophisticated communication, and that extended from community printshops into all areas of print and publishing, the use of computers, sound recording and video. The other dominant media in the early years of community arts - theatre, photography, writing and multi-media events among them - were equally capable of carrying a message.

Those art forms which were perceived, rightly or wrongly, as being more abstract than narrative, had been less comprehensively addressed. Perhaps the first people to appreciate that community arts wasn't doing all it could in their field were dance practitioners. Between 1976 and 1986 dance practitioners not only established the validity of their work in a community context, but in exploring the role and function of the animateur, created a new model for the development of community-based arts work. By then the economic climate did not favour the establishment of large, building-based projects: often the best that could be won was the creation of a single post. Dance practitioners made a virtue of necessity, creating a way of working which was flexible, sensitive to different communities and, by developing partnerships, maximised resources. The animateur model, as defined by its pioneering practitioners, won respect on all sides and showed how a relatively small investment could provide a valuable link between artists and arts organisations, local authorities and the general public. And where there were no arts organisations - as in many rural areas - animateurs became a sort of human arts infrastructure, reaching places and people that others could not.

Community dance

The first three dance animateur posts were created in 1976 in Cardiff, Swindon and Cheshire. At the same time, new companies with a community focus were being formed and existing dance companies were beginning to explore new models for residencies and education projects. In some areas individual dancers took the initiative as freelance practitioners, running classes and workshops and gradually gaining the interest and support of funders. In 1985 the Arts Council devolved funding of dance animateur posts to the Regional Arts Associations, and a year later the National Association of Dance and Mime

9.1 Community Dance & Mime Foundation
10 Community dance projects
14.8 ☛ *Community Dance - A Progress Report;*
14.12 ☛ *Animated*

Animateurs (NADMA) was formed. By then there were about 35 animateurs, spread fairly evenly across the country. 1986 saw the first national evaluation of the dance and mime animateur movement by the Arts Council, and the publication of the first handbook for animateurs by NADMA.

Since then the movement has grown substantially in strength, range and numbers. The progress report published by the Arts Council in 1993 identified a total of 262 community dance workers and practitioners, though it used a looser definition of the role than in the past. The creation of National Dance Agencies - often as a direct result of the ground-breaking work of dance animateurs - had also made significant inroads into the development of an embryonic infrastructure for dance, despite continuing problems with spaces. In their turn, national and regional performance companies have developed and extended their education and community programmes. NADMA was succeeded in 1989 by the Community Dance & Mime Foundation (CDMF), whose mission is to support practitioners and represent the area of work at regional and national level. *Animated*, the quarterly magazine published by CDMF, is an important tool in achieving both of these aims. Supported by Arts Council funding CDMF has ambitious plans to develop its work and services over the next few years. From April 1994, CDMF will have relinquished its responsibility for community mime to Mime Action Group, following increased separation of the two artforms. CDMF will therefore be adopting a new name to reflect its changed role.

Over the past fifteen years community dance has come a very long way, and has clearly established itself and its value. Its diversity is reflected in the many individuals and companies that are now part of this growing movement. It includes freelance and employed practitioners, education units of dance companies, programmes run by the NDAs and work promoted through local authorities and other partners at a local and national level. But, while the movement as a whole is strong, individual posts often remain vulnerable to the winds of economic change. There is a recognition that everything must be done both to consolidate existing posts and to work towards greater consistency in terms and conditions of employment. There is also work to be done in clarifying the aesthetics and definitions of community dance and in developing its public profile and identity.

Community literature

The first literature development worker was appointed in 1986, ten years after the first dance animateur, and the movement is

---

By late 1993 there were seven National Dance Agencies in England
10.1 From Animateur to National Dance Agency

6,000,000 people in Britain dance regularly. 30,000 people earn their living from dance, of whom 1,000 are full-time performers. There are 1,200 folk dance clubs in Britain. The Arts Council's dance budget in 1992/93 was £20,359,000, of which half went to the Royal Opera House.

9.3 National Association for Literature Development
11 Community literature projects
14.9 ☞ *Report on the Literature Development Worker Movement in England*

consequently at an earlier stage in its development. Its origins lie in the work of community arts projects and the various writer-in-residence schemes promoted by arts organisations, local authorities and others. Development was initially slow but the movement received an important boost as a result of the Ings report and by 1993 there were about 30 different posts, though most were part-time and limited to fixed terms. As with other artforms, they range widely in their aims, geographical brief, management structures and size, though they all exist to promote access to literature through reading, writing and oracy. The commonest model is perhaps the literature worker serving a county or city, but there are also notable projects serving particular ethnic communities. Local authorities (and specifically library services) often act as sponsors and hosts, while some posts are based in arts centres, community arts projects and other organisations.

Literature development workers have made consistent efforts to meet together and support each other, though they have been hampered in this by the demands of their work and limited budgets. The movement was evaluated by the Arts Council in 1992 and the evidence presented in the subsequent report helped strengthen the Council's commitment to the area of work. This involved a commitment to part-funding of at least one post in each Regional Arts Board area, and supporting established posts at risk where possible. In addition, early in 1994, the first steps were taken towards the establishment of the National Association for Literature Development with the recruitment of a part-time co-ordinator. Attention has also been given to the development of practice and training for literature development workers.

Community mime

Community mime, in the early years, was closely linked to the community dance movement partly, perhaps, because mime was dealt with by the Arts Council through the dance department set up in 1979. Three years later the first mime artist-in-residence was appointed at the Brewery Arts Centre in Kendal: the post was the only one of its kind for several years. The formation in 1984 of Mime Action Group (MAG) marked the first step in the creation of an infrastructure to support mime and physical theatre, and it coincided with a marked growth in the number of companies and practitioners and of public interest in their work. In 1987 this was recognised by the Cork Report of the Enquiry into Professional Theatre in England which noted that mime was 'one of the fastest growing and most popular forms of small scale touring theatre of the last decade.'

Two-thirds of adults in Britain read at least one book each month. There are 20,000 libraries in Britain, issuing an average of ten books a year for every person in the country. Twice as many books (70,000) are published annually in Britain as in the USA. The Poetry Society National Poetry Competition received 14,000 entries in 1990, and has on at least one occasion received over 30,000. BBC radio receives up to 13,000 play scripts each year. The Federation of Worker Writers and Community Publishers has over 50 member groups. There are about 400 small presses in Britain. The Arts Council's literature budget in 1992/93 was £1,472,000.

The Arts Council's drama budget in 1992/93 was £39,706,000. Franchise funding to mime companies was £590,000; other mime companies received project funding, and companies whose work include mime and visual theatre elements were also funded.

An important recommendation of the report - reinforced three years later in Naseem Khan's *Mime Training Report* - was that funding of mime and physical theatre should be transferred from the dance to the drama department of the Arts Council. This change, which was effected in 1991, marked a gradual separation of dance and mime over the 1980s, as the latter strove to gain recognition and funding for its unique area of work.

12.1 A college residency by a performance company

The growth of community mime has been slower than the comparable development of community dance for a variety of reasons. In 1992 the progress report into community dance identified twelve animateurs, though this included more companies than individuals. Compared to dance, music or literature, there have been few dedicated mime development workers (though some dance animateur posts have included mime), with much work being undertaken by freelance mime practitioners. Performance companies have played an important role in extending and developing their work through residencies and workshops. Mime Action Group is a focal point for this activity, though its concerns are with mime and physical theatre in general, of which community-based work forms only a part. In 1992 a research project supported by the Arts Council, and using the case study undertaken in the South East Arts area, produced the *Blueprint for Regional Mime Development*, to date the most comprehensive source material addressing the establishment of community mime projects and infrastructure. The following year Blitz Mime brought community mime to the South Bank for a day as part of the Ballroom Blitz dance event. In April 1994 CDMF relinquished its responsibility for community mime which was taken up by Mime Action Group.

MAG has been very successful in raising awareness of the artform among both funding bodies and the wider public. It has been active in promoting conferences and training opportunities in the field, and publishes a training directory as well as the quarterly magazine, *Total Theatre*, which is now an established and vibrant platform and information source for mime and physical theatre. Regional mime, physical theatre and circus fora have begun to be established (eg West Midlands, Scotland) to support further development and strengthen regional identity and activity. Through the work of Mime Action Group and these regional organisations, the future of the artform seems to be assured.

9.4 Sound Sense
13 Community music projects
14.12 ☞ Sounding Board

Community music

The roots of community music are extraordinarily wide: music collectives, composers-in-residence, orchestral outreach, punk energy, community arts, school teaching, brass bands, folk clubs - all these and more have made their contribution over the years. Although much community music activity had been undertaken before then, the creation of the Arts Council's music education working party in 1984 proved to be something of a turning point, partly because it produced a commitment to the development of animateur posts to support community music. Some of these, generally termed education officer rather than animateur, were attached to orchestras and opera companies and forged strong links with local schools and colleges. The Performing Rights Society Composer in Education scheme was also influential in pushing forward the boundaries of community music within a broad educational framework. But the greater number of posts, with the usual wide range of aims and structures, were based in arts organisations, local authorities and other community situations, though there was not always the experience or resources to provide adequate support. Their work embraced jazz, rock, electronic music, folk, non-western traditions and much else, but their development, away from the relative stability of the orchestral world, has been more uneven, with some posts not being sustained. Nevertheless, both short and long-term community music residencies often left important legacies of work and a demand for further projects which was picked up in some cases by developmental music organisations and local initiatives.

In 1989 the first National Community Music Conference held in Manchester, led directly to the establishment of Sound Sense to represent and support community musicians and raise the profile of their work. Sound Sense as the national community music association has organised two further national conferences, promoted training events and publishes a quarterly magazine, *Sounding Board*. The future of community music seems to be assured, though funding continues to be a source of concern. There is also a continuing debate about definitions of the work, and what constitutes good practice, usually a sign of good health.

Nearly 300 organisations and individuals active in community music were included in the First National Directory of Community Music in 1993. 345,000 candidates took Associated Board music exams in 1989. Choirs affiliated to the National Federation of Music Societies gave 3,460 performances to 847,600 people. The Arts Council's music budget in 1992/93 was £36,027,000, of which over half went to the Royal Opera House and English National Opera.

1.4   A CHANGING AGENDA

The growth of community dance, literature, mime and music has taken place against a background of almost unprecedented change in Britain, affecting our values, our social structures and much else. The public sector, so closely tied to central government, has been at the forefront of this change. From the preservation of ancient monuments to truancy rates in primary schools, there is scarcely a corner of contemporary life which has not received the attention of Parliament since 1979. This has meant that anyone working in or with the public sector has had to make an almost continuous series of adjustments to their thinking and practice in recent years and there is no reason to expect a rapid alteration in that situation. A state of change appears to have become the norm in education, social services, the NHS, local authorities and the arts. Any arts practitioner, animateur or community-based arts worker will find their task affected by these changes.

This section gives some account of the most important changes which may affect animateurs and practitioners in coming months and years, and as such is likely to be out-of-date fairly quickly.

You can keep up-to-date with changes by reading a broadsheet newspaper, and the various magazines and newsletters produced by the arts and voluntary sector.

Changes to the arts funding system

The present round of changes to the arts funding system originate in 1989 when Richard Wilding was appointed to report on the structure of the arts funding system by the then arts minister, Richard Luce. It is unnecessary to recount the story of the *Wilding Report* and the changes made by a rapid succession of ministers. Suffice to say that the process led to the creation of ten Regional Arts Boards (RABs) to replace the twelve former RAAs, the granting of autonomy to the Arts Councils of Scotland, Wales and Northern Ireland, and the translation of the old ACGB into the Arts Council of England as from April 1994. The creation in April 1992 of the Department of National Heritage (DNH) to replace the Office of Arts and Libraries (OAL) may have more far-reaching consequences. Alongside these structural changes, there has been a period of financial restraint, including the first-ever cut in the arts budget (£3.2 million in 1994/95). The effect of these developments on artists and practitioners working in communities up and down the country remains to be seen.

6.2 Funding from the public sector

Contracts, grants and service level agreements

Most organisations funded by local authorities or RABs will have experienced changes in their funding relationships. The nature and extent of those changes will have varied, but the overall theme is consistent: a move away from the practice of giving grants to support voluntary organisations (whether arts-based or not) towards a relationship which is more contractual. The principle is that the funder and the recipient of funding should state their rights and obligations in the form of a legally-binding contract. This process often leads to a worth-

14.1 ☛ NCVO publishes a number of books on contracting for voluntary orgaisations including an introduction in the form of Guidance Notes 1 The Legal Context, 2 The Contract Culture and 3 The Impact on Management and Organisation and Getting Ready for Contracts

while review of both parties' aims and, for the arts organisation, a formalised planning process which, used imaginatively, supports its management and practice. Local authority and RAB officers are mostly understanding and agreements seem generally to be being reached without too much difficulty. And if, as is intended, the resulting relationship becomes more consistent and supportive, arts organisations can only benefit.

However there remain potential problems, mostly around the perceived inequality between the contracting partners. On one side is the funder with money and extensive experience of negotiating contracts, and on the other is the local arts organisation with no more than the quality of its work to bargain with. It is also uncertain to what extent contracts and service level agreements entered into by local authorities are enforceable, given the legal restraints on their own spending, their potential imminent demise and the difficulties which would be experienced by any small voluntary organisation trying to take legal action for breach of contract.

Local government reorganisation

The review of local government is looking at different parts of the country and receiving submissions from interested parties on possible changes to the existing structure. In principle the best solution should be found for each area, so that in some places the structure will remain unchanged, whilst in others one tier or another will be abolished. From evidence to date it would appear that unitary authorities will generally replace the existing two-tier structure, though, if newspaper reports are to be believed, no county councils will survive. These changes obviously have far-reaching implications for animateurs and development workers employed or funded by local authorities, especially where their remit is county-wide. However, since all local authorities are keen to demonstrate the quality of their services, it is possible to make a good case for the arts within that overall programme. Arts workers of all sorts will need good local authority contacts at both officer and elected member level, and should keep informed of the debate and perhaps make a submission when the local government commission is reviewing their area.

Changes to education

The Education Reform Act 1988 introduced far-reaching changes to the education system in this country, and further changes continue to be introduced. Under the Act all schools with more than 200 pupils became responsible for managing their own budgets, with the 126 local education authorities

Compulsory Competitive Tendering - the process whereby local authorities are obliged to put some in-house services out to tender - has also begun to have some impact on local authority-managed concert halls and theatres.

5.9 Working in schools

17

(LEAs) in England and Wales retaining less than 7% of the general schools budget for specific areas of work. Since 1992 some schools have continued to opt out of local authority control, becoming directly accountable to the Department for Education as Grant Maintained Schools - the number currently stands at about 1,000 out of a total of nearly 23,000 state schools in England. The role of advisers, many of whom had been the first point of contact for artists working in schools, has also changed, so that in some areas they are now principally concerned with monitoring the national curriculum, although elsewhere they continue to have an important advisory role.

The effect of these changes is that education work by artists and arts development agencies is increasingly the result of direct contact with the school rather than the LEA. The national curriculum introduced by the Education Reform Act has changed the way in which artists work in school insofar as there is a demand that arts input should directly support curriculum work. The national curriculum provides for the teaching of art, music and design as foundation subjects for children aged between five and sixteen, with drama, mime, creative writing and media studies incorporated in the English curriculum, and dance in the physical education curriculum. The delivery of some arts elements of the curriculum can be undertaken by artists. The national curriculum itself is currently under review, whilst the publication of exam results and truancy tables in 1992 and 1993 represent further changes in this area.

Changes within the charitable sector

3.2 Legal structures for organisations

The Charities Acts of 1992 and 1993 represented the biggest shake-up of the legal environment within which charities and charitable organisations operate for a generation. Parts of the acts are still to come into force, but their main effect is to strengthen the powers and duties of the Charity Commissioners and formalise the management and accountability of charities generally. Although the new legislation, which was developed in consultation with the charitable sector, is still being digested by those affected by it, government has already opened a new debate on much more radical changes, including the abolition of the concept of charitable status. The Home Office has funded and published a substantial report entitled *Voluntary Action* by the think-tank Centris, which advocates a separation of charities into service providers and pressure groups. According to many in the charitable sector this analysis represents a fundamental attack on the nature of British charities for whom service provision informs a campaigning role. Although no action on this report is currently being taken, there will undoubtedly be a lengthy debate should any be proposed.

Changes in the National Health Service and Social Services

In relation to the work of artists and arts development workers, the most significant change to the health service has been the creation of NHS trusts for services and units which have opted out of control by the district health authorities. In some ways this parallels the opting out of schools from LEA control, though the NHS trusts are much larger. It remains to be seen what effect this may have on hospital arts work. Evidence to date suggests that some NHS trusts are committed to this area of activity. The government's Care in the Community policy has meant - among other things - the closure of many psychiatric hospitals and the growth of community-based support services for people with mental health problems and other needs. This has created a significant expansion of day support services, many of which are very keen to involve artists and practitioners in their work. Finally, anyone working with children should be aware of the broad provisions of the Children Act, though the detail you need will vary depending on your work.

5.10 Working in institutions

SETTING UP 2

2 SETTING UP

Summary

2.1 raises issues for consideration prior to the recruitment of a worker. It then looks at the needs of a worker taking up a new post, especially if they are new to local arts development. Section 2.2 covers a range of practical ideas which should help make the early weeks a little less confusing: it will be of relevance whether the worker is employed or freelance. Section 2.3 looks at how to review progress and begin a longer-term planning process. The last section looks at the value of networking and creating partnerships to support the work.

2.1 PLANNING A NEW POST

Although some animateur posts, particularly in the early years of development, grew from the initiatives of individual practitioners, it is more usual for them to be established by arts organisations and local authorities, often in partnership. Since such posts generally represent new initiatives as well as being time-limited, they must be well-planned: a new worker should not be called on to spend time dealing with problems which could have been avoided or resolved before their appointment.

Research and consultation

If the post represents a new area of work for those involved, it is essential that they undertake some preliminary research into the rationale behind and practice within animateur posts. The model has been well-tried and there is no need for anyone to set about re-inventing it: there is much experience to draw on. The involvement of RAB officers is essential, since they will be familiar with similar posts elsewhere in the region or in other parts of the country. The advice and help of specialist organisations like the Community Dance & Mime Foundation, Sound Sense, Mime Action Group and the National Association for Literature Development will be equally valuable. Local research and consultation is also important if the project is to be a success. Discussions should be held with professional and amateur arts organisations and individuals who may be interested in the proposals and with local authorities and the voluntary sector as appropriate. Some attempt should be made to get a picture of the existing level of development of the artform in question. Detailed research is often the first task of a new postholder.

14.9 ☛ *Report on the Literature Development Worker Movement in England*

Setting an aim and objectives

3.5 Policy and planning The preliminary research will help clarify what the post is intended to achieve. It is impossible to overemphasise the importance of this. Unless those involved know what they are trying to achieve and why, they will be unable to recruit effectively and set tasks for the person appointed. The resulting lack of direction is probably the single most common cause of under-achievement in arts development posts. Although aims will vary from place to place all animateur posts are essentially about extending access to the arts. But within that overall aim, priorities should be established. Existing posts illustrate different ways of doing this:

- **Prioritising a geographical area**
  examples: a dance worker in rural North Kesteven; a animateur in the City of Derby; the literature development workers serving Dorset, Oxfordshire and Surrey. Some posts have no prioritisation beyond a geographical area; others have additional priorities within the area.

- **Prioritising a particular community**
  examples: the Bedfordshire South Asian dance and literature animateurs; the African people's drumming animateur in Bradford.

- **Prioritising a particular issue**
  example: the remit of the writer-in-residence at the Pastures Hospital, Mickleover was to work with people on creative writing which explored their experiences of mental health services in hospital and in the community.

- **Prioritising a particular area of service**
  examples: education officers linked to orchestras, community writers working closely with the library service as in Northamptonshire; animateurs linked to the education service.

- **Prioritising a particular artform or approach**
  example: the rock and pop co-ordinator appointed by East Midlands Arts to work with local musicians and bands.

Targets and monitoring

3.5 Policy and planning The aim of an animateur post should be established in the original discussions between the sponsoring organisations and/or funding bodies. However it will be necessary to focus the work more closely by setting precise targets for the work and ways of monitoring progress. Although the preliminary thinking for this can be done before appointment, it is best to involve the new worker in the process and gain their commitment to the targets set.

Different models

The great strength of animateur and arts development worker posts is their ability to respond to local circumstances and national trends. Over the years, and across the country, many different models for posts have been developed to meet particular needs within set resource limits. Defining one is largely a matter of making choices:

See chapters **10 - 13** for actual examples of different models.

- **Aim** - how does the aim of the project affect the model chosen to deliver it? How do the needs of the proposed target audience affect the model?

- **Staffing** - will the post be full-time or part-time, and if part-time what will the postholder do for the remainder of their working week? Will there be more than one worker? If so, how will responsibilities be divided?

- **Skills** - will the aim be better achieved by a practitioner, by someone with arts management skills, or by someone with both? If it is to be a practitioner, who will provide administrative support?

- **Base** - should the base be an office, or a building with working spaces? If the latter, what role will the building play in the project?

- **Scale** - how does the scale of the outcomes sought (eg geographical reach) affect the choice of structure?

- **Independence** - should the post be set up as part of an existing organisation (eg local authority, arts organisation), and if so which? If the post is to be wholly independent, how will that be achieved?

- **Management** - what management structure is most suitable, and who should be involved?

- **Timescale** - how long should the project run for? If it is time-limited what consequences follow for the nature of and approach to the work , and what is planned to happen after its completion?

Research and discussions with the RAB and specialist artform organisations will help identify projects on whose experience those setting up the project can draw.

The length of a post

Ideally posts should be set up as long-term commitments, in the same way as other arts initiatives. There is every reason to expect that a development worker, far from having outlived their usefulness after a couple of years, will have created an interest in and demand for more substantial artform activities. A decision to set up a post without time-limit does not preclude either appointing individuals on fixed-term contracts, or building in a structured review process to monitor its progress and value. Where the funders are unwilling to make a long-term commitment, a post will have to be funded for two or three years to be able to produce worthwhile outcomes. If there is a place for short-term posts - six to twelve months - it is as active research initiatives, designed to identify answers to particular questions and strategies for action. Such work is really a form of arts consultancy and is probably best undertaken by people with experience in research and consultancy. All of these timescales should be reconsidered if the post is not to be full-time.

Funding a post

Most animateur and arts development worker posts are funded by a partnership between various bodies. In the past and for different posts these have included: the Arts Council, Regional Arts Boards, Borough and District Councils, County Councils through Leisure, Education, Library and Social Services, Health Authorities, local arts councils and charitable trusts. The involvement of commercial sponsors has been a recent development. Partnerships make a post more achievable (since each partner's contribution is reduced) and offer a greater degree of security because the post is supported by more organisations. The amount of funding required will vary from post to post, but should be at least £20,000 a year (in 1994/5) for full-time posts. Thought must also be given to the costs of setting up and administering the post, and creating a budget for project development. It is crucial to get a common agreement between the funders of the legitimate expectations each can have of the post.

4.6 Finance
In Lincolnshire alone, music development workers were established by four district councils, with moneys freed-up following the demise of a regional orchestra.

Management and support

3.4 Working with a management committee
A clear management structure must be agreed with postholders reporting to a line manager or management committee, or both. The structure should be made clear in the job description for the post, together with the limits of authority attached to the post. Support groups - drawn from local practitioners and interested people - offer a useful foil independent of the man-

agement structure. In some cases it may be sensible to offer one-to-one support for a worker, perhaps by linking them with someone doing a similar job elsewhere, but these arrangements can be set up following appointment. Where there is more than one form of management input or support, the respective roles and responsibilities of the different elements must be clearly established.

3.7 Managing yourself

Employment

It will be necessary to decide whether to employ someone to do the job, or to look for a freelance worker who will undertake it on a self-employed basis. This is not simply a question of administrative convenience. A freelance worker on a contract for services should approach a job of this sort in a different way to someone who is actually employed by a local authority or arts centre. If the person is to be an employee the terms and conditions governing the post must be agreed, unless they are joining the staff of an organisation with existing agreements. The terms of a contract for a freelance worker will also need to be agreed.

4.3 Employment
CDMF publishes *Guidelines on Pay and Conditions*

Administration

There will be many issues to consider, starting with the base from which the person will work and the administrative support which can be made available. In addition to adequate office accommodation, some posts will also need access to resources including rehearsal or meeting space and equipment. Other questions to be considered include financial management, insurance, health and safety and marketing.

4. Administration

Recruitment

From the job description it will be possible to draw up a person specification to guide the recruitment process. For some posts it may be necessary to include a practical element in the interview. This could include leading a practical workshop (though consideration will have to be given as to who might be involved in the workshop), resolving a hypothetical problem, or giving a presentation. Provision will have to be made for an adequate induction and training programme following appointment.

4.3 Employment

Finally

It takes time to set up a new arts development worker post: time to research and consult, to bring partners together and raise finance, to agree common objectives, to sort out the managerial and administrative issues. It is attractive to act while the enthusiasm is there, or because money must be spent quickly, but it is much better to resolve problems before someone is in post, than waste time on them when the work should be happening. A well-planned post will be twice as effective as one which has been hurriedly-cobbled together for unclear reasons.

2.2 STARTING A NEW POST

Although this is written from the point of view of someone taking up a post, most of it is equally applicable to a freelance practitioner seeking to become established.

The arts world offers few more daunting prospects than that which greets a new animateur on their first day in post: a vast area and thousands of potential users but no obvious place to start. It's harder still for freelance practitioners trying to establish themselves without even the confidence-boosting sense of having been appointed. To acknowledge the size of the task is not to be negative - most animateurs would confirm that it's also a uniquely exhilarating experience - but simply to admit that many people find their first few months in post stressful and confusing. The sense of bewilderment arises largely from the nature of the job itself. Based as it usually is around a single person rather than an organisation, the job has no reality until someone takes it on. It is simply an idea, an aspiration until it is filled out and made concrete by the vision, energy and hard work of the practitioner or animateur.

At the start of a new post it is natural to feel that you are not in control of the situation: you are the new element, and you have an enormous amount of information to take in. You are learning fast while probably feeling the need to prove quickly that you were a good choice for the job. But you should feel confident in accepting the assessment made by the interviewing panel: you were appointed for definite skills and qualities. If your manager or management committee has planned a thorough induction process you are fortunate, not only because it will help you get established, but because it implies that they understand the difficulties you face. If they haven't - or you don't have any managerial support - you need to do what you can to take control of the situation yourself.

Arriving on day one to find nothing more than an empty desk is hard, but you can start planning what you are going to do. Look at your work under a number of headings, and set yourself tasks attached to each:

- **The area**
  Start a file for information about the area which your post serves. Note anything useful, from population sta

tistics to the phone number of the railway station. In particular look out for arts activities of all sorts, voluntary organisations, public buildings and spaces for hire, local authority services. Read the local paper, pick up leaflets and listen to local radio, especially if you are new to the area.

LEARNING RESOURCES CENTRE

HAVERING COLLEGE

- **Your artform**
  Whatever your artform, start finding out what has happened in the area to date. Talk to professionals, including the relevant RAB and local authority officers and people from arts organisations, but don't neglect non-professional and amateur activity. For instance phone calls to local leisure centres might put a dance worker in touch with many people involved in amateur dance of whom professionals were unaware. Get in touch with animateurs, practitioners or development workers in other areas for support and sharing experience. Contact professional bodies or companies outside the area and get yourself added to their mailing lists.

- **Management**
  Find out the management structure within which you operate, including who you report to, if there is a committee, what your limits of authority are, what supervision and support you are supposed to have.

- **Policy and planning**
  Find out what decisions have already been made about establishing policies to guide your work and what plans exist. Check on targets which have been set for the post, and if they do not yet exist begin thinking about a realistic framework to guide you.

- **Funding**
  Arrange meetings with the funding bodies for your post, and make sure you understand their expectations. Find out their requirements in terms of reporting and/or claiming grants and explore the possibilities of additional project funding from them and other funding sources.

6 Funding

- **Finance**
  Ask about the arrangements for financial management of your work: if you have a budget check the procedures you are expected to follow to use it.

- **Employment status and conditions**
  Check your employment status and the terms attached to it. If you are self-employed make sure you have a

4.3 Employment

contract and that it meets your needs. If you are an employee, read the terms and conditions of your employment carefully and ask about anything you don't understand: get a copy of your job description. Check when you will be paid and how, and what expenses you can reclaim.

- **Office and resources**

4.2 Setting up an office

Take the time to get your workspace organised and equipped: it will be worthwhile in the long run and the routine nature of the task may be a welcome relief from meetings, interviews and induction.

- **Colleagues**

Make arrangements to meet people working in related fields. Who you should try to meet and when will depend on your work and your own priorities, but - in addition to those involved in the arts - it could include people working for local authorities, in schools and colleges, in the voluntary sector and in local community and leisure centres.

- **Your skills**

7.2 Preparing a training plan

No-one can do everything, or is equally good at all the things that they can do. As you learn more about your job, keep a note of those areas you don't feel confident in, or need training to take on; some training needs may be met internally, others through short courses.

- **Making progress**

Because of the peculiar nature of the first weeks of a job, it's easy to feel that you're not getting anywhere, and that all the managerial and administrative tasks are not what you took the job on to do. So it's a good idea to set up some practical work as soon as you can, perhaps through an existing arts organisation. Ask the local arts centre or college if you can set up a workshop or class in their premises, and invite the people already using the facilities to attend; or ask a school if you can do some free workshops with the children. It won't matter if it isn't the best work you've ever done: it will be good to be working with people, you'll make contacts, and it will provide an antidote to a surfeit of meetings.

- **Meeting your needs**

Don't neglect your own personal and professional life, especially if you have moved to the area to take up the post. Look out for classes or opportunities to work creatively with other artists, good suppliers and shops, physiotherapists etc as appropriate.

In general, make lists of your tasks and decide what you're going to do the next day each evening before you leave. Prepare for meetings you have set up by deciding what you want to get out of them and preparing questions you want to ask or areas you want to discuss. Make notes of your meetings when you get back to the office.

Making contacts in the community

One of your most important tasks will be making contact with people. You need to develop an understanding of the networks and lines of communication which knit individuals, groups and communities together. Make use of the local press to try to get known, and try to get mentioned or even to advertise in local community publications. Among those you may be able to interest are:

- the local evening or weekly paper

- local free newspapers

- community newsletters published by voluntary organisations, Council for Voluntary Service (CVS), charities, parishes, church groups, community organisations, local authorities etc

- talking newspapers for the blind

Make contact with journalists in local radio and television, but they may be more interested in covering the story when a project is actually happening. If you want to get in touch with a certain group of people - eg parents with young children, or people with learning difficulties - contacting them through the services and networks they use may be more productive than general publicity. But, whilst it is sometimes necessary to think of people in terms of social groups you should be cautious: people may belong to more than one group, and they may also not think of themselves in those terms. In short, whilst it is unwise to place too much reliance on any of these structures or networks in carrying out your work, each may provide a useful route to getting in touch with people. The following notes may help in thinking about how to publicise work to particular people:

Social Services departments and Health Authorities

contacts with people with learning difficulties; people with

One arts development worker, moving several hundred miles to a new job, made a rule for herself never to turn down a (reasonable) invitation. Three or four years later, she felt that, although she'd spent one or two dull evenings, she had made friends and established personal support networks much more quickly as a result.
3.7 Managing yourself - Time management

In some circumstances your appointment may in itself be newsworthy.

physical disabilities; people with mental health problems; people with dependency problems; people in hospitals and hospices.

Education authorities
contacts with school-age children and their parents; students and people studying through adult education; and people who use the premises outside school hours.

Voluntary organisations and charities
contacts with all sorts of people, depending on the particular interest of the organisation. The local CVS is a good place to start finding about this area.

Self-help, campaigning and pressure groups
as with voluntary organisations, but if they are run by the people they exist to serve, they may have a different ethos.

In addition to these important networks there are many others which are used by the whole community, including libraries, leisure and community centres, sports facilities, shops, trades unions, etc. You will find addresses and contacts through the local library, and the phone book which will also help you find out who is out there - for instance all the local schools will be listed - and give you ideas about who you should get in touch with. In some areas local directories of useful organisations have been published.

2.3 REVIEWING PROGRESS

It is possible to do this by following the well-known 'SWOT' analysis. SWOT is an acronym for Strengths, Weaknesses, Opportunities and Threats, and it simply represents a way of organising your thinking about an organisation or project into those four categories.

When you have been in post for about three months it will be useful to step back a little and review progress before making solid plans for future development. Ideally your management committee, support group and funders will all be involved in this process, though you will usually have to do the bulk of the preliminary thinking.

Think about the area in terms of:

its nature and identity, and recent changes

existing arts activities, organisations, practitioners and enthusiasts

access to existing artistic provision and gaps in it

voluntary organisations and local authority services

support and information networks

Think about your resources in terms of:

local artists and arts organisations

finances and potential for increasing them

facilities, spaces and equipment

time (on a weekly basis and overall)

management and funders

support, contacts, offers of help etc

Think about yourself in terms of

your strengths and weaknesses

your aspirations and vision

your training needs

Review the expectations of the funders and other people involved in setting up the post, and look at the aim and objectives originally drawn up. Consider whether they are still applicable and whether they have been set too high or too low. Think about your short- and long-term aims for the post and discuss them with management, funders and local people you have begun to involve. Try to agree a series of concrete targets for the next six or nine months. This review process is not intended to be an alternative to the more substantial policy development and planning process described in the next chapter, just a provisional process designed to support your work while the more permanent management structures and practice are established for the post.

2.4 PARTNERSHIPS AND NETWORKING

Many animateurs and development workers have the sole responsibility for their artform in a particular area, but whether this is the case or not, all find the creation of partnerships with other professionals and organisations a fundamental part of their work. Not only does it make the most effective use of resources, ideas and energy available, it also ensures that the work has a lasting impact on the permanent structures - an essential aim for any time-limited post.

The art of creating good partnerships is understanding the aims and concerns of the organisations you are trying to work with. The degree of congruence between your own objectives and those of your potential partners will vary from the close correspondence between people working in the arts to the very different concerns of social services departments or prisons. You must help those working in other areas to see how the arts can assist them in achieving their objectives, if they are to commit time and resources to arts projects. So talking to a social services department about the aesthetic qualities of contemporary dance, or the excitement of world music is likely to elicit, in the context, a mildly-puzzled response. But if you talk about the ways in which an arts project can help participants increase their confidence and advocacy skills, build links with mainstream community activities, and develop their independence, the response is likely to be much more positive.

Partnerships can be established with the following bodies among others:

- arts organisations and venues from national companies to local collectives

- local authority arts departments and the RAB

- social services departments including day and residential centres

- youth and community services

- health authorities and NHS trusts

- education authorities, schools, special schools and colleges

- voluntary organisations and charities

- the media and publishing industries

Many of these are already involved in partnership initiatives - for instance voluntary organisations, social services, education and health authorities share an interest in and a responsibility towards young disabled people - and it is often possible to become involved in existing partnerships. Such relationships make the most of available resources - time, money and energy and experience. Projects which would be too costly for a single organisation to promote are often within reach of three or four. But the most important factor for an animateur or arts development worker is that partnerships offer opportunities to have a lasting impact on attitudes to the arts generally and one artform specifically. A good arts project in a school can permanently change its policy towards involvement in the arts (though that is equally true of bad projects). There are many schools and day centres - to say nothing of education authorities and social services departments - which are now running imaginative arts programmes because of their contact with practitioners and development agencies over the past decade or two.

Networking

It is easy for people working on their own, perhaps based in an organisation which has little direct connection with their field of experience, to end up feeling very much alone. A sense of isolation can undermine a worker's confidence, but the problem is not confined to how people feel. Without regular contacts with other professionals, and through them access to a large body of experience, a practitioner or animateur is likely to be less effective in their work. The networks you can tap into will vary depending on where you are based and what your artform is. Community dance, now well established since its inception over ten years ago, has built effective organisations and networks both nationally and regionally. Mime is building its limbs through the creation of regional fora. Literature development workers, whose numbers are limited but growing fast, are now creating a national organisation. There are three main levels at which networks operate:

National organisations

Although they vary in their resources and the nature of their work, the Community Dance & Mime Foundation, Mime Action Group, the National Association for Literature Development and Sound Sense all exist primarily to support practitioners and work in their fields, and to raise the profile of the work at national level. Each produces a quarterly publication which must count as essential reading for any practitioner, as well as promoting conferences and training events. They produce guidelines and recommendations in different areas, including contracts and payscales, and form a natural first point of enquiry about problems for their membership. Last, and certainly not least, is their role in fostering a sense of identity and community among practitioners.

In addition to the artform-specific organisations mentioned, there are other national organisations which may be of interest to individual workers, including the National Campaign for the Arts, the National Artists Association, the National Disability Arts Forum and many others: the Arts Council or RAB will help you find out more.

Regional organisations

It has long been natural for practitioners in many fields to organise and meet regionally, usually within the boundaries of an RAB. Such regional organisations tend to be informal, and dependent on the energy and commitment of those involved. They can provide a valuable opportunity to share information, develop co-operative projects and training, publicise work and organise effective lobbying.

9 National artform organisations

Eastern Arts places a high value on the regional meetings of dance animateurs and makes participation a condition of funding posts, because it believes that the work of local people is greatly strengthened by regional co-operation.

They also offer support and opportunities to discuss problems and difficulties. Not all regional fora work well, however, and it is not unusual for numbers to dwindle after an enthusiastic launch simply because people have many demands on their time and energy. The key to success is probably to have a clear aim or focus for bringing people together - perhaps to work on an event, tour or festival, or to lobby the RAB or a local authority.

Local organisations

Local organisations - perhaps based on a town or district - vary greatly depending on the area and the people involved. In some parts of the country, you may be the only professional in your artform, so a local group is likely to involve anybody active in the arts, whether professionally or not. But in a city with an art college or university and a number of arts organisations it may well be possible to bring together a number of practitioners to form a group. As with regional organisations, having a clear aim is essential to harnessing people's enthusiasm.

It may also be worth thinking about becoming a member of a trade union. Check with other practitioners, professional workers and union offices to identify one which would suit your needs.

To an over-worked practitioner, struggling to carry out their programme and meet their funders' expectations, participating in meetings and networking can seem at best a luxury, and at worst an irrelevance. But there are decisive advantages which make networking not just worthwhile but essential to arts development workers. In particular, networking makes it possible

- to learn from other people's experience and so avoid making unnecessary mistakes or spending time discovering things other people have already found;

- to build links and work on joint projects, sharing the costs of touring input or buying equipment;

- to assess joint training and other needs and develop common strategies for meeting them;

- to avoid the dangers that arise from working too much in isolation, and to help individuals get known as practitioners;

- to keep informed of key issues - eg changes in arts policy - and develop coherent responses or lobbying;

- to support the confidence and morale of individual workers through contact with others who face similar problems and share similar ideas;

- to raise the profile of individual work, practice or organisations;

- to help ensure all practitioners share a common understanding of best practice and work towards it;

- to raise the profile of the artform, and express its aims and ideals coherently in appropriate fora.

It is essential for funders, management and the workers themselves to plan their work in such a way as to leave time and resources for networking and participation in regional and national organisations and meetings. The alternative is a potentially damaging insularity which undermines both the individual practitioner and the work they are carrying out. As an animateur, a practitioner or arts development worker, you are part of a large and growing movement. You are involved in pushing out the boundaries of art, creativity and practice, and your involvement with your peers is essential to developing interest in and support for the whole area of work.

MANAGEMENT 3

3   MANAGEMENT

Summary

The chapter begins by explaining the importance of good management procedures, before looking at different legal management structures and, in section 3.3, at the relative advantages of working towards democracy or accountability. Section 3.4 looks at working with a management committee, advisory group or similar structure. Sections 3.5 and 3.6 form the core of the chapter and cover the essential business of using management processes to plan work, and monitor progress. Section 3.7 looks at how to keep control of work by managing time. The remaining three sections deal with management relationships, with staff and with outside consultants, and how to deal with problems in those relationships when they arise.

3.1   WHO NEEDS MANAGEMENT?

Management is sometimes seen as separate from the work of arts development, and consequently its demands may be resented as getting in the way of the practice. But good management practice is central to the creation and execution of worthwhile arts work because it offers a structured way of planning and controlling what you do. Consequently it should underlie everything you do, whether you are employed or freelance, and provide a framework of procedures to guide and support you and those you work with. Good management is not mysterious - on the contrary one of its primary results is to introduce clarity into people's work - and developing skills is a matter partly of training, and partly of experience. It can be analysed in terms of five key objectives which any well-managed organisation should be working towards:

- Effectiveness - the achievement of your stated aims.

- Efficiency - the maximisation of results.

- Economy - the best use of resources, time and energy.

- Equity - the fair conduct of your work.

- Excellence - the achievement of quality in your work.

More traditional definition of management sees it as a series of functions: Setting direction; Forecasting; Planning; Organising; Directing; Co-ordinating and Controlling.

Apart from this analysis of the purpose of management, there are three simple reasons why organisations need good management:

- because they have to agree their aim and how to achieve it, monitor and assess the progress of their activities, and maintain control of their staff, resources and, ultimately, destinies;

- because they operate within a legal framework which makes demands on them which can only be satisfied through good management procedures;

- because they are accountable to funders, users and others.

The first step in building good management procedures is to establish the right legal structures to support them. Since law affects everyone, albeit in different ways depending on their own legal entity, it is essential to work within a legal framework which meets your needs and those of the bodies and organisations with whom you want to work.

3.2   LEGAL STRUCTURES FOR ORGANISATIONS

4.7 Legal matters
The Directory of Social Change and the National Council for Voluntary Organisations both publish useful books on aspects of management.
14.3 ☛ *Management of Voluntary Organisations* (Croner) is strong on the legal aspects.
15.8 The InterChange Legal Advisory Service is used by many arts and voluntary organisations. Among other services, it offers advice on legal structures, constitutions and applying for charitable status.

Every organisation needs a formal structure: this section provides a brief summary of the legal structures available to arts organisations. It offers no more than an introduction to the different options: the field is one of the most legally complex which concerns arts organisations and you should undertake more specialised research or seek professional advice if you have responsibilities in this area. You should not feel that you have to understand these issues without guidance. All of these legal structures - provided that they are properly constituted - are generally acceptable to funders, though some charitable trusts are restricted to funding registered charities.

Unincorporated associations

Two or more people who agree to work together for other than commercial reasons can constitute themselves as an unincorporated association, governed by a written constitution or set of rules. It is the simplest and most basic form of body, and is often, in fact, the status of most new organisations until they constitute themselves in other terms. Unincorporated associations are subject to the general law - that is, there are no specific acts of parliament governing their nature or procedures. Their advantages largely lie in the speed, ease and cheapness of their constitution, but in most cases these are outweighed by the significant drawback that they do not have, for most practical purposes a corporate existence. The association cannot in itself hold property, borrow money, or enter into contracts: these things can only be done by individual members of the management committee acting on behalf of the association. The existence of the management committee usually has the effect of indemnifying members of the association who are not elected to it, but places a heavy burden on the management committee itself since its members have (jointly and individually) unlimited personal responsibility for all debts, charges or liabilities of the association. This is therefore not a structure which recommends itself in most cases as a long-term solution.

If the people involved plan to carry on a business and make a profit - for instance a group of practitioners working together - they would probably need to set up a partnership or co-operative.

Charitable trusts

A trust is a legal mechanism created by one person or group of people to benefit another person or group of people and, as such, is another form of unincorporated organisation. There are two forms of trust: private trusts which are set up for various purposes (eg family benefit or tax efficiency) and charitable trusts, intended to benefit society at large, or a significant sector of the community. Charitable trusts whose conduct is enforced by the Attorney General, provide a legal structure for a number of voluntary and arts organisations. They are created by a deed of trust, which becomes the governing instrument dictating how the organisation must operate. The deed names trustees, generally between three and six people, who are then empowered, within the framework of the deed, to act on behalf of the trust and to apply its resources to its stated objects. The liability of the trustees is not limited in itself although where they can show that they have acted legally, jointly and in good faith, trustees are unlikely to be held personally liable.

14.3 ☞ *The Effective Trustee Parts 1, 2 & 3*

Charitable trusts are a well-established part of the voluntary and charitable sector, and they work well for many purposes. Because they have existed for many years, there is a substantial body of case law concerning them, and most solicitors have experience of establishing and running them. They provide a recognised framework and some limitation of liability to the trustees in normal circumstances. However they can be idiosyncratic, depending on the original deed of trust, with an inbuilt conservatism and reluctance to take risks. The expectations of trustees about their involvement in direct management is also likely to vary greatly, and there are grey areas around the delegation of responsibilities to employees. It can also prove difficult for charitable trusts to negotiate commercial loans.

Industrial and Provident Societies (IPS)

Industrial and Provident Societies are part of a group of organisations which grew up in the 19th century from a range of working class self-help initiatives. (The other members of this class are friendly societies, building societies and trades unions, none of which is relevant in this context.) An IPS is a form of co-operative and is relevant in this context only if it is established for the benefit of the community in general. An IPS is an incorporated body with a membership whose liability is limited to the share value of the society (generally £1). It is created on the approval of an application for registration by the Registrar of Friendly Societies, who must also approve its rules (constitution). Although establishing an IPS can be time-consuming, its administration thereafter is fairly straightforward. It offers the benefits of limited liability enjoyed by directors of a limited company, but is subject to separate legislation (the Industrial and Provident Societies Acts 1965 to 1975). In some ways the philosophy of the IPS sits more comfortably with that of an arts organisation than the profit-driven philosophy of companies, but it is becoming unusual for arts organisations to be established in this way.

Companies limited by guarantee

Arts organisations have increasingly sought to constitute themselves as companies limited by guarantee, as their operations, the commercial world around them, and the demands made upon them have grown and become more complex. (There are a number of other types of company, depending on their public or private status, and the nature and extent of their liabilities, but they are rarely used by arts organisations.) A company limited by guarantee is a legal body separate from its members, who agree to contribute a nominal sum (usually £1) to the settlement of its debts should it be wound up. It is established by a Memorandum of Association which defines its objects, and the conduct of its business is governed by its Articles of Association, or rules. To create a company limited by guarantee the memorandum and articles must be submitted, together with other items and a fee, for acceptance by the Registrar of Companies. The form of the documents and other matters concerning companies limited by guarantee are governed by the Companies Act 1985 and other related legislation.

The liability of members of a company limited by guarantee is the sum specified in the memorandum of association so that, in the event of insolvency, there can be no call on the personal assets of the members to meet the debts of the company. There is an important exception however: if it can be proved that the directors of the company continued to trade without reasonable expectation of the company being able to meet its debts, they become personally liable for those debts. This situation can occur in badly-managed companies, particularly when the faith of those involved in their ability to redress a bad financial situation is seriously misplaced. Thus, although the personal liability of those involved with a company limited by guarantee is much less than, say that of members of an unincorporated association, their responsibilities and duties - in respect of which the limitation of their liability is granted - are substantial and must be properly understood by them.

> Insolvency legislation has been strengthened by the Insolvency Act 1986 and the Company Directors Disqualification Act 1986.

There are many advantages to this structure for arts organisations, since it creates a recognised legal personality for the organisation, independent of its members or staff. Consequently a company limited by guarantee can own property, enter into contracts, borrow money and so on. The framework it provides can be useful for an organisation and the demands made upon it, such as independent auditing of accounts, strengthen rather than burden it. It will, however, need a knowledgeable and effective company secretary to operate properly within the law, since strict rules govern company procedures and there are substantial fines for non-compliance.

Registered charities

Britain is exceptional among its European neighbours in having a distinct legal class of body known as charities where status is determined only by the purposes of the organisation. In England and Wales charities are registered and regulated by the Charity Commission. Status as a registered charity is independent from the foregoing legal structures - though all registered charities need a legal structure and written constitution - and not all voluntary or arts organisations are registered charities. However, it is a legal duty for organisations which have charitable objects to register if their income is over £1,000 a year. An organisation seeking to register as a charity must

> The jurisdiction of the Charity Commissioners extends only over England and Wales. In Scotland and Northern Ireland, charities are subject to different legislation and regulation.

- have charitable objects as defined in law, (work in the arts is acceptable within certain frameworks, but there are other objects touching on education or social welfare which could apply to some arts organisations);
- be of public benefit;
- and be wholly and exclusively charitable in its aims.

There are a number of advantages to an arts organisation in being a registered charity:

- exemption from income tax, corporation tax and capital gains tax;

- mandatory non-domestic rate relief of 80% (and discretionary relief of 100%) on buildings ;

- the ability to receive grants from charitable trusts which may be empowered to donate only to registered charities;

- the ability to reclaim income tax from Government on donations made through Gift Aid or Deed of Covenant.

4.6 Finance - VAT

There are further advantages of a more technical nature, particularly with regard to some areas of taxation. (It is not the case, as is sometimes thought, that charities do not have to pay VAT, though there are some particular areas in which supplies to or by a registered charity can be zero-rated for VAT. This is a technical area liable to change and advice should be sought.) Charitable status may also have intangible benefits in reassuring potential funders and others that the organisation is non-profit making, of benefit to the wider community and accountable.

Registered charities are also obliged to mention their status and registration on all publicity material and certain other items like cheque-books and letterhead.
4.2 Setting up an office

Naturally charitable status imposes some constraints which, depending on the nature and purpose of your work, may or may not be considered disadvantages. Of these the most important are:

- restrictions on the ability to trade;

- a duty to secure the best reasonable return on capital and investments;

- a duty to submit annual returns and accounts to the Charity Commissioners: (these must be independently examined in the case of charities with an income of more than £1,000 a year, or audited where income exceeds £100,000 a year;

- a restriction on certain types of political activity.

The Charity Commission can also investigate individual charities where it has reason to suspect maladministration or dishonesty. On the other hand, registered charities can themselves seek the advice of the Charity Commissioners.

An organisation can only become a registered charity by registering with the Charity Commission. This can be a time-consuming process and will not be achieved overnight, even if the organisation's objects, structure and management are acceptable to the Commission. If it is intended to apply for status as a registered charity, it is sensible to get the agreement of the Charity Commission to the proposed legal structure and constitution before they are adopted. Advice and guidance can be sought from a solicitor or from the Charity Commission itself, who can be contacted by phone and who also publish useful leaflets. The National Council for Voluntary Organisations (NCVO) publishes examples of governing instruments which may help in drafting your own.

3.3   DEMOCRATIC OR ACCOUNTABLE

Although all organisations have, *de facto*, a legal status, not every structure allows for participation of users or accountability. Management structures should not be set up for the sole convenience either of legislators or of those involved in an arts organisation. There is always a need to consider the expectations and potential contribution which can be made by the users or audience. This is doubly important in the case of arts organisations which exist to work with local communities.

Many locally-based organisations have sought to address this by setting up a democratic structure, based on a membership, something which can be done through any of the structures above except charitable trusts. In fact this course will not necessarily achieve real involvement by local people. Take for example a music project in a small city, with 150,000 people living in its catchment area. It can be set up as a membership organisation with a management committee elected at the annual general meeting. On one level this seems a good way of giving control to the local community, but there are problems.

- Even if the organisation can attract 200 or 300 members, it will only involve a fraction of the total.

- The higher the membership, the greater the burden which will be placed on the organisation, potentially distracting it from its work.

- The membership - and consequently the management committee - may be unrepresentative of the local community.

- Those elected to the management committee may not have the skills required to do the job effectively.

Registered charities are regulated by the Commission through the Charities Act 1992 and 1993. The latter is a significant piece of legislation in this area, not all of whose provisions have yet come into force. Its principal effect is to improve the accountability of charities to the community, through the Commission, and, although new responsibilities and duties are imposed on charity trustees, well-run charities will not find the new system difficult to adjust to.

4.7 Legal matters

1.2 Basic principles

- Those who turn up to the annual general meeting, and those who stand for election may be only those who are confident in those formal situations.

- It is relatively easy for small groups to seize control of the organisation by manipulating the democratic process.

- There are many people who would like to have an input into the work, but not at the expense of discussing the business matters that necessarily form the bulk of the work of a management committee.

Even with these problems, the structure remains unavailable to sole freelance workers, or those already working within other structures such as local authorities.

The alternative is to build accountability into your structures, whatever they are. Making your work accountable means discussing it with representative members of the local community on a regular, formalised and open basis. There are a number of ways you can do this:

5.11 Feedback

- Put effort into getting real feedback during and after projects;

- Hold open meetings to discuss the work more broadly;

- Set up specific days which offer a mixture of discussion and workshops;

- Set up advisory committees or groups for specific projects, for geographical areas, for types of work, even to help with difficult things like fundraising;

- Co-opt people onto your management group;

- Make sure that people can get hold of you, and that they know you are interested in what they think.

It can be argued that this approach, though without the superficial attractions of democratic control, is actually much more effective at creating a real partnership between an arts organisation and its audience. The key advantages it offers are:

- It is possible to involve all sections of the community, and all sorts of people, on their own terms;

- Everyone can contribute their voice to the area of work or concern which is of most interest to them;

- The desire to manage the organisation's affairs are seldom a motive for people's involvement, yet this necessarily comprises 90% of the business of a management committee;

- It is not necessary to impose legal responsibilities on people who may not want them in order to involve them in the management of the organisation;

- The agenda can be set by the people you are consulting, because it need no longer be determined by management requirements;

- You can set up a separate management structure which not only represents your constituency, but has the skills required by the task.

It is of course possible to supplement and strengthen an existing democratic structure with further systems to improve an organisation's accountability to its users.

3.4 WORKING WITH A MANAGEMENT COMMITTEE

Many animateurs and arts development workers report to a management committee of some sort, though they may have different names, including board, support group, advisory committee etc. It is important to understand their legal relationship to you, however, and this should be explained when you take up a post. If you are reporting to a management committee or board in an organisation such as those described above, your relationship is defined in a legal context: the committee is in legal control and possibly ownership of the organisation, and your role is to carry out their instructions. Your direct line management may be conducted by a senior member of staff, but you will still be accountable in the wider sense to the management committee which is your employer.

In addition to reporting to a line manager and/or management committee, you may work with a support group or advisory committee which has no legal control over your work. This can work well, so long as both the worker and support group understand the limits of such a group in terms of controlling the work. It is essential that any worker should understand properly the management context in which they operate, and their role and duties within it. To this end, you should be familiar with the constitution and any other rules which relate to the management structure.

A good and supportive relationship with a management committee is one of the most essential things an arts worker can have, so it's worth the effort to get it right. The most common causes of friction in that relationship are different expectations between the two parties (generally expecting too much of each other), and confusion about areas of authority and responsibility. This section looks at how to avoid some of those problems and more generally how to make the most of your relationship with a management committee.

Getting people involved

14.2 ☛ *Care, Diligence and Skill; Board Member Manual*

A management committee is only as good as the people who sit on it, but in practice there are people sitting on management committees who don't contribute much in that particular forum. Most arts workers inherit, rather than bring together their management committees: indeed they're likely to have been appointed by them. If the latter is true, your relationship should be able to start on a good footing, since in selecting you the committee will have expressed its confidence in your abilities.

You may feel, however, as your work progresses, that the committee is not fully able to advise and support you in the way you would like. That may not be anybody's fault: the needs of an organisation change over time, as do the skills required to meet them. It's quite possible that your management committee doesn't include any representatives from the local community, or is perhaps weak in financial expertise or marketing experience. For any of these reasons, you may need to look at ways of bringing in new people. Naturally, you can only achieve this with the support and co-operation of the existing committee. Depending on whether this has come together by election or appointment, you may be able to invite new members. Alternatively, you may have to co-opt new members, perhaps without voting rights.

A skills audit or review for the management committee may be a good way to identify gaps in the existing skills.

Members of a management committee should all have:

- a commitment to and interest in the work;

- enough time to prepare for and attend meetings, at least, and preferably time to meet with staff and see the work;

- a willingness to work co-operatively with others and a respect for confidentiality;

- a relevant area of expertise or experience.

Depending on the precise circumstances, areas of expertise or experience could include:

- financial management, accounting, law, marketing, fundraising, public relations or the media;

- a particular art form, the arts world generally or arts development work specifically;

- local authority, governmental, private sector or voluntary sector operations;

- knowledge of a particular section of the community, or representation of a particular interest group.

A good management committee will include all sorts of different people with different skills and approaches to problem solving. They will naturally find their own roles, so that a solicitor may only attend the formal meetings, but offer crucial advice then, whilst a local artist or activist may be quieter in meetings but get involved directly in your work on a day-to-day basis. Both approaches are valuable in a balanced team of people who, between them, offer a range of skills and attributes. Some management committees are set up with membership limited to fixed periods: this can be good in forcing the committee to renew and refresh itself, but it can also be frustrating to have to lose the involvement of active and valuable members. Indeed it can take people several years to become fully active committee members.

New members will need proper induction if they are to be able to carry out their duties effectively. CDMF has sample job descriptions and contracts for committee members and other useful material.

It is your role as the employed person to facilitate and support the involvement of your unpaid management committee. Put yourself in their shoes and consider how much of your limited leisure time you would be prepared to give to another voluntary organisation. Don't expect the same investment in the organisation from them as you put in yourself. Try to agree with individual people what they can do, and don't expect or ask for more. Some organisations have job descriptions for management committee members, and these can help make sure that everyone knows what their commitments are.

Defining responsibilities

The way in which responsibilities are apportioned depends largely on whether the management committee is part of the legal structure of the organisation or an advisory group with no legal status. In the former case its responsibilities will be defined in broad terms by law and the governing instrument, and the main area of concern for an employee will be their duties, responsibilities and limits of authority. In other words, what action can you properly take without reference to the management committee, what can you do on the chair's authority, and what can only be agreed by the full committee. These should be specified in your job description, and the basic principles will be the same whether you report to a committee or a line manager. Once again, the crucial thing is that you know what they are. Ideally, they will give you reasonable scope for independent action, but if they don't, you can do little about it except negotiate with your management.

The situation in respect of support groups and advisory committees is quite different, since they have no legal authority over you. A support group will need to define its own function and tasks - since these are not imposed by a constitution - if it is to make a valid contribution. The most serious potential problem is that the support group recommends a course of action which is rejected by your management, leaving you caught in the middle. The only way to avoid this is to make it clear to everyone involved in the support group exactly what their role is from the start, preferably establishing the group's terms of reference in writing, and its intended duration.

Working with a chair

The chair of an organisation is one of the key positions, and it is essential to have it filled by someone who has the right attributes and is prepared to offer the commitment it demands. A good chair will act as the cornerstone of the management committee, ensuring that all the members are able to contribute in their own way. They will be involved in supporting the staff, discussing problems and offering advice. They will take on a public relations role, and will fight the organisation's corner where appropriate. Finally, they will not try to do their employees' job. In order to do and be all those things, they will need to be kept informed of what is happening in regular meetings and discussions. You should discuss the business of each management committee meeting with the chair beforehand, so that they are fully informed of the issues underlying each item. You should take the chair into your confidence and seek to build an effective working relationship.

Managing formal meetings

Meetings generally have a bad reputation because they are often thought of as tedious, self-serving and irrelevant. That is largely because of the way many meetings are run, and it can be avoided by ensuring that everyone attending knows what they are there for, and what their role is.

The first thing to sort out is the legal framework of a meeting. Regular management committee meetings in an organisation will have clear legal duties and procedures laid down in

This is a typical agenda for the management committee meeting of an arts organisation:

7.00pm	Apologies	*(from people who can't be there)*
	Present	*(people who are there, whether they are members or observers)*
	Agreement of the agenda	*(a chance to add any important items which have arisen since the agenda was circulated)*
	Minutes of the last meeting	*(agreement of their accuracy)*
	Matters arising	*(short reports on developments since the last meeting which won't otherwise come up in the main business)*
7.15pm	**1 Financial report**	*(a good first item since it will affect other decisions)*
	Papers previously circulated	
	(pink sheets)	*(using colour helps people find papers)*
	The treasurer	*(the person presenting the item)*
7.50pm	Break	
8.00pm	**2 Fundraising programme**	*(take items which need discussion early in the meeting)*
	The chair	
8.15pm	**3 Programme report**	*(the discussion on present and future work will interest most people,*
	Papers previously circulated	*so it can fit well into the latter half of the meeting)*
	(blue sheets)	
	Edith Sitwell, dance animateur	
8.45pm	**4 Any other business**	*(use only for small items of information, or minor queries)*
9.00pm	Close of meeting	

the constitution. There will be a certain amount of business - of which perhaps the most important is financial control - which must be dealt with on each occasion. Similarly those attending will have different rights - some to speak and vote, others to speak only, and still others just to observe.

The key to a successful meeting is a clear and detailed agenda, prepared by staff in consultation with the chair. This should itemise all the business to be dealt with, referring to any supporting papers and perhaps naming the people who will introduce the item. The agenda can allocate a certain amount of time to each item. In certain cases where important decisions are to be taken, it may be worth stating the decision to be made on the agenda. Make sure that the agenda and any supporting papers are sent out about a week in advance (assuming that people already know about the meeting).

Successful management of the meeting itself lies in the chair's ability to move discussion forward, avoid repetition, keep attention focused on the matter in hand, and ensure that everyone can make a contribution. If it is necessary to prepare minutes of the meeting, keep notes as you go. If possible get someone who is not participating in the meeting to take notes, even if you have to write them up afterwards. Generally speaking, minutes will record the following information:

- where and when the meeting took place;

- which members were present or absent and who else was at the meeting;

- that the minutes of the previous meeting were accepted as a true record and signed by the chair;

- separate numbered items (the minutes) stating what was discussed and what decisions were made, if any. The person whose responsibility it is to take action may also be named. In some cases or classes of meeting, minutes will record the actual text of resolutions agreed;

- date, time and venue of the next meeting.

In a well-run organisation, the last item will be known, since meetings should be scheduled at least twelve months in advance, so that people can ensure they are available. When setting up meetings, try to ensure that the room is quiet and pleasant, that people are able to sit around a table, and that refreshments are available. Meetings which last over two hours become decreasingly productive, as people tire, but scheduling breaks can be useful, even in short meetings.

The role of sub-committees
Even if management committees meet monthly, they may find it difficult to conduct all the business of an organisation in 24 hours a year. Sometimes it is necessary to create sub-committees or working parties to look at particular areas in more detail. Common examples include finance, employment, recruitment, equal opportunities and fundraising, but there are various others. Alternatively sub-committees may be created to oversee the management of specific projects or events. Sub-committees are a useful addition to management structures, but it is essential to set out their terms of reference carefully, and to ensure that their links with the full committee and staff are clear. It is also a good idea to set them up for a limited period, with a focused task, so that their role can be easily reviewed.

The role of observers
Many management committees invite representatives of other organisations (often, but by no means always, funding bodies) to observe their meetings - indeed in many cases the right to observe meetings is stipulated as a condition of funding. The contribution made by observers is often invaluable since they generally bring expertise, experience and a particular object-

ivity which committee members may lose. However, problems can arise where the role of an observer is unclear, or disregarded. Each committee will establish its own code of practice in this area, but the ground rule is that observers are there to observe: they may be allowed to speak freely, or through the chair, but they may not vote. If the matter being discussed is controversial, or simply private, the chair is entitled to ask the observer to leave while it is discussed. It is particularly important that the role of observers from an organisations' funders should be carefully thought about and mutually agreed.

Communication

In a well-run organisation there will be a planned structure for ensuring that all staff receive key information and feel connected to the work of the management committee. Information, ideas and views should also be able to pass effectively from staff back to the committee: good communication is the basis of a successful relationship. Informal meetings, making minutes available throughout the organisation, visits to see work and inviting all staff to observe board meetings are all useful ways of making sure that people throughout the organisation share a common understanding of what they are doing and why.

3.5   POLICY AND PLANNING

Any organisation, or any post, needs a policy statement which describes its aims, and a planning structure to guide it towards that aim, and both should be written down. The process of writing things down not only ensures that all those involved understand and agree what is happening, it also provides a fixed point against which progress can be measured. A general policy, covering the principal values and objectives of the organisation or the post, is fundamental. In some cases this will be supplemented by policy statements in specific areas like programming, employment or training. Many organisations have an equal opportunities policy, but it can be argued that this isolates issues and values which should permeate through the whole organisation.

Sorting out policy should be a collective process to which all members of the staff and management can contribute, as well as the audience or users, if only through systems of consultation and accountability. It will generally be undertaken by the management committee with senior staff, or by sole workers and their support groups as the case may be. It is possible

There are 3 levels of policy.
1. Overall organisational policy which encapsulates the values and aim of the organisation.
2. Policy which is specific to ongoing aspects or situations like employment or training.
3. Policy which is specific to events (like racism or harassment) which may arise but are not ongoing.

that the task of drafting a policy statement is too difficult to launch into straight away, and that everyone needs more experience of what they are doing before it can be done. In this case a simpler alternative is to agree the aim and objectives.

Setting aims, objectives and targets

Any new animateur or arts development project must define their aim and objectives, as indeed should freelance practitioners. The difference between the two can be easily summarised: an aim is what you exist to achieve and the objectives are the things you have to do in order to achieve it. So an aim is a single, clear statement of what you are there for, like this, which might fit a community music project:

> *Our aim is to promote participation in contemporary music in Huntingdonshire.*

The objectives show how the project proposes to achieve its aim:

> *We will do this by:*
>
> a. *creating accessible opportunities for people to hear, perform, compose and record music throughout the county;*
>
> b. *running music workshops throughout the county;*
>
> c. *promoting regular performances by local musicians and bands, and launching a tape production arm;*
>
> d. *liaising with local musicians, bands, music societies and other arts organisations to support and influence their work;*
>
> e. *offering an advice and information service to residents.*

This structure enables the organisation and other people to understand easily what it is trying to achieve, and to assess whether the steps it intends to take form a realistic route to its goal.

The aim of the post is often set by the funders before recruitment, but the objectives may not have been. Whatever the case, you will need to draft or review your aim and objectives to make sure that you, the person responsible for delivering them, understand and support the statements. Any drafting or review should involve consultation with key people about what the post is expected to achieve. These are likely to include your line manager and/or management committee, relevant officers in the local authority and RAB, any other funders (such as trusts), arts organisations and professionals with an interest in your field. At this stage, desirable as it would be,

---

The aims and objectives structure can be applied to projects of all types and sizes

Our aim is to offer a music information and advisory service to local residents.
We will achieve this by:

> a. *establishing a computer database of local musicians, music organisations, venues, classes, workshops and events;*

> b. *ensuring that it is available through the library information service, and by telephone at regular times;*

> c. *producing a free monthly newsletter to cover local music news;*

> d. *advertising the service through local radio, schools and colleges, the county council, musicians, venues etc.*

Or:

Our aim is to enable young black people in Huntingdon to explore music of their choice:
We will achieve this by:

> a. *contacting the local black community through community organisations, youth clubs, schools and colleges and discussing the project with them to agree if and how to go ahead;*

> b. *researching other black music projects in other parts of the country;*

> c. *setting up an advisory group to help inform the project;*

> d. *beginning discussions with local black musicians and bands.*

---

you may not be able to undertake effective consultation with local people or organisations, but this should be borne in mind for later review. Don't be afraid to take some time getting this right: you will have to live with the statements you agree, and your performance will be measured against them. The consultation about the post will in any case provide a useful starting point for establishing some of your most important relationships.

Try to make sure that your aim and objectives are

- clear and easy to read

- presented appropriately for a public statement

- comprehensive but not over-long

- precise but not restrictive

- logical and useful

Always take account of your actual and potential resources when setting your aim and objectives.

Targets, priorities and deadlines

When you have drafted your aim and objectives, you have a useful statement of what you are going to do, but it remains vague. How will you know whether you have promoted enough events, liaised with enough people, or run enough

If the aim and objectives have already been drawn up, they will normally have been included in the information about the post sent to applicants, so you should have seen them already. It may be that, on reflection, you feel they need revision in which case you will need to negotiate with your management and/or funders. It may not be easy to persuade them to agree to changes at this stage, but you should be able to reach a solution if your reasons for seeking them are well thought-out.
2.2 Starting a new post

2.3 Reviewing progress

workshops? What should you try to do first? The answer to that is to draw up a set of targets for each objective, linked to deadlines - ie the point by which you propose to have met your target. As before, consider your resources as you consider your targets. So the music project used as an example above could draw up targets as follows:

Objective: *to create accessible opportunities for people to hear, perform, compose and record music throughout the county;*

Target: *over the next twelve months we will liaise with representative sections of the community, including disabled people, ethnic minority communities and other interest groups to identify ways in which they wish to be involved in music activity .*

Objective: *to run music workshops throughout the county;*

Target: *in the next two years we will run ten - sixteen major music workshops, of at least ten sessions each and involving local musicians, evenly distributed between schools, community centres and other venues.*

Objective: *to promote regular performances by local musicians and bands, and launching a tape production arm;*

Target: *in the next two years we will promote up to ten music performances and produce a recorded collection of local music.*

Objective: *to liaise with local musicians, bands, music societies and other arts organisations to support and influence their work;*

Target: *we will establish co-operative working relationships with five arts organisations, and involve at least ten new musicians in our work during the course of each year.*

Objective: *to offer an advice and information service to residents;*

Target: *in the next nine months we will research music activity and provision in the area and build a database to hold the information; within eighteen months we will have publicised the service, and be distributing 200 copies of a music newsletter to interested people, rising to 500 at the end of the third year.*

The targets - which in reality would probably be more detailed and precise than those above - translate objectives into clear goals against which you, your funders, and anyone else with an interest will be able to measure your performance. But even within the targets, you will need to prioritise: which sections of the community are to be consulted first, in which order should you approach arts organisations? You cannot do every-thing at once, and setting priorities is the best way to ensure that you control how you proceed.

It will help to recast this thinking in the form of a plan, preferably spanning two or three years, and showing the pre-cise tasks and projects to be undertaken in each year, together with the internal developments which the organisation needs to carry out. Once it is supported by budgets, this plan, which need only run to three or four sides of A4, will provide suc-cinct but reliable information about what your post is intended to achieve, how and when it will do so, and at what cost.

Setting aside the wisdom or otherwise of the objectives and targets above, which serve a purely illustrative function, it should be clear how an apparently huge task can be cut down into manageable sections. Don't expect to achieve it straight-away: it's a gradual procedure which will become easier as all those involved become more familiar with it. This planning process can provide you, your management and your funders with an agreed road map to follow, and although it might appear to be a bureaucratic way of getting down to a job, it will help immensely in the months and years to come. It will also serve as a structure through which you and your manage-ment can actually define, carry out and monitor the tasks you have set yourselves.

Business planning
In recent years arts organisations have given increasing atten-tion to the planning process, partly at the behest of the funding system. In large and medium-sized organisations three or five year business planning (also known as strategic planning or three year planning) has become commonplace. Its value as a management tool for single posts or small community-based arts organisation remains open to question. If such a planning process can be undertaken without taking up a disproportion-ate amount of staff and management time, and if the skills and commitment to it exist, then it can contribute significantly to the organisation's understanding and control of its work. On the other hand, it can become a burden much heavier than it is useful, like an electric blanket on a camping holiday.

Business planning is a thinking process, not the achievement of a fat document which nobody looks at again. Most business plans will cover, in addition to detailed financial information, the following areas:

- The name of the company
- The objects described in the governing instrument
- Its aim and objectives
- Its structure and organisation, including legal status
- Information about board and staff members
- Its products and services (ie the work you do)
- The size of its market (ie potential audience)
- Any competition it faces (ie other people offering a similar service)
- A marketing plan
- An analysis of its strengths and weaknesses
- A list of its premises and equipment

This analysis and presentation reflects commercial thinking, and you will need to consider carefully what a business planning exercise will achieve for you. If it is a condition of funding you may need to take advice on how to make it work in your situation.

3.6   MONITORING AND EVALUATION

The planning process above will only help you keep control of your work if you keep a record of what you do and compare it with your intentions. This is usually referred to as monitoring (keeping track of the work) and evaluation (assessing its worth). The difficulties in this process arise from the judgements which necessarily underlie any concept of value. Like planning, this should be a continuous process, something that you do regularly. So each project will be monitored and evaluated, with a report presented to your management, and, perhaps every three or six months, you will set time aside to step back from the work and look at progress as a whole. At this stage the information gathered from separate projects can be collated to bring out the critical information which will make management decisions possible.

For instance, if you have collected figures on each of the projects you have undertaken in the preceding six month period, you will be able to determine how many people, on average, attend your workshops, and whether some types of work or locations attract more people than others.

You may find that, without realising it, most of your energy has gone into one or two areas to the detriment of others, or that you have actually exceeded the targets you set yourself. Whatever you discover, you will know better what you are doing, and consequently be able to make informed decisions about whether you need to make changes to your work.

You should put effort into monitoring and evaluation because it enables you to:

- assess the worth of your work to your audience

- demonstrate its worth to management and funders

- measure your performance against your targets

- use the facts learned to inform your policy and planning

The monitoring process
Monitoring is about generating quantitative and qualitative information with which to assess your work. The first, being essentially factual, is fairly straightforward to collect. It could include:

- the number of workshops, performances or events

- the length and duration of workshops, performances or events

- the location of work (geographical reach)

- the numbers of participants

- the cost of events

This basic information will reveal how much work is going on, but in most cases there will be a need for further information if you are going to look at the work in the context of specific policy objectives. Among the most important of these is equal opportunities commitments. The achievement of targets in relation to programming and freelance practitioners should be monitored. This can show, for example, that black or disabled people form a disproportionately small part of the audience, despite stated policy priorities. Only by collecting statistics is it

8.2 Developing good practice - Monitoring

possible to know, rather than sense, what is happening in practice.

The use of averaging can produce simple statistics like the average attendance at a workshop, or the average cost of workshops, or the average cost per head of different types of event. But playing with statistics can become addictive, so avoid giving undue weight to the facts produced by this sort of exercise. Quantative information can only take you so far, since in these terms a well-attended but terrible workshop is better than a poorly-attended but very good workshop. Consequently, to its two dimensions must be added a third through the use of qualitative information.

5.11 Feedback   This, because it is essentially subjective and based on value judgements, is more difficult to gather and to collate. It is looking for answers to questions like:

- What artistic qualities did the workshop/event/ performance have?

- Was it well managed and supported?

- What did the audience feel about it?

- Would they do the same thing again, or something different, or are they reluctant to get involved in the arts at all?

- How much did the audience enjoy the workshop/event?

- What did they like or dislike about it?

The answers are found by seeing the work and using your experience to make comparisons with other projects; by talking to the audience, participants and artists, and trying to hear what people want to tell you, not just what you planned to find out. Sound and image recording can help to capture the intangible qualities of a piece of work and contribute to the final reporting process. But the answers to these questions are naturally subjective, so good evaluation links them with the quantitative information described above.

In conducting a monitoring and evaluation process, it's important to be open and clear about what is happening. People should be told why you are recording facts, views and opinions, and what you intend to do with them. This is not just fair, it will encourage people to participate.

Making use of the results
The results of the monitoring and evaluation process need using, not filing. If the subject is a single event, a short report,

supported by figures and photographs should be given to your management and funders. In many circumstances, though not always, it will be right to give it to those involved in the project; in others you can discuss the results verbally. Where a project has been particularly innovative or important, or where you want to raise the profile of the work, it may be worth widening the circle of those to whom you report through a seminar or conference or by publishing a report.

All the projects and separate pieces of work need collating at regular intervals into the basic information with which management decisions are made: the work in practice needs relating constantly to your stated policy objectives. Monitoring and evaluation are an integral part of a management cycle: begin by determining policy and planning how to carry it out, do the work, and then monitor and evaluate it in order to revise your policy and planning in the light of experience.

5.4 Residencies, workshops and classes
5.5 Performances, publishing and festivals - Publications
5.6 Training courses and conferences

3.7 MANAGING YOURSELF

The basic management structures already discussed above form the best framework through which you can manage your own work. If your post, whether it is independent or part of a team, is supported by good, clear management structures, it will be much easier to get on with your job.

Managing your work as an employee

If you are an employee you should have a job description, though its usefulness may vary. People still draw up job descriptions that consist only of a long list of undifferentiated and vague duties which start with 'to promote literature in northern England' and end 'to share in office cleaning'. Even if you have a good basic job description, it will probably need revision following the agreement of objectives and targets for your post, because there should be a close connection between the two.

4.3 Employment
4.4 Self-employment

A good job description will include the following information:

- Job title and grade

- Base or location

- A single-sentence summary of the job's function

- The posts or people for which the postholder has responsibility, and the manager or committee to whom they are in turn responsible.

- The limits of authority of the post

- The key tasks, of which there should not usually be more than six or seven. They should focus on output or results rather than input, so it is clearer to define a duty as being 'To keep the building in good repair', since this is a clearly measurable objective, than to define it as 'Maintaining the office and building', since there is no objective measure of achievement in the second phrase.

- Additional tasks - two or three minor duties (like liaising with colleagues) which are part but not central to the purpose of the job

- Review procedure

Some job descriptions include the hours to be worked

Restricting the key tasks to six or seven makes them achievable and enables the postholder to prioritise the things that they are actually there to do. If the job really cannot be reduced to that number of principal tasks, it may need rethinking: perhaps two people are needed to do it. If the post has been well thought through the key tasks in the job description will correspond closely to the objectives and targets which have been set, particularly if they have been set for a single post, rather than an organisation.

Managing your work as a freelance worker

If you are working on a freelance, self-employed basis, agreement of the aim, objectives and targets of your work are essential since they should properly form the basis of your contract. No-one should accept a contract for services which does not specify exactly the nature and extent of the services which they are to provide. The best way to define those services is as a series of tasks, linked to clear targets, and based on the agreed aim and objectives for the post or piece of work. You will also need to know your limits of authority and accountability.

Time management

4.4 Self-employment - Contracts for services

In practice most animateurs and arts development workers have jobs which are really too big to be done by one person. The consequence is that they often find themselves under pressure, rarely able to do more than respond to the most urgent demands on their time, and less effective than they could be.

2.2 Starting a new post

The first step in dealing with this problem is to assess whether a job can be done. You can only respond to a task in one of four ways:

- Do it well
- Pass it on
- Do it less well
- Don't do it

It is only discouraging to have tasks which, in fact, you either never do or do badly, so where they exist in your job, try to weed them out. If they are essential or can't be passed on, make sure you get training to be able to do them. With a coherent statement of tasks you can begin to prioritise.

Although most workers keep a list of work they need to do, they don't necessarily prioritise the tasks on that list effectively. If you recognise that there are two different types of pressure behind any task: urgency and importance, then you can begin to prioritise. Everything you have to do can be classed as to whether it is urgent, important, both or neither. It will generally be obvious whether or not something is urgent, but it's easy to mistake urgency for importance. Your targets and/or job description will help you identify the tasks that are actually important, because they are the ones that further your overall aim.

In that context you can start to create a sensible order in which to deal with your tasks, starting with those which are both urgent and important. There are some basic ideas which may help you organise your time, and relieve the stress of having so much to do:

- Decide when you work best (eg morning, afternoon, evening etc) and keep those times for your most important tasks.

- Set aside blocks of time to do important tasks, if necessary by switching on the answerphone or working away from the office.

- Deal with incoming mail and messages straight away, but quickly, sorting it into important or urgent things for which you will set aside time, information which you will look at, and things which should go into the bin.

- Don't be afraid to throw things in the bin when you've dealt with them.

- Don't put off jobs you don't enjoy; don't spend a long time doing things you do enjoy but which aren't important.

- If you have regular routine tasks to deal with - eg financial records - set aside a regular part of the week to do them in, and stick to it.

- Have places in the office for things, and file as you go along.

- Set aside regular time for reading publications etc, and one afternoon a month for things which are neither important nor urgent.

- Review your work list and keep it up to date.

- Try to leave your desk clear before you leave: it'll look better in the morning.

- Don't take work home on a regular basis.

3.8   MANAGING OTHER PEOPLE

Managing staff is a large subject on which much has been written. Alternatively it could be argued that it is all fundamentally a matter of common-sense and respect between people. If you are working within an organisation with an established management structure, you will need to make sure that you understand the rules and procedures by which you are to operate. If that is not the case, you will have to establish procedures to codify your management structures so that everyone knows where they stand. Your management committee should certainly take the lead in this area, since terms of employment are their responsibility. If you are new to managing staff it would be wise to go on a short training course to strengthen your knowledge and confidence in the field.

Good management systems will ensure that staff

- have a clear understanding of what is expected of them - their job description should specify not only their duties, but their limits of authority, standards of performance and process for reviewing their work;

- feel that they understand the organisation, its plans, opportunities and difficulties, and that they can contribute to decisions about its overall direction;

- feel that they have the encouragement, advice and support of their manager, that he or she has an interest in their work and wants them to succeed;

- receive proper recognition of their successes, and understanding, support, and guidance when they fail;

- are treated with consistency, reliability and fairness, and feel confident that they can raise a problem or grievance with the appropriate person.

In addition to regular one-to-one meetings with their line manager, staff should also have their work reviewed in an annual or bi-annual appraisal involving members of their management committee. This should consider not only the individual's work and performance, but their training needs and other issues which they wish to raise. This appraisal should result in a written report to be given to (and agreed with) the member of staff. To some extent staff management systems, like constitutions, remain invisible except when something goes wrong. But when it does, the quality of those systems will determine how quickly and effectively the problem can be resolved.

7.2 Preparing a training plan

3.9   USING CONSULTANTS

Independent consultants have been used increasingly by arts organisations in recent years, with mixed results. Sometimes bringing in an outsider with a fresh perspective and particular skills can be just what is needed to tackle a particular job or resolve a problem within an organisation. But an inappropriate consultant or mismanaged process can leave those involved confused and resentful, and wishing the money had been better spent. If you think that using a consultant might help your current situation, ask for advice from your RAB or Arts Council officer, and talk to other people who have used consultants.

The Arts Council has a database of consultants and will supply a number of possible names in response to an enquiry.

The advantages of consultancies are:

- they can bring in new skills, new ideas or experienced advice

- they can offer training and support for staff and management committees

- the task-centred nature of the consultancy focuses people's minds

- outsiders can sometimes see situations more objectively and deal with problems more directly

- outsiders can sometimes be neutral and help heal rifts

Against these benefits are some potential drawbacks:

- they can be expensive and time-consuming

- bringing in outside 'experts' can cause resentment

- if your work or organisation is unusual you can spend a lot of the time teaching a consultant to understand it

- they may not achieve what you hoped

If you do decide to use a consultant, the following groundrules may help:

14.2 ☞ *Managing Consultancy*

- define the task you want done, and how much you can pay

- get several people to submit tenders, and interview them

- draw up a precise contract for the work

5.3 Commissioning other practitioners

Try to have reasonable expectations of what the consultant can do for you. Communicate effectively with them, because the information you provide will form the raw material with which they will work. Finally, try to choose someone whose input will leave you with better skills to tackle your own problems. Some of the best consultancies are in effect a form of tailor-made training to integrate new skills permanently into the organisation.

7.3 Types of training - Tailor-made training

3.10   DEALING WITH PROBLEMS

The best-managed organisations are not exempt from problems and disputes, but good management systems come into their own at such times. Disputes can arise in any of the relationships which characterise your work - with your funders, with contracted practitioners, with companies - or internally, between members of staff or between staff and management. The quality of the various decisions made in the past, and the rules and procedures established, will go a long way towards determining the way in which matters proceed. If you have a good staff management system, if you have drafted good contracts, if the plans on which your funding has been secured are good, you will be able to deal with most problems effectively.

However you will still need to negotiate a solution. Many people think they are better at negotiation than they really are, because they don't see themselves from the other side of the table. It is hard to judge how you come across to someone who is at best neutral and at worst hostile, but it is important to try to look at yourself objectively. You may find, when it comes to negotiation, that you adopt an unnecessarily hard position, based on an adversarial approach which finds success only in the defeat of your opponent. Alternatively you may overvalue the avoidance of conflict, and so be prepared to concede more than you should. Either of these approaches is likely to create, out of resentment, deeper problems.

It doesn't really matter who is in the 'right': you have only to look at present conflicts to see how their sense of being right leads politicians to prefer slaughter to peace. All that really matters is finding a solution which everyone finds acceptable - if not ideal. The best agreements are those which leave both parties satisfied, because they will work to make them succeed. If one party is forced into an agreement which is basically unacceptable to them, their commitment to it will be negligible, and the solution temporary. In some cases that is unavoidable: if the conduct of a member of staff requires dismissal, nothing is going to make that easier for those involved. But where a lesser problem arises between members of staff, or you are trying to resolve difficulties at organisational level, you need to find a solution which is acceptable to everyone.

This approach, which has been termed 'principled negotiation', has gained ground in recent years. It sees the parties not as opponents looking for victory, but as people looking for a mutually acceptable solution to their problems. Principled negotiation helps remove the personalities from consideration because it focuses on the problem, and on the interests of each party. It involves considering a range of possible solutions - rather than trying to get what you have already decided you want - and working to find the best in the circumstances for everyone involved. It demands that negotiators be more objective, governed by reason rather than feelings, and co-operative rather than confrontational. It is not immediately easy to shift your thinking in this way, and you may still be negotiating with someone whose stance remains confrontational. Even so, your principled approach will help you resist unreasonable pressure and work towards a better solution. Similarly, although the power of negotiators may be unequal, adopting the right approach can only help your case.

14.2 ☞ *Getting to Yes*

Where negotiation cannot provide a solution, you may need to use an arbitrator, though such situations are fortunately very rare. However, planning an arbitration procedure can be a useful safeguard where you are negotiating an important contract or agreement. In general, the use of good management practices and procedures will help depersonalise disagreement and create fair strategies to address problems when they arise.

5.3 Commissioning other practitioners

ADMINISTRATION

4

4.1 EFFECTIVE ADMINISTRATION

4.2 SETTING UP AN OFFICE
Getting the office working ◆ Simple systems and ideas ◆ Computers

4.3 EMPLOYMENT
Employed or self-employed? ◆ Recruitment ◆ Person specification
◆ Recruitment timetable and advertising ◆ Application procedures
◆ Shortlisting and interviewing ◆ References and checks ◆ Induction
for new employees ◆ Contracts of employment ◆ Salaries and
expenses ◆ Terminating employment

4.4 SELF-EMPLOYMENT
Self-employment and being paid ◆ Tax and National Insurance
◆ Contracts for services

4.5 WORKING WITH VOLUNTEERS

4.6 FINANCE
Budgets ◆ Keeping financial records ◆ Pay As You Earn (PAYE)
◆ Value Added Tax (VAT) ◆ Security and fraud ◆ Management
accounts and bank reconciliation ◆ Accounts and Auditing
◆ Bank and building society accounts

4.7 LEGAL MATTERS
Professional advice ◆ Health and safety at work
◆ Insurance ◆ Copyright

4.8 MARKETING
The role and value of marketing ◆ Defining the
target audience ◆ Public image ◆ Marketing tools
◆ Writing copy ◆ Working with designers and
printers ◆ Distribution ◆ Working with the press
and broadcast media ◆ Personal contacts

4   ADMINISTRATION

Summary
This chapter deals with practical administrative matters, starting with basic principles and setting up an efficient workspace. Sections 4.3, 4.4 and 4.5 look at the principles and practicalities of being at work, covering employment, freelance work and the situation of volunteers. The next section covers financial management, budgeting, bookkeeping, VAT, and accounting, while section 4.7 looks at legal matters like insurance, health and safety and copyright. The final, long section looks at the whole question of marketing work.

4.1   EFFECTIVE ADMINISTRATION

The mere thought of administration can be enough to send some people into quiet depression. This section doesn't aim to convert you into an enthusiast for office life, but it will try to show you that administering your work effectively is straightforward, good practice and very good for your peace of mind. Administration is part of everyone's working life, and doing it well is hugely preferable to doing it badly.

Administration is a means to an end: the administrative systems you use should be designed to help you organise and keep control of the relationships which are central to your work. Setting up an efficient filing system is only useful because it enables you (or anyone else) to find a letter or document without wasting time. Sometimes - as in the case of financial controls - the administrative structures also ensure that other people (management or funders) can see that the work is being undertaken as agreed, and to acceptable standards. The administrative needs of different organisations and individuals vary because of the nature of their work. There is no single right approach, but there are some ground rules to bear in mind.

Administrative systems should

- be clear, simple and understood by everyone involved

- ensure and show proper control of resources

- support staff in the achievement of their objectives

- support good management practice and provide a day-by-day framework through which policy is executed

• occupy an appropriate amount of time relative to the main purpose of the organisation or post

The rest of this section deals with some of the key areas which animateurs, development workers and practitioners are likely to have to deal with: as in other parts of the book, not all of it is relevant in all cases.

4.2   SETTING UP AN OFFICE

The first thing to think about is the location of your office: is it in the right building, in the right area, or even in the right town? Can people find you easily? Are meeting rooms and catering facilities available? There is a lot to be said for an office space you don't have to pay for, but not if it means that you become inaccessible to the people you are trying to work with. If you have any flexibility, consider the relative merits of sharing office space with another arts organisation, being based in the community or local authority sector, or finding space on your own. There are advantages and disadvantages to each situation, which you and your management group are best placed to assess.

> Taking on premises is a complicated business, and you will need legal advice, particularly if you are signing a lease.
> **4.7 Legal matters**

Once you have the location - whether by choice or not - do what you can about its image. Try to make sure that your office is well signposted, or if there's a reception area, that the staff know what you want them to do when people arrive to see you. Imagine the effect which the building in general, and your office in particular, will have on visitors. You need them to see you as efficient, competent and professional: it will be much easier if your office projects the same image.

The space you use should be comfortable. Look at the existing lighting, and simple ways to improve it. Try to make sure that the temperature and ventilation are adequate throughout the year. If you are getting furniture, you will find secondhand office equipment relatively cheap and plentiful. If you don't have any money, you may find that the local authority or other large organisations are prepared to pass on surplus furniture, or that there is a local furniture recycling store open to voluntary organisations. Putting up pictures and bringing in plants is not a waste of time if it makes your workspace more pleasant. Make sure you have facilities to make tea, coffee etc, and adequate sanitary and washing facilities.

> Provision of toilets and washing facilities, and much else is governed in law by the Offices, Shops and Railway Premises Act 1963. If you are responsible for the premises you use, you should be aware of its provisions and any future legislation which may be enacted.

You will also need to think about safety and security in your offices. Again, if you are based in someone else's premises, you will only need to familiarise yourself (and colleagues as appropriate) with the existing fire precautions and security procedures. If your offices are self-contained or independent, you will need to establish procedures and equipment to comply with the relevant legislation.

Getting the office working

You will need a certain amount of basic equipment to make your office an efficient workspace. Some things - like a telephone - you'll need immediately, but others, particularly expensive items like photocopiers or computers, can wait. Some equipment can be leased, but it is wise to be cautious - not all leasing arrangements are good for small organisations: if possible, deal through the local authority or its supplier. As always, take advice: ask other arts or voluntary organisations what equipment they use and how they acquired it. You can divide your needs into basic equipment and desirable additions which would improve your office management, for example:

Basic	Desirable
Telephone and answerphone	Fax and minicom
Typewriter	Word processor or computer
Comfortable chair and desk	Informal seating area
Filing cabinet	Cupboards
Good lighting	Natural light
Diary and address book	Wall planner
Tea-making facilities	Fridge
Access to a photocopier	Your own photocopier

In addition to the equipment, you will need stationery and other consumable supplies like paper, folders etc: try to find an office supplies wholesaler rather than using high street stores. Unless you are working within another organisation like a local authority, you will need to get letterhead printed. Remember to include all the important information - credits to funders, charity registration number, registered office - as appropriate. A single-sentence summary of your work on your letterhead may help potential funders or users understand its nature more quickly.

The legislation includes the Health & Safety at Work, etc Act 1974, and the Offices, Shops and Railway Premises Act 1963. The former covers such areas as safety of the working environment and equipment, provision of information and training for employees, and safety policies. The latter covers questions of overcrowding, ventilation, temperature, lighting, cleanliness and maintenance. First aid is covered by the Health and Safety (First-Aid) Regulations 1981.
14.3 ☞ *Management of Voluntary Organisations*

If you need to get a telephone line installed, ask BT which numbers are currently available and choose one which is easy to remember.

3.2 Legal structures for organisations

Simple systems and ideas

A post-book should help you keep a track (and potentially show an auditor) of where your stamp purchases go. If you have substantial mailings it may be worth talking to the Post Office about franking machines.

Establishing some basic systems will help make life easier. Keep a post book, recording the incoming and outgoing mail; use a date stamp to mark the date you received letters or items through the post. This is particularly important if you are receiving money through the post. If you work with other people, keep a message book, and a board or office diary to say where people are. Keep an address book or card index and add new names to it. As your work grows you will need to establish mailing lists sorted into groups - eg audience, artists, funders, education etc - and you may be able to set up a computer database. Databases - which organise addresses on computer and retrieve them according to set categories - can be very useful, but they are expensive and can use a lot of time.

Keep files of projects and your contacts with key organisations and funders. Simple ring binders in which you put papers in chronological order will do, though you can use a filing cabinet for the same purpose. Keep notes of important meetings and file them for future reference. Begin to build a reference library of useful books. As a rough guide you need to spend at least £100 a year for books and subscriptions, but a small investment of this sort will pay for itself many times over. Particularly useful are the publications of the Directory of Social Change, Bedford Square Press (the imprint of NCVO) and the Arts Council. You will need to subscribe to specialist publications and organisations in your field: your artform organisation will be able to advise you on these. Get your name added to the mailing lists of relevant organisations - the RAB, the local authorities, arts organisations - to help you keep up with what other people are doing.

Computers

If you are storing information on computer you must comply with the provisions of the Data Protection Act 1984. In particular if you hold information of certain types, you will need to register with the Office of the Data Protection Registrar. **15.10 Contacts.** The Registrar publishes free guidelines and advice can be obtained over the phone (0625) 535777. See also **14.3** ☞ CDMF Information Pamphlet 1 *The Data Protection Act*

If you can afford one, or have regular access to someone else's, a computer will be enormously helpful in managing and administering your work. They can make some common tasks - writing, bookkeeping, mailing lists etc - much quicker and easier and, through programmes like desktop publishing (DTP), they can significantly improve your presentation. If you are new to computers, you will need training to get started: many colleges offer short courses. You should also have experience of different systems before you decide which of the various types you should invest in: visit the dealers, try things out, read relevant magazines and ask for advice from enthusiasts. The world of computers is changing very fast, so it is often worthwhile buying second-hand equipment; it will meet your needs, but be much cheaper because it does not have the latest features. Whether you are buying new or second-hand, choose an established dealer who will offer after-sales service.

4.3   EMPLOYMENT

Employed or self-employed?

Employment is closely regulated by complex and wide-ranging legislation, and only basic guidance is given here. The first issue which some workers have to face is whether they are employed or self-employed. This is not always straightforward, and may have nothing to do with the views of the person or organisation offering the job: it will ultimately be decided by the Inland Revenue. There are ground rules you can use to assess your position.

You **are** employed if:

- you have a contract of employment

- your contract is not limited to a fixed term (though you may have a fixed-term contract of employment)

- your hours and place of work are specified

- space and equipment for you to work with are provided

- the terms of your employment include holidays, sickness, maternity and redundancy rights

- you receive a wage or salary and a pay advice or payslip

- tax and national insurance contributions are deducted from your salary

You **may** be self-employed if

- you have a contract for services

- your contract is limited to a fixed term

- you are responsible for delivering a service, not for a specified number of hours worked

- you are responsible for your own workspace and equipment

- your contract does not mention holidays, sickness, maternity and redundancy rights

- you receive a fee

- no deductions are made from your fees

Key employment legislation includes:
Trade Union Reform and Employment Act 1993
Employment Act 1989
Wages Act 1986
Employment Protection (Consolidation) Act 1978
Race Relations Act 1976
Sex Discrimination Acts 1975 and 1986
Equal Pay Act 1970 (and Amendment Regulations 1983)
Disabled Persons (Employment) Acts 1944 and 1958
Children and Young Persons Acts 1933-1969
8.1 Basic principles - The legislative framework

14.3 ☞ *Guidelines for Contracts, Working Conditions & Payscales* (CDMF 1991) and *Employed or Self-Employed?* IR56/NI39 available from Inland Revenue or DSS offices.

- you pay tax on your annual earnings and national insurance contributions under classes 2 and 4

- your income in fees comes from several sources

4.4 Self-employment

Not all of these factors are decisive, and each case will be considered by the Inland Revenue on its merits. However, their presumption will be that you are employed unless you can clearly demonstrate that you are not. The rules have been applied quite rigorously in recent years, and the Inland Revenue is more reluctant to accept some workers as being genuinely self-employed. It is, of course, possible to be employed and self-employed at the same time. For instance, a worker may be employed part-time by a local authority, and supplement that income with self-employed income as a freelance practitioner. If you are uncertain of your situation or are experiencing difficulties in this area, you should discuss the problems with your management group or supervisor or consult an accountant.

Recruitment

3.7 Managing yourself - Managing your work as an employee

Once it has been decided to take on staff it will be necessary - unless you are working within a large organisation with a personnel department - to begin a recruitment process. The first step is to decide who is going to be involved - management, other staff and funders - and get them together to discuss the post. Careful thought at this stage can avoid serious problems at interview or even during employment, so it is worth spending time getting things right. The need for the post will have been identified by the organisational planning process. From this you can draw up a job description, and decide other matters like the management structure and terms and conditions of employment.

8.1 Basic principles

There is an important legal framework designed to prevent certain types of discrimination in employment, and any employer should be aware of this. But, in addition to any legal obligations they may have, an employer with a commitment to equal opportunities will consider how to ensure that the post can be made accessible to all suitable applicants. This is not as straightforward as it might appear: the removal of unnecessary barriers to employment requires training, experience and imagination. It means asking of candidates everything that is essential to the job, and nothing which is not. The difficulties arise in deciding what is essential: for example, the ability to drive a car (even to own one) is frequently attached to arts development and animateur posts. This excludes many people who cannot drive, including many disabled people, from applying for the post even though they might have much more important skills and qualities to offer.

Person specification

Although a job description defines a post and is the guiding document for an employee, it is not necessarily the best tool for selecting the right candidate. Consequently more and more organisations are using person specifications. This is a list of attributes and skills which a person will need to do a job and is based on the tasks specified in the job description. Its use can help minimise subjective (and potentially unfair) assessments in recruitment. The person specification for a music development worker might - for example - include the following points:

Attributes:

- experience of music promotion, and public performances

- familiarity with a wide range of contemporary and world music

- self-confidence and the ability to be self-motivating

- experience of the arts funding system

Skills:

- experience of running music workshops

- proficiency in at least one musical instrument

- working knowledge of sound technology including recording skills

- good verbal and written communication skills

- good planning, management and administrative skills

Using a list of skills and attributes which the job demands makes it easier to assess candidates on what they can *do* rather than who they *are* . Skills and attributes are sometimes divided between those considered essential, and others which are desirable, but some would argue that fair assessments should only be made on the basis of essential factors.

Recruitment timetable and advertising

Having agreed the job description, person specification and associated matters, you can draw up a timetable for advertising the post, including a deadline for submission of applica-

One arts development worker promoted events throughout two rural counties for eight years, making use of public transport to get about. When she did learn to drive, her employer observed no change to the way her work was carried out since her real effectiveness lay in her abilities as a development worker, not a driver.

3.7 Managing yourself

tions. It's helpful to set dates for shortlisting and interviewing at this stage as well. The interview date can be included in the advertisement, and should certainly be included in the information which is sent out to people who enquire.

Decisions about where to advertise a post will depend on its nature and the size of the budget that is available. The *Guardian* is probably the single most effective outlet for a full-time arts job. Other possibilities include the local press and national publications with distinct readerships (*Asian Times, Disability Now, Disability Arts In London, Arts Management Weekly* etc). Circulation of the advert through the RABs, agencies like CDMF and Sound Sense and relevant arts organisations is also important.

Application procedures

It is bad practice to ask questions which are not relevant to the post partly because the answers obscure the matters legitimately under consideration, and partly because it implies that a particular sort of person is required, rather than the best person to do the job. One national charity asks applicants whether or not they are home owners, a question whose relevance to their suitability for employment is hard to identify.

Whatever application procedure is adopted, the information - including background information about the organisation offering the job - which goes out to potential candidates should be full, clear and well-presented, if it is to encourage them to apply and help them present the best application. Offering to discuss the post informally with potential candidates can also help improve the quality of the applications received, though such a discussion should not involve anyone who will be on the interview panel.

Application is generally by letter and CV or by application form. The use of application forms enables you to request the information you want, and makes comparison - and fair treatment - of candidates easier. Some organisations use numbered application forms: the first page, with personal details and qualifications is removed, and shortlisting is done on the basis of the information which specifically applies to the job. Consequently, those involved in shortlisting do not know the names, gender, age or education of the candidates, and base their assessments only on the relationship between the answers given and the person specification.

8.2 Developing good practice - Monitoring

It is good practice to request information to carry out equal opportunities monitoring. This should be in the form of a questionnaire with boxes to tick, and it must explain why the information is sought, that it will be used statistically for monitoring purposes only, and that candidates do not have to provide it unless they wish to do so. Such forms should have no identifying features and should be separated, unseen, from the applications on receipt. The Commission for Racial Equality has monitoring forms which can be adapted and extended, as do some local authorities and RABs.

Shortlisting and interviewing

It is rarely necessary to interview more than six candidates, so the first stage is for the interviewing panel to agree a shortlist from the applications received. Interviews will form the basis on which the final decision will be reached and they must therefore be planned appropriately. The following suggestions may help:

- communicate well with candidates - write to them promptly, and if they are invited for interview tell them not only when and where, but who will be interviewing, how to reach the venue, what expenses you will pay etc;

- ask whether candidates have any access requirements and ensure that you can meet them;

- timetable the day so that each candidate has long enough, interviews will not overrun, and the panel has adequate breaks;

- arrange for someone to greet candidates when they arrive, perhaps show them round, and answer their questions;

- use a light, comfortable room and think about the seating arrangement;

- ensure that the interviewing panel is well-balanced, skilled and informed of their task;

- use the same format of questions testing elements of the person specification for all candidates, and make sure that the panel has an agreed and consistent system for scoring candidates;

- if it is appropriate to set a practical exercise, or request candidates to prepare a presentation, they should be told in advance and sufficient time should be allowed;

- allow time for the candidates to ask questions;

- set aside adequate time to consider candidates, even if you have to meet again the next day;

- agree a second choice candidate (if possible) in case the first declines the offer;

- contact the successful candidate by phone as soon as possible, and write promptly to other candidates.

Some employers give unsuccessful candidates reasons why they were not successful, with some positive comments on their good qualities. Alternatively, if you are prepared to give honest and constructive feedback, you can invite people to phone you to discuss the interview. But these options, despite being helpful to unsuccessful candidates, do require considerable sensitivity on the part of the employer.

References and checks

The Rehabilitation of Offenders Act 1974 entitles people with convictions of less than 30 months custody legally to deny those convictions according to a set scale depending on the gravity of the offence and the passage of time since conviction. People who are members of some professions (eg doctors, accountants, solicitors) and people seeking certain types of employment (including work with people under 18, over 65 and/or those with disabilities or mental health problems) are never entitled to withhold information about criminal convictions.

References can be sought before or after interview, and a job can be offered subject to satisfactory references. In practice references are usually sought simply by writing and enclosing a job description, but asking specific questions, or using a form can elicit better responses. In either case, the main point is to demand and take up references; general statements (as in *to whom it may concern*) are of no value. In the case of certain sensitive posts - for instance in work with children - it may be necessary to make further enquiries. You should seek the advice of the police or social services department before beginning the recruitment process in such situations.

Induction for new employees

The advantages of putting energy into a proper induction programme for a person taking up a new post are obvious. They will settle in more quickly, avoid unnecessary errors and misunderstandings and become more confident and so more effective. If induction is neglected, new workers who arrive with enthusiasm can find their energies dissipated by the scale of their task, and consequently become frustrated and resentful. An induction programme should initially be aimed at relieving the stress of the first day in a new job, and then at gradually equipping the new worker for their task.

A new worker should be met by a member of the management committee or an appropriate colleague - probably their line manager - and shown where they are to work, and where the facilities are. They should be introduced to colleagues and other staff with whom they may come into contact, and later to representatives of funders and other arts organisations. Over the coming days and weeks time should be made to take the person through their job description and any planning targets set for their post. Particular attention should be given to ensuring that the worker understands their position within the management structure, and what provisions have been made to offer support in the early days. The terms and conditions of their employment should be dealt with by going through their contract. It would also be sensible to look at the training needs of the new worker and begin to establish a training plan.

7.2 Preparing a training plan

82

Contracts of employment

All employees are entitled to receive, within eight weeks of the start of employment, a written statement of the terms and conditions of their employment (though it is better to include that statement with any offer of a job, so that it is clear on what basis the job is offered and accepted).

14.3 ☞ *Guidelines* published by CDMF, and *Executive Survival*

Such a statement must in law cover the following principal matters:

- **Names** - of the employer and employee.

- **Dates** - on which employment (and continuous service) began.

- **Duration** - of employment if temporary.

- **Salary** - stating the amount and scale (if applicable), and arrangements for payment.

- **Title** - the actual title of the post.

- **Hours** - stating the regular hours of work.

- **Place of work** - and address of employer if different.

- **Leave** - stating leave entitlement (including statutory holidays).

- **Pension** - stating what pension arrangements exist (if any).

- **Collective agreements** - details of any such agreements (eg trade union negotiations) which affect the employee.

- **Sickness and Statutory Sick Pay** - dealing with the rights and responsibilities of the employee and employer in the eventuality of sickness.

- **Notice** - stating the period of notice to which each party to the contract is entitled.

- **Grievance and disciplinary procedure** - outlining the rights and responsibilities of the employee and employer and the systems in operation.

In the case of an arts development worker or animateur, a good contract (or statement of terms) of employment, would also cover the following points:

- **Duties** - the job description should form an appendix to the contract, which should state how it can be reviewed.

- **Leave** - stating the arrangements for taking leave, and for carrying unused leave forward from one year to the next.

- **Compassionate leave** - covering arrangements in appropriate circumstances (eg family bereavement).

- **Maternity leave** - covering rights and duties of employee and employer in appropriate circumstances.

- **Parental leave** - covering arrangements in appropriate circumstances (including paternity and adoption).

- **Expenses** - stating entitlement and arrangements for claiming expenses incurred.

An employer will not normally seek to control the outside interests of an employee but may legitimately wish to be informed of some of them. For instance, an employer whose resources were provided in part by an RAB might reasonably wish to be informed if an employee became a member of the board of the RAB.

- **Outside interests** - dealing with the employee's rights to take on other paid or honorary work.

- **Union membership** - the employee's rights to be a member of a trade union or professional association.

- **Training** - covering entitlement to training through courses, short placements and unpaid leave.

- **Health and Safety** - covering the employee's and the employer's responsibilities under the relevant legislation.

- **Equal opportunities** - covering the rights and responsibilities of employee and employer within the organisation's equal opportunities policy or statement; (this is sometimes given as an appendix).

4.7 Legal matters - Copyright

- **Copyright** - dealing with the copyright position of art and other work undertaken by the employee during their period of employment.

- **Redundancy** - describing the situations in which redundancies may be declared and the procedure to be followed.

Salaries and expenses

4.6 Finance - PAYE Payments to employees are regulated by the Wages Act 1986 and the Equal Pay Act 1970.

The tax and national insurance contributions of employees are deducted from their gross pay by their employer, who sends it to the Inland Revenue, with additional contributions. The money paid to employees after deductions is net pay, and belongs entirely to the employee. Whether they are paid by cheque, in cash or by bank transfer, all employees must be given an itemised pay slip on or before their pay day. These are important since they provide details of any deductions from salary. A copy of the end of year statement (P60, showing annual total pay and deductions for tax and NI) sent by the employer to the Inland Revenue must also be given to the employee.

Generally speaking, legitimate expenses reimbursed by an employer are not taxed, but the rules in relation to mileage allowances in particular have been tightened up in recent years, and the Inland Revenue tax the so-called 'profit' element of some allowances. Guidance leaflets are available from the Inland Revenue.

Terminating employment

There are a number of reasons for which employment may be terminated, other than by mutual consent. But employees who have been continuously employed for at least a month and who work more than sixteen hours a week (eight hours once they have been employed for five years) have statutory rights which an employer must observe. An employee who believes that they have been dismissed unfairly, or that their rights have in some other way been denied them, is entitled to seek redress through an industrial tribunal. If they are seeking damages in respect of financial losses resulting from breach of contract, the case will be heard in the County Court or the High Court: this is also the case for a freelance worker with a contract.

An employee may be fairly dismissed for reasons relating to their ability to do the job (including health) or their conduct; because of redundancy (or other substantial reason such as organisational restructuring or the expiry of a fixed-term contract); or because they could not continue their work without infringing the law. In addition, the employer must show that their procedure in implementing the dismissal was fair. In practice, where there is a thorough and fair disciplinary procedure, it will be necessary to show that this was properly followed, and that the employee was dismissed fairly.

> The reasons for fair dismissal are outlined in the Employment Protection (Consolidation) Act 1978.

4.4 SELF-EMPLOYMENT

Self-employment and being paid

Some arts development workers and animateurs are freelance contractors providing services to a number of clients. Others, working as part-time employees, supplement their work with freelance work undertaken on a self-employed basis. Both can experience difficulties convincing others of their self-employed position. The Inland Revenue is the first, but not always the

> For the difference between employment and self employment see **4.3.**

Employees have many rights which self-employed people contracting for services do not have. These vary depending on the period of continuous employment, although some are automatic for all employees. Among the most significant are the right to:

• protection against discrimination on grounds of sex or race

• a statement of the terms and conditions of their employment

• itemised pay slips

• sick pay and maternity benefits

• time off work for various reasons

• fair treatment of grievances

• not to be unfairly dismissed.

hardest to deal with: if you are genuinely self-employed the Inland Revenue will accept this.

Problems sometimes arise because the worker concerned is, in terms of their duties and management relationships, treated as an employee by an organisation which, for whatever reasons, is not prepared to take on the responsibilities of employment. Since employment confers rights on the employee, and imposes responsibilities and additional costs on the employer, there will always be some organisations which will seek to keep workers self-employed. If you find yourself in this ambiguous position, the best course is to operate in accordance with the employment status you are granted. In other words, if the organisation which has offered you the post insists that you should work on a self-employed basis, you should follow that through in terms of providing a service, rather than a number of hours, and building a client-contractor relationship.

Even if you have persuaded the Inland Revenue that you are genuinely self-employed, it can be much more difficult to persuade some organisations - among whom education authorities are notable - to pay you as a self-employed contractor. This is because, in the event that you default on your income tax and national insurance liability, the Inland Revenue will seek to recover that liability from the employer who paid you without making deductions. Some people will accept your Schedule D tax number (ie the tax reference given by the Inland Revenue to your self-employed work) as proof, others will require a letter from a chartered accountant or even confirmation from the relevant tax authority. How far you take this will depend on the amount of money you are due, and the length of the contract.

Tax and National Insurance

As a self-employed person you are still liable for income tax and national insurance contributions. The only difference is that they are not deducted at source by an employer, but paid by you at the end of the financial year (in the case of income tax), or on an ongoing basis (in the case of national insurance).

It is illegal to avoid paying income tax if you are liable. Income from work undertaken as a self-employed person is taxed under Schedule D. You are personally responsible for notifying the Inland Revenue of this income whether or not they send you an income tax return. You must notify your local Inspector of Taxes as soon as you start self-employment, and you must submit accounts (usually for twelve month periods) without undue delay. Failure to do so may result in interest and penalties being charged in addition to any tax liability.

As a self-employed person, you will be taxed on your profits (once certain allowances for earnings free of tax have been made). Some expenses, incurred wholly and exclusively in the pursuit of the work, can be set against the profits, thus reducing the total on which tax is ultimately payable. These include materials, equipment and some - but not all - travel costs and are termed tax-deductible expenses. It is important to understand that they are not deducted from the tax liability, but from the gross profits, *before* assessment of tax liability is calculated. Take for example, an artist whose annual profit after personal allowances is £10,000. At the current 25% basic tax rate, they would have to pay the Inland Revenue £2,500. But, if they had allowable expenses of £2,000, the profit would be reduced to £8,000, and the income tax liability to £2,000.

This area of regulation is complex, and an accountant - whose fees are themselves tax-deductible - can offer good advice, and help in discussions with the Inland Revenue. Whether you employ an accountant or not you must keep full records of all earnings and expenditure, including receipts and payment advices so that you can prepare your accounts and justify their accuracy. If you are paying tax through PAYE as **4.6 Finance - PAYE** well as doing freelance work you still have to complete tax returns for the latter.

Liability for national insurance exists on both employed and self-employed work: the former is paid through PAYE, but if you are self-employed you have to arrange your own payments. Self employed people are liable for two different types of NI contribution - Class 2 and Class 4. The Class 2 contribution is a weekly sum and may be paid four-weekly by direct debit from a bank account, or by stamping a card. You are liable for these contributions unless you hold a 'small earnings exemption certificate'. This is given to people expecting to earn less than a given figure each year, and must be applied for in advance and not at the end of each financial year. The Class 4 contribution is calculated on your income tax assessment after deducting capital allowances and losses, but before deducting personal allowances. It is charged at rates and to levels determined annually by Government.

Contracts for services

As a self-employed person, you will need to agree contracts with clients, to specify the services you are providing, the fees you are due, and any other relevant arrangements. This sort of contract will be similar to those discussed in connection with contracting artists in section 5.3. In different circumstances you will provide your own contract, or be required to sign one

See the *Guidelines* published by CDMF

drawn up by someone else. In either case the contract should properly cover the following matters:

- **Names** - of the parties to the contract.

- **Dates** - specifying the period of the contract.

- **Service** - in respect of which fee is to be paid.

- **Fees** - stating the amount and arrangements for payment.

- **Expenses** - stating entitlement and arrangements for claiming expenses incurred.

- **Hours** - although some statement of the number of hours or days to be worked can be made, care must be taken to ensure that this is not done so as to imply employment rather than delivery of a service.

- **Insurance** - the respective arrangements and liabilities for public liability and personal insurance of the parties.

- **Sickness** - arrangements and liabilities in the case short and long-term sickness.

- **Copyright** - dealing with the copyright position of art and other work undertaken by the worker under contract.

- **Termination of contract** - stating the circumstances in which the contract may be terminated by either party and the notice due.

In some circumstances it may be appropriate to include a clause on:

3.10 Dealing with problems
5.3 Commissioning other
practitioners

- **Arbitration procedure** - outlining the procedure to be followed in the case of a dispute which cannot be resolved by the parties.

In a contract for services there may legitimately be no provision for leave, training, or many of the other matters which should be covered in a contract of employment. Contracts for services vary considerably depending both on the services involved and the parties to the contract.

4.5 WORKING WITH VOLUNTEERS

In community-based arts work - as in much other community work - the dividing line between a user of the service and a volunteer can be hard to establish. A rule of thumb could be the degree of commitment offered - if someone agrees to come and help for a regular time each week, you should perhaps be thinking of them as a volunteer rather than a user. Other volunteers may become involved in specific areas of your work - like basic administration - because they have time and or skills in that area. The local Council for Voluntary Service (CVS) will help you contact people interested in voluntary work. Students looking for work experience placements can also make a useful contribution. In any of these situations, it's important not to underestimate the time involved in managing a volunteer, or to fall into the trap of using them as cheap labour. The successful involvement of volunteers depends on the activity being worthwhile to both parties.

Some of the legal considerations which affect employees - for instance concerning health and safety at work - apply equally to volunteers, and adopting high standards will benefit everyone. It is quite normal to pay expenses incurred by volunteers - for instance travel costs - but you will need to establish and follow clear guidelines on this to avoid problems. It is important that expenses should not be able to be construed as payment for services, since this can affect the entire nature of the relationship between yourself and the volunteer. It could also have important repercussions for any volunteer entitled to state benefits. Guidelines should be drawn up by your management committee with advice from an accountant, Council for Voluntary Service (CVS) or other suitably experienced adviser.

You should consult your insurers about the way in which your cover may be affected by the involvement of volunteers, and whether you need to extend cover in some areas (for example to include their personal property). It may also be sensible to prepare a short contract or letter of agreement for volunteers, stating the nature of their involvement with the organisation, and the commitments each party is making. This can be supplemented by an information pack covering such things as management structures, health and safety, insurance and so on. The extent to which you need to consider these points will depend entirely on the role of volunteers (if any) within your work.

Apart from the practical matters which you have to consider, you need to look at the underlying principles of using

Advice on working with volunteers can be sought from the local Council for Voluntary Service, or The Volunteer Centre UK. It is also worth talking to other arts and voluntary sector organisations in your area. NCVO publishes a number of relevant books and pamphlets.

An elderly woman living in a residential home memorably asserted her right to have access to professional tuition in the arts in the same way as if she were able to attend the local college. She had paid her taxes and her rates all her life and didn't see why she should have a service in any way different to that offered to anyone else.

volunteers. Whilst you might welcome the various offers of voluntary help that come in, you have to ask yourself whether it is appropriate to use volunteers in all situations. For instance, would it be right to use a practitioner as a volunteer to run sessions which you would normally pay someone to run? To what extent, if at all, is it fair to expect participants to access the arts through the good will of a volunteer? One workable rule is to make use of volunteers only in areas which support your core work - for instance in tasks like marketing, driving, administration - but not in the delivery of the programme itself. But each voluntary organisation must establish its own code of practice with reference to its aim and philosophy.

4.6   FINANCE

14.3 ☞ *Organising Your Finances*

If you are responsible for keeping financial records, but do not already have experience in this area, training should be arranged either within the organisation or through an appropriate external training course. Keeping control of financial affairs need not be difficult and is at the heart of effective management, but it is essential to be equipped for the task. It may help to look at financial records as another way of explaining what is expected to happen, or has happened within an organisation. Accounts and financial records use figures instead of words, but to anyone who has learnt the language, they can provide a clear and complete picture of one aspect of an organisation.

Budgets
A budget is simply a list of projected income and expenditure, drawn up in advance of an accounting period. Its complexity - perhaps extending to sub-budgets - will depend on its subject, but the principles remain the same. It shows how much money is expected to come in, and from where, and how much is expected to be paid out, and for what. A budget is a key management tool, since it records what was expected to happen and, by comparison with what actually did happen, it highlights operational successes and failures. Getting a budget right is a matter of experience and judgement, and you will need help and advice if you have not done it before. If you are new to a post, and are presented with a budget drawn up by someone else, discuss it with them or your management, in order to find out what knowledge and assumptions underlie the figures. A budget is no help unless you understand the facts or aspirations it represents.

See **Table 1**

A typical, simple budget for an adequately-funded animateur post:			Table 1
Income	Year 1	Year 2	
Regional Arts Board	7,000	6,000	
County Council	7,000	7,000	
Borough Council	2,000	4,000	
Project grants	3,000	4,000	
Earned income	500	1,000	
Total income £	19,500	22,000	
Expenditure			
Salary	12,500	13,000	
National insurance (ENI)	1,450	1,500	
Training	750	800	
Office costs	500	600	
Travel	750	800	
Telephone & postage	500	600	
Programme budget	3,000	4,500	
Total expenditure £	19,450	21,800	
Surplus/(deficit)	50	200	
Brought forward		50	
Reserves	50	250	

Keeping financial records

This is often referred to as bookkeeping and is the basis of all financial management. An accountant can make sense of a disorganised jumble (though with justifiable complaint), but if the records do not exist at all, there is nothing anybody can do. Bookkeeping is like a project diary - it is a way of recording on a daily basis what happened - but it is essential that the diary is kept up-to-date and accurate, in order for the organisation to fulfil its legal obligations and justify the trust placed in it.

Day by day, money goes into an organisation, and is paid out by it. Each transaction is recorded in a ledger or analysis book or, in more sophisticated cases, on computer. The record will show the date of the transaction, who it was made with (ie who paid or was paid money), the amount and the budget item to which it relates. As time passes, it is then possible to assess how the earlier forecast matches reality.

See **Table 2** at the end of this chapter - note that income records must always be kept separate from expenditure records.

The simple recording of transactions must be supported by documentary evidence. For arts organisations money will usually come in through bank transfers, cheques or cash (from box office receipts and other sales). In the case of the first two there will be records like bank statements, remittance advices and the paying-in book. In the case of cash income particular safeguards must be adopted, such as counting money in the

Bands are perhaps the most important exception, since they often want to be paid in cash after the performance. This can be a problem, especially if it means that you have to attend an event with several hundred pounds in your pocket. Every organisation which encounters this problem will need to seek its own solution, but paying people out of the box office takings is never good practice, since it distorts the transactions.

presence of more than one person. Cash should always be banked and never used for paying expenses. Money paid out will almost always be in the form of cheques, which in themselves form a documentary record (supported by the bank statements) of the transactions. However since they do not explain why a payment was made, an invoice or receipt is also needed for each item.

All the documentation supporting transactions must be carefully kept to justify the transactions to any person or body entitled to enquire, including your management, funders and accountants. The simplest way to look after these papers is to put them in ring-binders with the date of the transaction and the cheque or reference number written on each. Income records should be kept in chronological order from the date they were banked. Expenditure records must be kept in the order of payment - ie corresponding to the cheque number. This is required of anyone registered for VAT but is best practice in any organisation. Separate ring binders are needed for income records, expenditure records, bank statements, and other documentation (eg official orders) which don't belong elsewhere.

If you have to handle the finances and pay bills yourself, you will need the following items as a start:

- a file for bills to be paid

- a file for invoices you have issued

- a secure place to keep the chequebook and paying-in book

- a ledger or analysis book

- separate ring-binders for income and expenditure records (ie remittance advices and paid invoices), bank statements and odds and ends

- office equipment like a calculator, stapler, hole punch and date stamp

You may need to run a petty cash system, alongside the main bank account, to cover small payments (eg travel expenses to volunteers). Petty cash accounts are straightforward if properly run, and you can get advice from your manager or accountant on setting up a system if necessary.

Keeping control of the finances is not difficult so long as you follow some basic rules:

- set aside a regular time each week to do the work and don't let the work accumulate;

- keep everything in numerical order or, for income, date order;

- always complete cheque stubs and paying-in books;

- be methodical and clear in what you do;

- keep all the documentation and records; if in doubt, file it until you can show the accountant.

Pay As You Earn (PAYE)

Employees pay income tax and national insurance contributions through Pay As You Earn. If you are employed in an established organisation, you will be put on the payroll and will probably have no contact with PAYE except through your payslip. However, you may have to operate a PAYE system yourself, or oversee someone else who does that work. If staff are to be employed and a PAYE system is not already in place, you should contact the local tax office who will allocate a reference number and provide you with the forms and instructions on setting up and operating PAYE.

See Inland Revenue Booklet P7, Employer's Guide to PAYE, available from any tax office.

Value Added Tax (VAT)

VAT is a tax levied on supplies (including services and goods) made by someone registered for VAT in the course of their business. Different rates of VAT apply to different supplies: most attract the standard rate (currently 17.5%), some a zero rate, and some are exempt. In simple terms people who are registered must submit quarterly returns, showing how much VAT they have charged and paid, and passing over any surplus of tax charged to the Customs and Excise. Where they have paid more VAT than they have collected, they can claim a refund.

VAT is covered by the Value Added Tax Act 1983

Items currently zero-rated for VAT range from food and water to gold and banknotes.

Whilst everyone - including registered charities - must pay VAT where it is due, there are some reliefs available to voluntary organisations generally, and further reliefs available to registered charities. An organisation or individual must register for VAT if their earnings from relevant supplies exceed an annual limit (£45,000 from December 1993, but liable to change). Some types of grants may be considered earnings by Customs & Excise, but this is a technically complicated area. It is possible to register voluntarily for VAT, even if earnings do not exceed the registration threshold but it is unlikely that any

See Customs and Excise booklet 700/1/88, Should I Be Registered for VAT? and Public Notice 700, VAT General Guide.

freelance practitioners, animateurs, or small arts organisations would find it beneficial to do so.

Security and fraud

30% of larger private companies and nearly 10% of local authorities detected frauds of more than £50,000 in the last two years, and the trend is upward. **14.3** ☛ *Protecting the Public Purse.*

People who are honest sometimes forget that others may not be. Good financial systems do not rely on individual integrity, but have inbuilt safeguards against fraud or dishonesty. Such safeguards not only protect the money, they protect those who are responsible for it. The first and principal safeguard for any arts organisation is to have their accounts audited annually by a qualified accountant. Since financial security is unlikely to be an area of expertise you possess, it is worth employing an accountant who can keep you in touch with good practice and advise on improvements to the financial management systems.

Management accounts and bank reconciliation

Never assume that the balance on your bank statement represents the money you actually have, since it will not take account of income you have received but not yet banked, or cheques which have not yet been cashed.

It will usually be necessary to review the financial situation monthly, and the bank statement provides a good opportunity. When it arrives, you should check every item on it against your own records, so that you can be sure that no errors have been made, and that your records of how much money you have coincides with the bank's. This task is called a bank reconciliation, and you may need help the first time you try to do it.

At the end of each month, or perhaps once a quarter, it will be necessary to prepare management accounts, either for your own information or for your management or funders. Management accounts simply compare the total income (actual or guaranteed) and expenditure (actual or committed) with the budget in order to identify potential discrepancies. Sometimes these will be easily explained: a grant is received late, or a training budget is used up because of a recent course. Sometimes they show that there is a problem which needs action: perhaps forecasts of earned income were too optimistic, so money will have to be found elsewhere or expenditure reduced.

This sort of information underlies the financial juggling imposed on all publicly-funded organisations. Unlike commercial enterprises which seek to maximise their profits and build reserves for reinvestment or payments to shareholders, publicly-funded organisations have to operate annually without building 'excessive' reserves which would justify cutting their grants in the next year, or deficits which could bring the same result on the grounds of mismanagement. Because they are obliged to walk this financial tightrope, the management teams of small arts organisations need regular and accurate management accounts to guide their decision-making.

Accounts and Auditing

At the end of its financial year (which will probably, but does not have to, run from April to March), the organisation will need to draw up its annual accounts. These consist of two elements: an income and expenditure account and a balance sheet. The first presents the total figures for everything that happened in the preceding twelve months, while the second presents a picture of the organisation's finances on the last day of the accounting period. Neither gives, on its own, an adequate account of what has happened, though the two taken together should do so. The income and expenditure account should not be confused with a receipts and payments account (which will sometimes form part of the final accounts). A receipts and payments account simply says what money has gone through the account during the past year. An income and expenditure account is based on that, but takes into account the organisation's debtors and creditors, thus providing a truer picture of its financial affairs.

The money owed to the organisation by its debtors, and the money owed by it to its creditors, will also appear in the balance sheet as assets and liabilities respectively. This is the part of the accounts which people often find harder to understand. In fact it is simply a table which offsets liabilities (mostly creditors) against assets (which will include debtors, cash at the bank or in hand, items - like insurance - paid in advance, and capital items like equipments and buildings) at a given point in time. Given the need for non-profit making organisations to keep close to a breakeven point, this is not always a very informative document, beyond signalling lack of working capital and potential consequent cash flow problems.

An organisation's accounts are drawn up from the financial records maintained during the preceding accounting period. The accounts can be drafted by anyone with the skills to do so, but in many cases are drawn up by an external accountant. But whether they are drawn up internally or externally, they do not have any independent authority unless they are audited. An auditor is an independent qualified person who examines the accounts, records and management committee minutes of an organisation, in order to satisfy themselves that the accounts drawn up present a true picture of its financial situation. Having done so they will provide a statement to that effect to accompany the accounts. Occasionally they will advise the organisation on ways in which its financial management can be improved or made more secure.

Not every arts organisation will be legally obliged to have their accounts audited but it is strongly recommended. The auditing of accounts may be a condition of grant aid and is required of organisations with certain classes of legal structure but, in any case, it inspires confidence in those with whom the organisation has dealings.

Bank and building society accounts

There is considerable high street competition in the financial services, and you may find it worthwhile to shop around for the best deal. You need to consider a number of factors including the rate of bank charges (ie what business customers pay on each transaction), the interest paid and charged, convenience in relation to your offices, the other services offered, and the institution's willingness to offer overdraft facilities should they be required. Some banks and building societies will offer more generous terms to charities or non-profit-making organisations, while others operate special accounts designed for charities. Decisions will have to be taken by the management committee and properly recorded, and named individuals appointed as signatories. Business accounts should always require signatures from two people on cheques and instructions to the bank. It is common for the chair, treasurer and principal staff member to be signatories, but whoever is chosen must be easily accessible.

4.7   LEGAL MATTERS

Professional advice

There are a number of areas in which you will need professional advice, principally from a solicitor or an accountant. Establishing a good relationship with an individual whose advice you can seek both formally and informally can be a great help. The better they know you, your organisation and your work, the better their help will be. Sometimes it will be possible to invite people with financial or legal expertise to join your management committee, though for some services - such as auditing - you will still require an independent person. If you need to find a solicitor or accountant, discuss their experiences with other arts or voluntary organisations in the area, and see if any firm can be recommended. Always have a preliminary discussion with the person or firm you choose - for which you should not have to pay - to discuss your needs and the service they offer before agreeing to use them. You will be a small client to most of these professionals, so it will help to find someone who has an interest in what you do: it will help ensure that your business is not always dealt with last. If you are working within a local authority, you may be able to make use of the internal professional staff.

Health and safety at work

The law relating to health and safety at work is covered principally in the Offices, Shops and Railway Premises Act 1963, and the Health & Safety at Work, etc Act 1974, together with a number of statutory instruments. The legislation covers the provision of toilets and washing facilities, ventilation, temperature, safety of the working environment and equipment (including the use of VDUs), first aid and much else. It covers not only employees but volunteers and visitors, and anybody responsible for building-based projects should be aware of the broad principles of the law. The Health and Safety Executive produces leaflets and guidance notes on this area.

15.10 Contacts

Insurance

Any arts organisation needs to review its insurance needs with an experienced broker or other suitable adviser on a regular basis, to ensure that it is complete and adequate to meet the risks associated with its work. Areas of risk against which any arts organisation should protect itself through insurance include:

Only insurance agents registered with the Insurance Brokers Registration Council are entitled to term themselves 'brokers'.

- **Public liability insurance** - to cover legal liability for injury to third parties arising from the organisation's activities.

- **Employer's liability insurance** - all employers are legally obliged to insure against liability arising from injury to their employees in the course or as a result of their work.

- **Buildings and contents insurance** - to cover the structure and/or contents, depending on requirements. If this includes computer equipment it may be worth extending it to cover the cost of replacing any software or data lost as a result of fire or theft.

- **Motor vehicle insurance** - to cover any vehicles owned or operated by the organisation.

- **Equipment insurance** - to cover the property of the organisation away from its premises against a range of risks.

- **Money insurance** - to cover a wide range of risks relating to cash.

The first four items are legal requirements. More specialist areas of insurance appropriate to some arts organisations or freelance workers include:

- **Professional liability insurance** - to cover against liability arising from advice or information given to the public or to other bodies.

- **Fidelity guarantee insurance** - to cover against the consequences of dishonesty in employees.

In addition to the basic insurance cover maintained at all times, it may be necessary to extend existing policies to cover short-term situations (eg to cover losses arising from cancellation of a particular event), or to take out additional policies for short periods (eg for an event involving pyrotechnics).

Freelance workers will need to arrange their own cover for some of the classes of risk above, particularly public liability insurance, but should also consider:

- **Injury or sickness insurance** - to protect their income in the case of injury, sickness or disability.

- **Motor insurance** - if a vehicle is to be used for work purposes, the insurers must be aware of that use.

All workers, whether employed or not, should consider whether or not to take out personal pension plans to provide for them in retirement. Personal pension funds operate independently of occupational pensions, and are unaffected by changes in employment.

Copyright

Covered by the Copyright Act 1956 and the Copyright, Designs and Patents Act 1988

Copyright law affects practitioners, animateurs and arts development organisations in two ways: in using material to which other people hold copyright, and in the copyright of original material created. Copyright applies to the creation of a piece of artwork, not to the idea. So, if Shakespeare were writing today, he would hold the copyright to his text of Hamlet, but could not prevent another person from retelling the story in their own words. Copyright can be held in original literary, dramatic, musical or art works; sound recordings, films, videos and TV programmes; and specific published editions. Copyright expires fifty years after the death of the creator of the work - or fifty years after it was first made available to the public, if no author is known. Different time limits apply to works which have been marketed industrially.

If you want to use material which is protected by copyright you have to obtain the permission of the copyright holder, for which you may have to pay a fee. Permission to use work is obtained from different sources depending on the type of work:

Music	The Performing Right Society	**15.1, 15.10 Contacts**
Film/video	The British Film Institute	
Books	The publisher	
Records/tapes	Phonographic Performance Ltd	

Establishing copyright in your own work can be achieved simply by producing it in some tangible form - as a typescript, video, tape recording, photograph etc. There is no need to go through any more formal procedure than this. But in relation to the work of animateurs and practitioners, the more important question is who holds the copyright - the employer, the practitioner, the participant, or someone else. In the case of work produced singly by a member of the public - such as a song or play - there can be no claim by anyone other than that person to the copyright. The difficulties lie more in jointly-produced work - such as dance pieces - or work produced by a practitioner in the course of their duties - such as a piece of music. The situation can be very complicated, and the potential rewards attached to holding copyright may be slight. However, some thought should be given to establishing common-sense and fair agreements so that everyone knows where they stand.

4.8   MARKETING

The role and value of marketing

Marketing in the arts has become increasingly sophisticated in recent years, as people struggle to keep and develop their audiences. There are so many competing leisure attractions hoping to win audiences who themselves often have less money to spend than in the past, that there is a real advantage in getting your message across. Marketing is, in the end, about selling, and that is not something which all artists, practitioners or administrators feel comfortable with. Consequently, in larger arts organisations, marketing is generally placed in the hands of people with real selling skills. Although some animateurs and development workers working in local authorities may have access to marketing support through the publicity department, most retain responsibility for marketing their own work. This is even more true of freelance practitioners. Whatever your situation, it is essential that you understand the underlying principles of arts marketing, and develop your skills in this area.

14.10 ☞ *Marketing Mime*

Your work may be excellent and your management of it exemplary, but unless you are maximising its audience you are doing it, yourself, and the funders no service. Marketing should be seen in an equal opportunity context: policy and practice should be guided and informed by your commitment to extending access to your work to everyone in your area. If your marketing is not reaching or not persuading large parts of the potential audience - including perhaps many of those you have prioritised - it is failing.

1.2 Basic principles

Defining the target audience

Before planning your marketing strategy, it is essential to define the target of that strategy - the audience. Nothing interests everyone: there are different audiences for different arts activities. Most promoters and arts centres today are able to send information about dance, or classical music, or contemporary literature just to those people on their mailing lists whom they know to be interested in that area. But audiences also have differing degrees of interest, from the committed enthusiast, past the mildly curious to the defiantly hostile: marketing strategies will be different for each target audience. Areas of interest also overlap: a new Kathakali dance performance with contemporary music and using themes and stories about birds could attract audiences with interests ranging from contemporary Indian culture to ornithology.

An animateur, practitioner or arts development worker has to begin by defining the audience for their work in general terms. If the audience, as defined by the post itself, is simply the population of a particular area, it will probably be necessary to prioritise. So, a literature development worker with a county-wide remit may prioritise, in policy discussions with their management, work in schools, or libraries, or with particular sections of the community or in particular locations. General marketing strategies, and the organisation's public image, will be influenced by the basic target audience, but

3.5 Policy and planning

individual elements of the programme - for instance, work with the deaf community or with older people - will need distinct approaches in order to be successful.

Public image

To present yourself, or your organisation, effectively to your audience and to the wider public you need a consistent style for your publicity material, so that it is recognised quickly. It should also be flexible so that it can be applied to a wide range of printed and other publicity material. If your budget allows, work with an experienced graphic designer, but before you do so, think about what appeals to you and what may appeal to your target audience by looking at:

If you are working in a local authority, try to establish good links with someone in their print department. If you need an independent designer, ask other arts organisations who they use. In some areas there are good community print facilities, and some colleges may be interested in a partnership approach.

- printed publicity material you like the look of, from arts and other organisations, trying to identify the common elements;

- printed publicity material produced by other people and aimed at the audience you are trying to interest.

The latter is actually more important since, though you need to project a public image you are comfortable with, how other people read it is what matters. Look at the material produced by leisure centres, local authorities, voluntary sector organisations, doctors, dentists and other professionals, the commercial sector, government agencies, clubs, societies and pressure groups and the magazines and newspapers read by your target audience. Not all will be well-produced or effective and much will be inappropriate to your needs, but it will help you understand some approaches which work.

Marketing tools

Having defined your target audience you can look at the range of marketing tools at your disposal:

- **Personal contact** - you will be trying to encourage interest and participation in your work on a daily basis through contact with groups and individuals. It may be possible to make presentations at meetings of key people - district librarians, associations of arts officers - or to talk directly to potential audiences. You should have some printed material with your name and contact details - a business card or leaflet.

- **Leaflets and flyers** - these can be linked to a specific event, or be about your work in general. They are relatively cheap and easy to produce, and can reach all sorts of places. They also give people a tangible reminder.

- **Videos and tapes** - a short video, explaining the event or project, perhaps showing the location or the type of work, can be much more effective in some situations than traditional leaflets. For instance, in promoting an event within the deaf community a BSL video would not only give the information, but also reassure the potential audience that their needs will be met. Similarly an audio tape for blind people and non-readers generally can be circulated to appropriate outlets.

14.3 ☛ *Charity Annual Reports*

- **Annual reports** - although the precise nature of the information to be included will depend on the legal status of the organisation, there is scope for making an annual report work for you. Annual reports are often produced with a view to impressing funders, but they should also aim to report to the users and audience of an organisation. An annual report which is readable, well-illustrated and interesting can explain the work to the audience, arts officers and charity trustees and will have a much longer shelf-life.

- **Newsletters** - can vary widely in style and sophistication, and their production and distribution can be a substantial drain on resources. But they can be a very effective way of creating a community of interest.

If you have high mailing volumes it may be worth talking to the post office about discounted postage rates.

- **Mailing lists** - anyone working in community-based arts promotion needs to build and maintain mailing lists of supporters and interested people. They are a precious asset, enabling you not only to carry out the work effectively, but forming a tangible pool of allies. Make sure your budget allows for the cost of direct mail.

Automated mailings using computerised records can prove expensive: it's not uncommon for six or seven identical pieces of mail to be received at one address in the names of different staff, many of whom may have left.

- **Databases** - or computerised mailing lists offer a significant step forward on simple mailing lists, but only if you have the equipment, and the time to manage them.

Writing copy

The text of publicity material is crucial to its effectiveness, but getting it right is difficult. Language which is clear to one person is off-putting to another; English is not everyone's first language. Many people will not even pick up a leaflet covered in text, so it is essential to keep information brief, to the point and approachable. Some basic rules can help:

- use short sentences

- use short, common words

- avoid padding, indirect language and artspeak

- use design to make text clearer

- use positive language

- say what, when, where and who (how and why are rarely relevant to publicity material, though they may interest you)

In 1989 the Plain English Campaign produced *The Plain English Course* which is designed to help organisations produce clear, well-written English.

When people have understood what you are trying to tell them, you have to ensure that they can take action as a result. So a publicity leaflet should never neglect to include information on what to do next - how to book tickets, register an interest or see further details.

None of these ideas implies writing 'down' or writing badly: clear simple language helps everyone understand your message in a world over-charged with information. Short training course are available in this area, but good copywriting is a skill which develops with practice and which depends ultimately on a good relationship with your target audience.

Working with designers and printers

The cost of computer desktop publishing has fallen dramatically in recent years, and if you have access to the facilities and an interest in designing your own publicity, they can offer control and cost-effectiveness. But they cannot give you a good eye for graphic design if you don't have one already so, if you have the resources, you may still wish to work with a designer. Ideally you will be able to establish an ongoing relationship with someone who understands your work, so that it is not necessary to keep going over the same ground. The same is true of a printer, who will also find it easier to work with the same designer over a period of time. You should think about the following points:

- **brief** - discuss the work you want doing carefully before the designer starts working, including style, format, content, method of printing, print materials, print run, estimated costs and timescale

- **roughs** - ask to see rough ideas before going ahead

- **proofs** - look at proofs at all stages, and check them carefully for typing errors and for other mistakes or omissions. Remember to check titles and headlines, and photo credits

- **photos** - use the best you can, and put the photographer, subject, with your name and address on the back

- **computers** - you will save time and money if you, the designer and the printer all work from compatible computer systems

- **quantity** - get the size of print run right to avoid waste or shortages

- **print ethics** - printing on recycled paper is becoming common, and some printers can also offer high environmental standards in use of inks and other areas

- **quality** - look at other work produced by the printer before choosing them. The Quality Assurance Standard (BS5750) provides some guarantee of the work

4.6 Finance - VAT

- **estimates** - get proper written quotes from the designer and printer, with full specifications of the work and costs, and check whether you have to pay VAT

You may be able to use a community printshop in some areas and this can be a good way both to keep costs down and build useful contacts. The growth of high-street printshops has made it easier to get basic design and print work done, and this can be a good first step if you are starting a new post. The field is very competitive, so shop around to get the service that suits you best.

Distribution
Having produced the leaflets, posters or other information you need to get them out to people. Obviously, some will be mailed out to your supporters, but others need to be distributed through some of the following outlets:

- shops, cafés, pubs and restaurants

- other arts venues, museums, and libraries

- schools and colleges

- doctor's and dentist's surgeries and health centres

- leisure centres

- voluntary sector organisations, CVS, CABs

- local authority buildings (eg community centres)

- day centres, welfare services, social clubs

- tourist information centres

The choice of venues will naturally be dictated in part by the target audience. If you are committed to involving people who do not use the existing arts provision, putting leaflets in the local arts centre will not be very relevant. Likewise if you are planning a youth project, you will leaflet schools, colleges, cafés and pubs before social clubs or tourist information centres.

For particular projects it is possible to tap into other networks. If you are running a project aimed at people with learning difficulties, you may be able to distribute material through Social Services, Education and voluntary agency networks. A school may agree to distribute information about youth music activities to its pupils. As a rule people will distribute information for you to their members or the people they are in contact with, rather than give you direct access to a mailing list.

Working with the press and broadcast media

It is not always easy to interest the press in community-based arts work though the more local the media outlet, the more interested they are likely to be. So the local paper, community radio and cable television will usually be more receptive to your approaches than regional or national organisations. It is also easier to build relationships with local reporters and editors and, as always, personal contacts can make your work much more effective.

The Arts Council publishes press lists (as do most RABs) with information on publications, press, TV and radio contacts for people seeking to publicise arts events.

To get general coverage of your work, you will need to prepare a press release, possibly with additional material like photos. A press release should be kept short (not more than two sides of A4, double-spaced) and to the point. Your copy writing skills will come in useful in presenting the information clearly, concisely and comprehensively. Give thought to the first sentence, since this is the hook which will get people to read on, and try to express the heart of the project or event. Press releases normally read a bit like the articles they eventually become - in other words they are written in the third person (he, she, it or they, rather than I or we), and often in the past tense. You may include a quote - even from yourself - which can be used by the journalists. If so, end the press release with it, and put it in quotation marks and preface it as: *Literature development worker, Herbert Lom, said: "We are particularly pleased by...."*

Local and regional listings magazines and diaries are a useful way of getting in touch with a potential audience. In different areas they are published by the local authority, the RAB, or independent companies, both non-profit-making and commercial. You will need to plan your work in good time to meet the copy deadlines.

Your finished information can be sent out to whichever press, TV or radio outlets you think may be interested in covering the project, but try to send it to a named person whenever possible. If local or regional TV is interested you will need to allow sufficient time to facilitate their coverage. More common, in community-based arts work, is local radio interest, and this may entail you visiting the radio station, or a journalist with a tape recorder visiting your project.

Personal contacts

The importance of personal contacts has been mentioned several times already, but it is worth stressing again in two contexts. It can be of the greatest importance to get funders to see your work. Certainly this is true of the officers with whom you have day-to-day contact, but it is almost more important to involve the ultimate decision-makers where you can: councillors, board members, mayors etc. The choice of events to which you invite them will depend on the person, but the time spent in doing it will be of great value in securing your work. There is a world of difference in the support a councillor may give to something they feel is basically worthwhile, and the support they will give when they know the people involved and have *seen* the value of the work at first hand. Take time to invite people personally, encourage them to come, and when they do, ensure you make time to speak to them.

The second area where personal contact is crucial is getting audiences or participants for your events. Some people are sufficiently self-confident to go and take part in a new activity with people they don't know as a result of reading some publicity, but many are not. Talking to people individually or in groups, letting them get to know you and trust you, is one of the most important marketing tools you have.

Table 2

The following table shows how a day's transactions can be recorded simply in an account book. Each line reads across the page showing the date, the source of income or payee, the reference or cheque number, the amount paid in or out, and the budget heading to which it is allocated. Each column can also be read downwards to give the total income or expenditure and the total for each budget heading, making the drawing up of management accounts relatively simple. Similarly the figures can be added horizontally or vertically to provide a check for accuracy. Naturally, bookkeeping systems can be much more complex than this, but keeping records in this simple format will be adequate for most small organisations and single posts.

INCOME

		Ref	Amount	RAB	County	Borough	Projects	Earned
	Brought Forward		9,678	4,000	3,000	1,000	1,200	478
3 Oct	Regional Arts Board		2,250	2,250				
3 Oct	County Council		1,500		1,500			
3 Oct	A Charitable Trust		250				250	
3 Oct	Workshop fees		20					20
	Carried Forward		13,698	6,250	4,500	1,000	1,450	498

EXPENDITURE

		Cheque	Amount	Salary	ENI	Training	Office	Travel	Tel/Post	Progrme
	Brought Forward		9,402	6,000	680	400	200	304	168	1,650
3 Oct	A course fee	000151	80			80				
3 Oct	Stationery	000152	15				15			
3 Oct	A Practitioner	000153	115							115
3 Oct	Room hire	000154	40							40
	Carried Forward		9,652	6,000	680	480	215	304	168	1,805

PROGRAMMING 5

5 PROGRAMMING

Summary

This chapter covers the whole business of setting up and carrying out community-based arts projects. Following a brief introduction, section 5.2 looks at planning and running sessions, and section 5.3 deals with commissioning other practitioners and companies. Section 5.4 covers practical, participatory work, while the next two deal in turn with presenting work - performances, publications, festivals etc - and running training courses and conference events. Section 5.7 is a project planning checklist which summarises much of the information in the preceding pages. Access issues are dealt with in section 5.8, work in schools and institutions in the next two, whilst the last section looks at getting feedback on work.

5.1 PLANNING PROJECTS

The planning process described elsewhere will help you identify and organise the programme of projects which are at the heart of your work. Even if you are starting a new post, and expect to be running every session yourself, it is sensible to set up a planned programme of distinct projects. It helps you keep control of your work, build proper management structures, and raise additional funds. The range of possibilities for projects is discussed in more detail below, but it includes:

2.3 Reviewing progress
3.5 Policy and planning
6.5 Planning a fund-raising strategy

- Workshops and classes

- Residencies

- Commissions

- Multi-media and inter-disciplinary projects

- Performances and promotions

- Festivals

- Training courses

Of course, none of these categories is rigid, and some projects will be two or more of these things at the same time. The exact nature of your programme will also depend on your own skills and ideas, the requirements of the funders, and the nature of the area in which you work. It is also likely to change over time as you gain experience, the community becomes more aware of the possibilities, and your work becomes established. For instance it is not uncommon for arts development workers to begin by doing all the work themselves, gradually building up to using other practitioners and companies to increase the range and scale of the programme.

Despite the endless scope for variation in the content of community-based arts projects, they will largely fall into two sorts: projects you actually run yourself, and projects where you are commissioning another practitioner or company to do the work. Although most of the ideas in this section apply to both types, the way in which they are considered and implemented will depend on your role in the project. If you are running projects yourself, their planning and execution will depend only on you. If, however, you are using other people, you will need to create structures through which you can ensure that people can deliver their best work and you can retain overall control of your project.

2.2 Starting a new post   **5.2   RUNNING YOUR OWN PROJECTS**

Planning

Planning a programme using the management techniques described in chapter 3 helps narrow your focus down from the large objectives and principles which inform your work, to the actual practicalities of running a two-hour workshop with a group of people in a community centre. If you approach your work in that methodical way, many of the questions arising from an individual project will have been resolved. You will already have decided:

- why you are doing the project

- who it is for, and how they will be involved

- what is the best format, timetable and content

- how it will be funded

- what will follow it and how it fits into your programme

By the time you have got this far, the things which still need thinking about will be the relatively minor practical problems of actually running the sessions. Much of this is a common-sense business of checking, and rechecking all the arrangements - date, times, venue etc - that have been made. By the time you turn up for the session, you should, if possible, have nothing to think about but the creative work itself and responding to the dynamics of the group and individual needs.

Running practical sessions

Approaches to workshop preparation vary, but few people turn up to lead a new class or workshop without having planned at least the first session. The content of the sessions will very often have come out of thinking about why they are being held in the first place. On the other hand, a willingness to adapt plans and respond to the interests that participants articulate on the day is essential. There are some general things to think about for all sessions:

- See the space beforehand if possible; if not, try to check that it meets your needs and those of participants.

- Get there before the participants if possible, so that you can welcome them: nothing is worse than rushing into a roomful of people who have already been waiting ten minutes and having to start without even catching your breath.

- Introduce yourself, the participants to each other (unless they already know one another) and try to remember their names.

- Talk about what is going to happen, reassure people about it: this may be their first experience of the arts since school.

- Try to help people focus on the expressive, creative side of the artform, rather than the technical: they will acquire as much or as little technique as they need to meet their own needs.

- Try to be aware of the different needs of participants, and ensure that no-one is causing problems for anyone else.

- Assess the risks that you ask people to take carefully, and try to create an atmosphere in which people feel it is safe to be adventurous. Many people give up the arts in later childhood because they are made to feel that they aren't good enough, that the gap between their aspiration and their achievement is so great as to render them foolish in trying. Few things are worse than feeling you've made a fool of yourself, and a good workshop leader will ensure that participants do not feel that.

Courses in developing dance leadership skills include the Laban Leaders Course and the Dance Leaders in the Community Scheme co-ordinated by Yorkshire Dance Centre. Short courses in running workshops are offered by a number of organisations including Regional Training Centres
7.4 Training providers

In the same way as a hurdler focuses on the finishing line, rather than the hurdles in front of it, it is often more productive to get people to think about the artwork they are interested in producing - however small-scale or personal it might be - rather than the technical stages they will have to jump over to get there. If people can become enthusiastic about a goal, they will take the difficulties in their stride.

- Try to imagine how you would feel in a room of strangers learning about an activity of which you know little.

Few practitioners or arts workers are able to run community-based sessions with a specific training to support and guide their work. Instead, practitioners draw on their general professional training and experience, their knowledge of the techniques and ideas of other people and their creativity and imagination to run sessions. The best training in this field is experience and working with people: you will learn from participants in workshops and from professionals in other fields. You will, of course, learn from other practitioners, so networking is essential. It can be very heartening to talk or work with colleagues, partly because you learn from them and partly because, seeing them learn from you, you realise that your own ideas and practice have much to offer. Working too much in isolation can sap the self-confidence of the most experienced practitioner.

Working through agencies
Some work may be set up and paid for by an agency - eg Arts Education Agencies, Shape/Artlink services - which commissions you to run a project for another organisation like a school, hospital or day centre. You may in turn contract other artists to carry out projects for you. In building such relationships decide whether the individual or organisation has similar objectives to your own, pays fairly and is proposing a sensible project. If its dealings with you are unprofessional, the chances of it being able to manage the project and support you properly may not be very good. Good contracts are equal, so you should not just accept the agenda presented by the agency if it doesn't cover all the things that you want to see agreed in writing. Don't be afraid to require people to match your standards of professionalism.

Working with venues and partners
2.2 Starting a new post - Making contacts in the community

You will often be working directly with venues - like schools or day centres -and creating partnerships with other people whose work interlocks with yours. Each of these contacts will be different, depending on the situation and the personalities, but despite good intentions real problems do arise either because of different expectations or because, when the project is actually happening, the organisation is under some sort of pressure (most commonly through staff absences). Where possible, draft a contract to cover the project, and get it signed by the head of the organisation. It should cover:

- the name of the parties to the contract

- the aim and a brief description of the project

- the names of the people who will carry out the work

- the date(s) of the work, the time of arrival, and the time(s) of the workshop or performance

- technical requirements and whose responsibility it is to meet them

- the numbers of participants and the number of staff present

- the respective insurance responsibilities of each party

- marketing arrangements and who will do what

- the financial contribution made by the host organisation (if any)

- the arrangements and liability if either side has to cancel the project

Where cancellation is no-one's fault - eg bad weather, industrial action - the arrangements will be different from those which apply when cancellation is due to one party to the contract.

The numbers of participants and number of staff present are the factors that change most often between agreeing a project and the day it starts, so be clear about your needs. You should not accept a situation where your agreements about numbers of participants and staff support are unreasonably disregarded since this will not only affect the viability of the whole project, it can, in some circumstances, leave you vulnerable and potentially infringing health and safety or care regulations. The best way to stress the importance of this point is to specify failure by the school, hospital or day centre to meet agreed numbers as a breach of the contract allowing you to terminate it. Where it is not possible to use a contract, a reasonable alternative is to write a letter after the planning meeting, confirming what has been agreed so that you can proceed with confidence.

You can create constructive partnerships with other artists and arts organisations, teachers, education advisers, social services staff, librarians, community centre managers, business and community leaders, voluntary sector workers and many more. Some of those partnerships will bring obvious benefits - perhaps in arranging joint projects, or getting free use of a public building - while others will bring less tangible, but not less valuable benefits, like understanding of the local community, ideas for new initiatives and so on. Making this sort of partnership helps you extend further into the community, and helps build support for your work.

5.3   COMMISSIONING OTHER PRACTITIONERS

It may be that part, or all, of your programme is to be undertaken by other artists, practitioners and companies working on a freelance basis. The first stage will be to identify people who can do the work through established networks:

- talk to people involved in arts development work and community arts

- talk with people doing the same job as you in other areas

- consult RAB and Arts Council officers, and their registers of artists and companies

- talk to local authority arts officers

- contact specialist artform agencies like CDMF, ADiTi, National Dance Agencies, Sound Sense, MAG, the Poetry Society, Theatre Writers Union, Independent Theatre Council etc

- see local performances and workshops

- keep in touch with local colleges and universities

The Visiting Arts Unit of the British Council can keep you informed about artists and companies from abroad who may be in your area.

Get yourself added to mailing lists of any relevant organisations and publications to keep up to date with new developments.

Choosing the right artist

From the many possibilities, you need to find the best match with the planned project. The most obvious factor will be the nature of the artist or company's work: if you need a writer, it will usually be clear whether it should be a poet, a theatre writer, a novelist or a storyteller, and so on. But to choose between their different strengths, approaches and experiences is more difficult. For instance, a writer who delivers stunning public readings, may not be an effective workshop leader, while another's strengths will lie in their ability to support and guide inexperienced writers. Even among those who specialise in workshops, different people will be more or less effective in different situations. Not everyone can help a group of writers with learning difficulties achieve their potential and not everyone is comfortable working in an inner-city youth club.

Although you will have to rely on your own experience and judgement, you should consider whether the artist or company has:

- previous experience of similar projects

- references you can follow up

- a demonstrable track record

- a professional approach to their administration and management

- high but reasonable expectations of you

- a flexible approach

- imagination and energy

- a quality you find exciting

In general

- Don't make assumptions about the artist, or about the participants or audience - discuss the project with them

- Don't be afraid to take a calculated risk by using someone with less experience, or in a context where they've haven't worked before - but if you do, make sure they have enough support

- Don't assume that the quality of their promotional material (high or low) reflects the quality of their work

- Don't be persuaded into making a choice you're not completely sure of

- Don't forget to take up references and seek other opinions

Working with practitioners and companies from abroad
Introducing practitioners from abroad into your programme can be a very exciting way to expand its range and to stimulate interest in your work. Unless you already have contacts with artists or companies working outside the UK, you will probably need to work with the Arts Council, British Council or your RAB perhaps to extend a visit, or to set up workshops or masterclasses alongside an existing tour. In such cases, the work permit required will be secured by the principal host organisation, but if you are inviting the artist yourself, don't forget to check that you can satisfy the legal requirements. Citizens of the European Union (the former European

A black senior citizens' club planning a writing project about the different Caribbean islands where the members grew up, specifically asked for a white writer to work with. The members explained that they wanted someone who didn't have any previous knowledge of Caribbean culture, so that they could have access to the person's skills as a writer while ensuring that the content of the work would not be influenced by anyone outside the group.

15.1 Contacts
Get advice from your art-form organisation, the Arts Council, British Council or your RAB.
14.4 ☛ *Europe, A Manual; Networking in Europe; Performing Arts Yearbook for Europe.*

Community) are able to reside and work freely in any EU country.

Contracting freelance practitioners

Advice on drawing up contracts for services can be obtained from the RAB, or from many of the organisations concerned with specific artforms - eg CDMF, ITC, etc. If your post is based in a local authority or arts organisation, check whether there are established guidelines for contracts.

When you have identified the artist or company you want to use, you need to fix the terms of your agreement. To avoid misunderstandings, or resolve disputes, the points agreed should be written down in the form of a contract. Contracts come in all shapes and sizes - a verbal agreement already constitutes a contract - from a simple letter to a long and complex document. There is no 'official' wording or format for a contract. It's only important that it should be clear, precise and comprehensive.

Contracts between a promoter or animateur and an artist or company will usually cover the following main points:

- the name of the organisation issuing the contract

- the aim and a brief description of the project

- the names of the people who will carry out the work (which, in the case of a company, may not be the same as the person signing the contract)

- the date(s) of the work, the time of arrival, and the time(s) of the workshop or performance

- how many people will be involved (in participatory work)

- technical requirements and whose responsibility it is to meet them

- the respective insurance responsibilities of each party (eg public liability, equipment insurance etc)

- marketing arrangements and who will do what

- the venue (and location within it if necessary, eg a room in a college)

- the fee, the services in respect of which it is being paid and the arrangements for payment (including when)

- the rates of travel and other allowed expenses

- the arrangements and liability if either side has to cancel the project

Avoid open-ended contracts where possible. If you are setting up a workshop which you expect to run weekly for say twelve months, you don't need to give an artist a contract for the whole period. A contract for ten or twelve sessions in the first instance is much more flexible since it creates a natural review period once the project is under way. At that point you may find that the artist isn't coping or delivering what was required, or the participants themselves may have expressed their desire for a change. A fixed-term contract enables changes to be made without either the acrimony or the sense of failure created by having to terminate a contract. Where you need to recruit for a large block of work - say for an artist-in-residence project - always include a three month probationary period which must be satisfactorily completed before the full contract is confirmed.

The contract should specify that it is a contract for services, not a contract of employment, and that the fee is paid on that basis. Don't be afraid to spell out clearly the tax and other obligations of each party. With larger projects it may be wise to include an arbitration procedure whereby both parties agree to abide by the decision of a mutually-acceptable third party in the event of a complete disagreement about the execution of the project. An RAB or local authority arts officer might agree to take on this role, though it will rarely be required.

The contract can be drawn up in the form of a letter, or as a separate document, but each copy should be signed and dated by the individuals or authorised representatives of the organisations involved. Each party must have a copy, and if there is an arbitrator, they should have a copy as well.

If you are very involved with contracting with practitioners or companies you may find it worthwhile to produce a standard form or, if you have one, to keep a basic contract on your computer.

Finally, although it's possible to work effectively by planning projects thoroughly, building strong relationships and using the minimum of formal contracts, it does not work the other way round: an impressive contract is no substitute for thinking a project through and discussing it carefully with everyone involved.

Fees and expenses

The payment of fees and expenses should be governed by policy, not individual judgement. If your post is part of a larger organisation - eg a local authority - there may already by policy guidelines in this area. If not, or if you are working independently, you will need to establish your own policy. Most RABs have recommended rates for artists, as do professional organisations like Equity; education authorities will have rates for adult education tutors. You can refer to these in

An artist-in-residence on a particularly sensitive project took on other work in another part of the country two months after appointment. His intention was to do both, but since this would have meant him working 60 hours a week, such an arrangement was deemed unacceptable since he would not be able to do justice to the first project. Fortunately, his contract included a three month probationary period, so it was possible to terminate it and recruit someone else.

working out your own rates, but whether you follow another body's or establish your own, it is essential that they are formalised. You should not pay an artist less than your basic fee - even if they themselves ask a lower fee. On the other hand, some artists and companies have their own charging policies, which may mean that you are asked to pay more than your agreed rates. A good fee policy will allow for this, by authorising fees above the standard rate in exceptional circumstances. If the artist's work or service is different, unique or of outstanding quality, and so will enable you to achieve your objectives better, you would be justified in paying more than the usual rate.

Troubleshooting and support

Greenwich Dance Agency operates a scheme which provides support and supervision for artists leading workshops, and which also ensures that their work fits within the organisation's philosophy. The scheme is described in a policy document, and the practitioner agrees with a staff member the criteria for observation. They then observe the session, and meet the artist individually to discuss the work, and offer support and ideas for development.

3.10 Dealing with problems

The process of writing and agreeing a contract is not only important in itself, it helps ensure that both you and the artist or company have thought through all aspects of the project you are undertaking. It will also provide a framework within which you can resolve problems. However, everyone will be happier if you can identify and deal with problems before they get to the point where people are reading the fine print of their contracts. Good planning is the foundation of a good project, and it is good practice to pay freelance artists or practitioners to attend a meeting to discuss the project beforehand. Ideally this will happen at the venue or host organisation and will involve any other relevant people. Once the project is under way, keep in regular contact with the artist, the participants and anyone else - such as the venue staff - involved in the project. Visit regularly, see what's happening and listen to what people have to say. Where necessary, try to help people understand each others' concerns, worries or doubts. Similarly, keep in touch with the artist away from the project: offering support, being someone to bounce ideas off or complain to, is not only good practice in itself, it will help you spot problems earlier and deal with them better.

Equal opportunities

Good equal opportunities practice should inform every part of your work. The contracting of freelance practitioners and companies is no different. However, it must be recognised that there are rarely adequate resources in community-based arts development to undertake a fully open and equal commissioning process for every minor contract.

On the other hand, a commitment to equality of access should translate into contracting the widest possible range of appropriate artists and companies. The best way to achieve that objective is to review your contracting annually, and check what work has been done and by whom. Monitoring enables you to assess how your stated policies are translated into practice, and so be properly in control of your work. Then, if you, your management or your funders are unhappy with the way things are developing, you can take action to bring about change.

5.4 RESIDENCIES, WORKSHOPS AND CLASSES

This section covers projects designed to enable people to participate actively in the artform in which you specialise or are promoting. There is a wide range of models which can deliver opportunities to participate and, as always, your choice will be dictated by what you are trying to achieve. Each offers different emphases and an effective programme is likely to use a combination of formats over a period of time. The following notes are intended for anyone not entirely familiar with the terms, but it should be remembered that they are used loosely in practice.

Residencies
The term was originally - and still is - applied to long-term placements of artists in specific situations, such as a college, which provided a bursary, accommodation and workspace in return for some teaching and/or community work. The idea of patronage - offering an artist a space in which they could develop their own work in a concentrated way - was central to the earlier schemes, as it often is today. The concept of the artist-in-residence has subsequently been extended to many settings, including hospitals, prisons, rural areas etc, where actual residence is not required by either party. In these cases - which usually last between three months and a year - the artist receives a bursary or fee in return for two or three days teaching or community-focused arts work. Some schemes simply offer a workspace with minimal demands being made on the artist's time.

But the term residency is also commonly used for projects which are more like long workshops. So a week's work by a musician or a mime company in a school is often called a residency, to differentiate it from a series of workshops. This structure has a number of advantages. An opportunity to concentrate on artwork for a clear and substantial period of time can help participants achieve a great deal - they can get somewhere fast. It is common for a week-long residency to end in the creation of an exciting piece of artwork, giving people an opportunity not only to explore their creativity, but to share that exploration with others. There are disadvantages, however. The most important is that unless further, perhaps more low-key, possibilities for work have been planned, all the positive achievements can evaporate quite quickly. It is not necessary for every project to go on for ever, so participants should know what the situation is, and how they could pursue an interest further if you cannot follow up a particular project.

Workshops and classes

Workshops and classes are shorter in duration than residencies, generally lasting an hour or two at a time, and usually running regularly over a period of months or years. Obvious examples are writers' workshops where people meet for an evening once a month, or Saturday morning music sessions for young people: there is no shortage of formats. Most workshops are run by a practitioner and to a greater or lesser extent are about passing on skills - though some writers' workshops provide an example of how to work successfully with only occasional professional input. Consequently their advantages over residencies lie in their ability to provide a framework through which people can build a firmer technical skill base and confidence over a period of time, and in their continuity of provision. On the other hand, a workshop programme can lose its focus, drift and get stale It can get bogged down in skill development to a degree which discourages people who don't see themselves as 'dancers' or 'musicians', but who want to say something through their artwork.

Perhaps there was once a clearly-understood distinction between workshops and classes, in which the first offered explorations of an artform by equal participants, and the second saw a teacher communicate knowledge and skills to students. If so, it doesn't exist today. There are people who operate like teachers in situations they call workshops, and others who have brought democracy into the classroom. The only reliable approach is to know what you want to achieve, and find the best means to achieve it, whether in your own work or in using other artists. In some ways the most important thing about the words is the effect they are going to have on the people you want to attract.

The term workshop is also used for one-off events lasting anything from half a day to three or four days: in other words, an event that seems too short to be called a residency. Likewise a residency by a dance or mime company in a particular town may result in a series of one-off workshops with different groups and communities in the area.

Taster or introductory workshops

In new areas, or working with people who have not had much experience of the arts before, taster workshops can provide a good opening. These can be one-off sessions to introduce an art form, or a series of separate sessions, perhaps run by different people, offering an insight into different artforms or styles. Taster workshops enable people to make an informed choice about the sort of work they want to be involved in, or the particular artist they want to work with. They work best when people know that the workshop is only an introduction and they are fully involved in deciding the range of work they would like to try. It would be unwise to run taster workshops without the resources and commitment to follow them up.

Commissions

Commissions are a relatively recent addition to the range of community-based arts work. Very successful projects have been run where an artist - composer, director, choreographer, writer - has been commissioned to work with a particular group or community specifically to produce a new work. The format and structure of the work varies, but the focus on production of a piece of artwork is constant. This naturally involves a degree of risk, since failure to produce something satisfying will colour people's perception of the whole project. When they work well commissions can combine the excitement and focus of a residency with the skill-sharing aspects of workshops. The key to success here - as in all such partnerships - is to ensure that everyone fully understands their role in the project, has realistic expectations of it, and is committed to learning from each other. You need to think as always about what will happen after the project.

Multi-media and inter-disciplinary projects

Collaborations between artists and practitioners in different fields can produce exciting opportunities to involve people in new and innovative areas of practice. Some collaborations - such as those between writer and actor, dancer and musician - are well-tried, but others offer the participating artists a chance to experiment within and test the boundaries of their form and technique. Performance groups have worked with video and film-makers to create new pieces of work drawing inspiration from both forms.

When the East Midlands was Region of Dance in 1993, a weekend open access dance event was built around creating informed choices. On Saturday, participants took part in contemporary, Kathak and African dance workshops, before choosing which style to explore in more depth on Sunday. In fact, the numbers choosing each of the three styles was almost equal.

During the South East Arts Mime Development Project, taster sessions were run for teachers to prepare for practitioners going to work in schools.

See **11.2** and **13.2** for examples of projects where artists were commissioned to create work.

The composer David Machel worked with Art to Art, a group of people with and without learning difficulties, to create a new piece of music inspired by a secluded valley in Derbyshire. The piece was performed by the East of England Orchestra, with Art to Art, during the 1991 Nottingham Festival.

11.2 Using literature in site-specific work
13.2 Community music in rural areas

Community-based artists and practitioners also excel in work which blurs the boundaries between performer and audience, teacher and pupil, professional and non-professional artist. There are many examples of approaches which achieve this: tea dances, for example, or scratch bands. Even simple writers' workshops, where everyone both presents their own work and responds to that of the other members, erode traditional concepts of artist and audience. There are no rules here, since such projects depend on individual imagination and enthusiasm.

5.5 PERFORMANCES, PUBLISHING AND FESTIVALS

Performances

See section **5.3** on identifying and contracting artists.
Performances can be an important part of your overall programme, both in extending access to good professional work in your field, and by showcasing the work that community groups have been developing. For some people performance is the nail that holds the entire programme together, and without which it would be a disjointed series of unfocused initiatives. The place of such events in your work will depend on your objectives and philosophy.

If you are planning a performance in an established venue - eg an arts centre - there will be an experienced team of people to help you get it right, whether you are performing yourself or acting as a promoter for a company. If you are new to promotion, you can do far worse than seek their advice and support.

For performances in less usual venues - for instance in a school as part of a residency by a dance company, or poetry readings in an art gallery - you will have to take on more responsibility for the arrangements, and particularly for getting an audience in. The following notes will help you plan the event:

- Avoid dates when there's anything similar happening in the same area: you'll split the audience.

- Keep in touch with your RAB, touring companies and regional promoters; you may be able to negotiate a lower-cost performance if a company is already in your area and has free time in its schedule.

4.7 Legal matters - Copyright
- Check the copyright status of any material you intend to use.

- Think carefully about your pricing policy, and the use of complimentary tickets: judge your pricing by the attitudes of the audience you are trying to attract.

- Agree the fee or box office split, between you, performance company and venue, before the performance.

- Order enough leaflets and posters, and get them distributed.

- Don't underestimate the amount of time and effort you need to put into getting your audience, both for one event, and to build it over the course of time.

- If there isn't a box office at the venue, you may be able to sell tickets in advance through local agencies (including the local authority, tourist office or established venues); if tickets are only available on the door you won't know if anyone is coming until fifteen minutes before the show.

- Use the press, radio and, if possible, local TV for publicity.

- Make sure that the technical requirements of the performance company (floor area, power points, sound system, lighting rig) are known to, and can be met by the venue.

- Make sure there's enough time for the performance company to get in, set up, do a technical run-through, have a break before the performance, and get out afterwards.

- Can you make sufficiently good use of programmes to justify the time and cost of their production?

- You can't expect people to turn out as a reward for the amount of work you've put in. If you don't get a good audience, don't get depressed - find out what attracted those who did come and how you can do better with the next event.

Pricing performances requires sensitivity. Although you will not want to undermine your commitment to access by charging a high ticket price, to make the event free can imply that it is not worth very much. It is possible to fix a fair price, but to make generous use of complimentary tickets to build an audience, particularly where the capacity of the venue is large. Giving someone a complimentary ticket can be good public relations and encourages them to attend the event. Depending on your skills as a promoter, it may be a choice between a full hall with many people seeing the performance free, or a half-empty hall with everyone paying the full price. However, extensive use of complimentary tickets requires sensitivity towards the paying members of the audience.

Performances by community groups

There are numerous examples of highly-professional ongoing performance groups which have come out of community-based workshops: Heart 'n' Soul, Amici Dance Co, Eye Contact etc

As a result of your work, or that of other arts development workers in the area, you may find yourself arranging performances or tours by community performance groups. This can be a very rewarding experience for performers and audience alike, though some basic principles should be adhered to. Control of the process must lie with the performance group: only they can decide if they want to perform, in what situations and for whom. You may need to act as a brake if you feel a group needs more experience before they perform in public, but you should never persuade them to perform if they don't feel ready. A first performance for a private audience of friends and relatives can be a good stepping stone to the wider world. It is sometimes the case that some members of the group want to perform while others do not, in which case the solution may entail the creation of a smaller performance group.

Control of the process, especially if it is going to lead to an increasingly independent role for the group, should extend to involvement in all aspects of planning and managing the performance or tour. The group should not remain dependent on a professional worker for access to a public arena. As the group becomes more professional and successful, it is worth thinking about the reasons why some people may be being paid and others not, and ensuring that this is not a source of friction.

Lastly, try to make sure that the content and style of their work is appropriate to the performance venue. An intimate dance piece which works in the day centre where it was created could look dangerously vulnerable on the public stage of the local media centre. On the other hand an older person's music group could find itself in great demand in local residential homes for the elderly; but as always be wary of making assumptions about the creative interests and attitudes of either partner in such links.

Publications and exhibitions

11.2 South Asian literature project
13.1 Music, animation and older people

Performances are not the only way of bringing good work to a wider audience. Publications of all sorts - books, sound recordings, videos - and exhibitions (eg a photographic exhibition of a physical theatre project) can also make an important contribution to validating people's work, and to gaining a place for it in the broader context of contemporary culture. Think about the following in planning a publication or exhibition:

- In judging where to pitch quality of presentation, look at commercial products at least as much as community publications, and decide what messages the work should be giving out.

- Think carefully about the market: who is the product aimed at, how will you reach them and how will you persuade them to buy it? How will they find out about it, and obtain it?

- Think about the finance: will the product be self-financing, and if so how many units do you need to sell to break even? What is the best price to achieve maximum sales *and* maximum income? How will commercial discounts affect your profit margins?

- How will the product be distributed, and how long will its shelf-life be?

The amount of time, energy and finance you put into such a project will depend on your own priorities, but try not to underestimate the demands it may make. As ever, talk to people who have experience of producing similar or related work, and set your sights high.

Festivals
Organising a festival can be a good way of raising the profile of an area of work or an art form, hence the number of established festivals around the country. It is also very hard work, and will tax your imagination, energy and resources to the limit - which is another good reason for doing it. If you are planning something substantial - say a ten-day literature or mime festival in a small city - you will need help. The best way to get it is probably to set up a festival committee to advise on and oversee the event. Invite representatives of arts organisations, local artists, people from the local authority and the voluntary sector, the RAB, community and business leaders and anyone else who wants to make a contribution. Get them enthusiastic about the idea, involve them in programming, identifying venues, fundraising, dreaming up new events, publicising the festival - anything else they are interested in. The best festivals are firmly rooted in the local communities where they happen. The nature and extent of the actual authority vested in the committee will be a decision for your own management committee.

Students on graphic design courses have sometimes taken on design projects as part of their work.

127

14.4 ☛ *The British Performing Arts Yearbook* lists all current festivals in Britain.

It is also worth visiting other festivals, getting their publicity material, and meeting with the organisers (at a quiet time) to get advice. You should start planning *at least* a year before the festival. Consider the festival timetable: if your literature festival happens at the same time as those in Hay, Cheltenham or Edinburgh, you might find it hard to get the involvement of the writers you want. On the other hand, you might find that media attention on a big festival elsewhere stimulates interest in what you are doing. If the festival is to combine professional and community-based work, the programming will require sensitivity to ensure that audiences have appropriate expectations. You should think of - and publicise - your first festival as a one-off: you may not want to be committed to repeating it until you have had time to consider its value. If it does become a recurrent event, you may find that a biennial (rather than annual) timetable allows time to work on other projects while preventing the festival itself from becoming stale.

Outdoor events

Given the British climate, promoting events out of doors is always hard on the nerves. It is essential to plan an outdoor event knowing what you will do if the skies open or the fog is so thick that no-one can see the bands. Depending on the nature and timing of the event, you can postpone, move to another venue, or carry on regardless, but everyone involved needs to know the contingency plan. Because of the complexity and work involved you may also feel it is worth setting up a committee or planning group to help make the event a success (see above). Again, if you have no experience of this sort of event, talk your plans through with people who have: local authority or RAB officers will help you contact them. There are a number of additional factors which you have to consider if planning an outdoor event:

- Ownership of and permission to use the site

- A performance licence from the local council

One annual music event taking place on a site near the Borough Council offices regularly got complaints about noise despite its council funding.

- Neighbouring premises (don't site a rock festival next to a hospital)

- Public liability and other insurance cover eg equipment, cancellation

- Site and equipment security

- Staging, sound system, lighting, power - everything has to be brought in and taken away again

- Traffic control, parking and emergency access

- Liaison with key organisations like the police, fire brigade, St John Ambulance, and the local authority

- Food and toilet facilities, marquees, table, chairs, fencing etc

- Timetable for setting up, technical run-throughs, event, packing up

- Cleaning up afterwards

5.6   TRAINING COURSES AND CONFERENCES

While there can be no rigid distinction between workshops, classes and training courses, the emphasis in training is firmly on learning, rather than on the practice and exploration of an art form. Arts training undertaken in community situations will largely seek to meet the needs of two different groups: people with a strong commitment to the arts, who can't or don't want to use mainstream education to pursue their interest, and professional people working in other areas - teachers, care workers etc.

Training in the community

Offering training can be an important element in a programme of community-based arts work because it is another mechanism for increasing access to the arts. Traditional educational routes to employment in the arts - through school and college - are not equally accessible to all people. The situation of disabled people illustrates this clearly. Segregated education, inaccessible buildings, course materials and teaching methods, and an externally-created culture of reduced expectations make it almost impossible for many disabled people to attain further education. Other people, for cultural, economic, social or other reasons find it very difficult to get access to further education in the arts. Others come to the arts later in life, perhaps without the educational qualifications which could secure a college place, or unable to get a grant from their LEA. Still others, whilst having a wholly professional approach to their work, are unable or unwilling to commit more than a certain amount of time. For these and many other people community-based arts work, and the training opportunities it offers, form a uniquely valuable route into the some areas of the professional arts.

One disabled student at a Midlands college was accepted on the condition that she should be accompanied at all times (not necessarily by a person of her choice) since she was deemed to constitute a fire risk. It is hard for non-disabled people to understand what it takes to overcome such institutionalised affronts to human dignity.

7.3 Types of training

129

Training professionals

Building training opportunities for professionals into your programme is a valuable way of passing on your ideas and practice, raising awareness of the artform and perhaps leaving
something behind. There is a wide range of people who may
want to learn from your experience and skills - teachers, librarians, community development workers, dance instructors,
other arts workers, care workers and many others. Some of
that training can be associated with projects in which they are
involved, either through direct participation, or through an
introductory training session before the project happens. Some
can be set up as distinct training courses, designed to address a
particular area of your work. Such courses can also be useful
ways of earning income for your work, particularly if you can
interest a local authority department or other organisation in
buying in the course for its staff.

Conferences and seminars

There are many reasons for running conferences or seminars,
from bringing people with shared concerns together to focusing attention on a particularly innovative or interesting project
or area of work. A well-planned and paced conference can provide an excellent framework for promoting understanding,
common interests or even planning action. If you are thinking
about running a conference you will need to decide how many
people need to attend to make it a success - conferences are
fundamentally about people talking - and try to judge whether
there are enough people who would come. It may be wise to
run the conference in partnership with another organisation -
perhaps a local authority - who can lend credibility and administrative support to your ideas. Similarly a keynote speaker
who is well-known in relation to the subject of the conference
can help attract people.

Running training courses and conferences

Planning and running conferences and training events is largely a matter of common sense, and drawing on your own experiences of attending such events. If there are general rules they
are:

- decide what you want to achieve, and the most
  appropriate format

- focus clearly on the matters to be considered

- build a timetable which offers variety of pace, activity
  and length

- supply adequate written material to guide people through the day, and produce a report - even if it is brief - promptly afterwards

- communicate effectively with participants

- make clear what expectations participants should have of the event

- make space for people to relax, mingle and network

- never underestimate the amount of attention which needs to be given to the domestic arrangements

Finally try to be alert to the different agendas and needs that people will bring with them. Where the subject of the conference is potentially controversial, plan your structure so as to minimise scope for confrontation whilst giving everyone the chance to contribute.

5.7   PROJECT PLANNING CHECKLIST

When planning the project, think about:

- **Aim** - you should be clear what your aim is, and how it is going to be achieved by the format, content and nature of the project you are planning.

- **Participants** - where possible, involve participants in discussions about the project from the beginning.

- **Access** - not just the physical access to premises, but the whole range of access issues, including the accessibility of the content to the intended audience and the appropriateness of your publicity.

  5.8 Access issues

- **Artists** - unless you are running the project yourself, identify the most appropriate person or company to take on the work and discuss it with them from the start.

  5.3 Commissioning other performers - Choosing the right artist

- **Finance** - work out a budget showing expenditure and income. You may have to pay for artists' fees and expenses (including travel and accommodation), room hire, equipment and materials, set and costumes, publicity, transport for participants, fees for BSL interpreters, refreshments, a crèche, documentation, security, and insurance. Remember to include the cost of your time and overheads if these are not already fully underwritten by revenue funding. Add 5% of the total to

  6.5 Planning a fundraising strategy

131

cover unforeseen difficulties or cost variations. If you don't know the costs, ask advice, or get quotes from suppliers; remember to check whether quotes or other costs include VAT or not.

- **Fundraising** - If you can't meet the project costs from your existing resources, begin your fundraising as soon as you know what you want to do, and how much it will cost.

- **Marketing** - plan your whole approach to promoting your project from the beginning.

- **Date** - there are obvious choices (weekend or weekday, term or holiday time) and obvious factors (the availability of artists). You need to think about the effect of community events (eg summer fair) or national events (eg FA cup final), cultural festivals etc.

- **Venue** - if the choice is not dictated by the project, or availability, think about the messages different venues give out. Remember also that where people regularly meet in one venue (eg a day centre) there can be benefits in relocating for the duration of the event, but do not forget the importance of accessibility.

5.8 Access issues

- **Insurance** - check that your public liability and other insurances will cover the project adequately.

- **Your time** - plan your work so that when the project happens, you can give it attention without another area of your work being neglected. Try to ensure that you have the practical help and moral support you need.

- **Follow up** - make sure that you know what your options for following up are, depending on the outcome of the project.

Before the project, check that

- **Participants** have been involved in discussions, know what is happening, when, where and why. If you are not in touch with the audience or participants beforehand, check that your marketing is effective.

1.2 Basic principles

- **Contracts** have been exchanged with the artist, and the work discussed informally again.

- **Funding** has been secured and there will be no cash-flow problems.

- **Representatives** of funding bodies have been invited to attend.

- **Facilities** are clean, private, accessible and ready for use, and that changing rooms, toilets, refreshments etc are available.

- **Technical requirements** (sound equipment, power points, materials, dance floor etc) have been met and equipment checked.

- **Safety** and security issues have been considered ie minimise the possibilities for accidents, know what to do if they occur, minimise the possibilities for a wide range of events including theft of belongings and disruption of the sessions.

- **Venue staff** (especially the caretaker) know what is happening and are willing to help sort out minor hitches.

- **Publicity** has been arranged which is appropriate to the nature of the event and its place within your programme.

- **Documentation** has been arranged.

During the project, check that

- **The work** itself is meeting everyone's needs and expectations.

- **Facilities** are proving adequate.

- **The artists** are coping with the work and are comfortable when they're not working.

- **Monitoring** arrangements are working in practice.

- **Documentation** is happening with people's consent as appropriate.

- **Invitations** to funders and other people are taken up.

- **You** can be contacted in case of problems.

After the project, ensure that

- **Participants** know what is happening next or of other opportunities (eg through colleges, community arts projects etc) they can take up.

- **Feedback** opportunities are created and used.

- **Reports** are written and sent to funders and management.

- **Funding** that has been promised is delivered.

- **Bills** are paid promptly.

- **Thanks** go to everyone who helped make it possible, and consideration is given to anything that will make the next project better.

5.8   ACCESS ISSUES

What is access?

It can be assumed that any artist or company working in the community is committed to broadening access to their work. Problems can arise, however, because of different perceptions of what the word means. Some people identify access issues with the needs of people with physical disabilities, while others think of it in terms of outreach or education programmes, and still others relate it to questions of cultural identity. All are right: access issues are wide-ranging and complex, and change as quickly as society's broader social and political expectations.

Working to ensure that everyone has real access to your work is more difficult than it might at first appear. For example, an open music workshop running from 7.30 to 9.30 on Thursday evenings in a college of further education could seem a good way to offer access to music to a neighbourhood. But different people might be put off coming for any of the following reasons, among others:

- streets around the college are poorly-lit

- public transport is too infrequent

- they're interested in other forms of music

- they're uncertain about physical access to the building

- it's too expensive (or, if it's free, they doubt it's any good)

- the publicity didn't go to the right places

- they associate school with failure in music

- they get paid on Thursday and do their shopping that evening

- there isn't a sign-language interpreter

If this list appears crushingly pessimistic, it is important to remember that there are two sorts of access issues: those you can do something about, and those which are beyond your control. Do what you can about the first, but don't get depressed about the second: it's counter-productive. Ideally your work is helping to make the community a better place to live in: it can't change society single-handedly.

Remember too that you are offering access to your work, not access for everyone to everything you do. There are situations where it would be wrong or impossible to offer general access - a workshop in a prison, for example, or some projects with people with mental health problems. What you need to ensure, through the planning and monitoring systems described in chapter 3, is that you are offering the best possible access to your work to the widest possible range of people over the course of a year's programme of work.

Basic access issues

Good access practice benefits everyone. Easy physical access, whilst it is essential for some disabled people, is helpful to all. No-one likes climbing endless stairs and pushing through heavy doors; similarly it is not just women who dislike walking down badly-lit alleyways. Consequently the ideas in this section, with a few obvious exceptions, are not organised to address the specific needs of 'sorts' of people, but to look at the range of access issues which you need to think about.

Not every question is relevant to every event: setting up an open access mime class is a different process to running a week-long residency in a special school. The aim is not to be prescriptive, but to offer a collection of ideas on which to draw. It is also important to remember that these are not comprehensive simply because they are set out here: the subject is too broad, and it changes too frequently; moreover our individual perceptions and attitudes develop. At the end of this section are some ideas on how to get advice, learn more, and improve your practice.

Premises

- What messages does the building give out?

- Is it associated with a particular section of the community?

- Is it in the right place for the people you want to reach?

- Is access by public transport good?

The best advice on the access requirements of disabled people comes from them. If your work already attracts disabled people, ask for their views of the current access situation. If you are not already in touch with disabled people, make contact with the local Coalition of Disabled People, or Access Group. It is generally preferable to seek advice directly from disabled people and their organisations, but where this is not possible other groups - such as local societies for blind people - will be able to help. Some local authorities have access sections or officers who can advise you, and RABs will also have some experience in this area - one at least has a part-time disability researcher

Access guides to various community facilities, from neighbourhood centres to cemeteries, are published by many local authorities, and the standard is improving all the time. Most RABs also have information about the accessibility of arts venues in their areas. In many areas disabled people are involved in Access Groups which promote and campaign for improved accessibility. There are also more general disabled people's organisations including coalitions.

- How will disabled people be able to get there?

- Who else uses the building, when and how?

- Is it already familiar, or easy to find?

- Is the part you are using clearly signposted?

- Is the building (and facilities such as café, bar, toilets etc) accessible to people with mobility impairments?

- How accessible is it to people with visual and/or hearing impairments?

- Is there a reception area, and if so, is it friendly?

Facilities

- Do you need to provide a crèche?

- Is it appropriate to provide refreshments, and if so, what would best suit the cultural or dietary needs of the audience or participants?

- Is there good car-parking, with reserved spaces for disabled people?

- What other things will have to be considered if the project is residential?

Publicity

14.4 ☞ *Marketing to Disabled Audiences*

- How is the event going to be publicised?

- How well will that publicity reach all sections of the community?

- How will people for whom English is not a first language (including many deaf people) respond to your publicity?

- Do you need to produce publicity in other languages than English?

- Do you need to make information available in different formats (eg large print, braille, tape, BSL video)?

- How will non-readers respond to your publicity?

- Is it appropriate to seek media coverage and other publicity, and if so in what form?

Format

- Is the event at the best time, day of the week, season?

- Is its length and timetable right for the audience you expect?

- Is the artist/tutor/company the right match for the situation?

- Is the pricing policy right?

Content

- How does the content relate to people who are not already familiar with the arts?

- How does the content relate to disabled people?

- How does the content relate to non-European cultures?

- Are the language and images used exclusive or inclusive?

- How can the potential audience or participants be involved in discussions around format and content?

Developing your experience

No-one knows it all; everyone has things to learn. In the context of making your work accessible, the best experts are the people you are trying to open it to. Make contacts in the community with the widest range of people and groups you can. Don't be afraid to ask for advice, to explain that you don't know. The leader of an Asian youth project will not expect a white literature worker to understand at once the complexities of Asian cultures, needs and experiences, any more than they would expect to understand the needs and concerns of a disability arts group. With sensitivity, a commitment to developing your skills through training, and a respect for other people's experiences, you will gradually be able to extend access to your work, and make it increasingly relevant to all sections of the community in which you work.

2.2 Starting a new post

The preceding section lists some of the issues that you need to consider, but it has deliberately avoided offering answers. Take, for example, the question of access to the arts by deaf people. It would be possible to produce a checklist which covered the use of BSL interpreters, induction loops, provision of information in BSL on video, the role of sign-supported English (SSE), the differing policies of education authorities about the use of BSL in teaching, the richness and vitality of deaf culture etc. Apart from the fact that it would certainly be incomplete, such a list could not offer a fraction of the understanding which talking to deaf people about their interests and

In the case of deaf people, the organisations to contact would include the British Deaf Association, the Royal National Institute for the Deaf and the local deaf organisation. It would also be worth contacting the relevant Shape organisation and the National Disability Arts Forum. The Arts and Disability Unit of the Arts Council and the RAB appropriate officer would be able to provide information. Finally most of the larger local authorities have officers or departments concerned with equal opportunities and access by disabled people.

The Arts Council Education Unit publishes a number of useful resource packs and other specialist publications. RABs are also involved in arts education and generally have an education officer.

1.4 Changes to education

needs will bring. Meeting with the communities you want to involve in your work is real, is the beginning of creating a working relationship, and is exciting. There is no substitute.

To some extent, the more community-based work you undertake or promote, the better at ensuring good access to it you will become. You will meet more and more people, who will tell you more and more about their concerns, needs and interests. Nobody can expect you to understand all these things at once, or to get them right all the time. What you should expect of yourself is an understanding of why they are central to what you are trying to do - not an irritating afterthought - and a commitment to continual improvement of access to your work. Extending access is not a problem - it's an opportunity to build a greater market for the arts.

5.9   WORKING IN SCHOOLS

The education system in England and Wales has undergone major changes in the past decade, and more are certainly in the pipeline. They have affected the way schools are managed and the way pupils are taught. The changes have made life harder in some respects for independent artists and practitioners seeking to work in schools, though there remains great scope for exciting work, and new approaches to arts education are now being developed to meet the changed situation.

Management of schools

Until 1988 education was provided through local education authorities (LEAs) which generally served a county or metropolitan borough, managing schools, allocating resources and providing various support services. Among these last were the encouragement and funding of a range of arts activities including visits to schools by artists, writers, dance and drama companies, and musicians. LEAs also provided equipment and instruments to schools from common pools. These services were co-ordinated by specialist LEA advisers who often had excellent relationships with the local arts community. The Education Reform Act 1988 introduced local management of schools (LMS), under which schools with more than 200 pupils became directly responsible for their own budgets. One consequence has been the loss of co-ordinated activities, and indeed the advisory service itself has become largely inspectorial in function in some areas. Now that school governors manage their own budgets they are necessarily more acutely aware of the competing claims on their limited resources. The arts do not always get a high priority in these circumstances, particularly without an experienced advisory service to articulate their value.

A further development has been the creation of grant-maintained status (GMS) for state schools wishing to opt out of LEA control. Grant-maintained schools are funded directly by the Department for Education, and accountable to the Secretary of State for Education. The fragmentation of the school management system has led smaller schools in some areas to form 'clusters' to share resources, but this is still the exception rather than the rule. The development of discrete arts education agencies (see below) is a further response to these changes.

The National Curriculum
The introduction of the national curriculum (which applies to a large part of the school day) has changed both what and how children are taught. In relation to the arts, only music and art are accorded the status of foundation subjects, though creative writing, mime and drama should be covered within the English curriculum, and dance is incorporated in the PE curriculum. No arts subject is compulsory after the age of 14, though they may still be available in school. However, used imaginatively arts activities - particularly in primary or junior schools - can support other parts of the curriculum. Themes and topics being dealt with in mathematics or history for instance can be explored through dance, music, mime or literature projects. If you are planning a specific project, check the national curriculum guidelines published by HMSO for that subject. The national curriculum is currently being reviewed by Sir Ron Dearing and further changes are to be expected.

Setting up projects
It can seem as if the hardest part of running projects in schools is knowing who to talk to first. The position varies across the country, so there is no absolute answer. Preliminary discussions with the education officer of the RAB, the relevant LEA adviser or arts education agency (if they exist), and with other arts organisations will help you get a feel for local conditions, what work has been done and with which schools. When you have some background you will be able to contact individual schools. In primary or special schools it is usually best to contact the head teacher, though you may be referred to another teacher with a particular interest or responsibility for the arts. In secondary schools an alternative is to contact the head of

Local arts organisations or venues may have education officers with whom you could discuss your plans and potentially set up working partnerships.

department if there is one in your field. Phone the school office to check who to contact.

Teachers are under pressure from all sorts of directions, and you will need to make sure that you are not adding to that pressure. Write first, explaining what you can offer and suggesting that they call you at a convenient time if they'd like to discuss a project. You will probably need to follow your letter with a phone call, so do it at lunchtime or preferably just after the end of the teaching day. You may still find it hard to get hold of the person you want to speak to. If the teacher is interested you will need to plan and set up the project with sensitivity to the school timetable, existing teaching programme, and current concerns. Gaining the support of the head teacher and, ideally, the governors is crucial to the long-term success of the work. A discussion with teachers or perhaps a short presentation at a governors' meeting can be very useful, especially if the school is to commit any of its financial resources. If your salary or fees are already met, and you are able to offer input at no cost, it will obviously be easier to promote your work. Alternatively a school project can be fundraised for in the same way as any other project you are planning. Primary schools will find it particularly hard to contribute to the cost of arts projects from their resources, though they are often well-aware of their value.

Special schools
Special schools - few of which are yet affected by LMS - run alongside the mainstream schools and cater for children with special educational needs. These may result from physical, sensory or mental impairments or from emotional or behavioural difficulties. Special schools tend to be small - with perhaps fifty pupils - and may cater for primary age children only, or span an age range from 2 to 18. They operate the national curriculum but, like primary schools, have a more flexible timetable than secondary schools. The value of the arts is often appreciated in special schools, though teachers do not always have the skills or time to develop this area.

Since the Education Act 1981 there have been increasing moves to integrate children with special educational needs into mainstream education, though this has not been supported by all of those concerned. Some mainstream schools now have support units to provided specialist assistance to disabled children attending regular classes.

Arts Education Agencies

The term Arts Education Agency has emerged recently to characterise a wide range of initiatives set up to act as a link between schools and colleges on the one hand and artists and arts organisations on the other. To some extent they have begun to fill the gap left by the reduction in the arts advisory services of LEAs. They vary enormously. They include independent organisations, those set up as educational trusts or as business units of the LEA and the education work of some arts organisations; some cover particular areas, others span the country; some specialise in artforms or, like Arts Education for a Multicultural Society (AEMS) in particular issues. Some animateur and development worker posts have such specific links to the education services that they themselves form arts education agencies. If there is such an organisation working in your area, it will be sensible to make contact with them before taking on school projects.

14.4 ☛ *Arts Education Agencies*

5.10 WORKING IN INSTITUTIONS

Introduction

An increasing number of arts projects take place in institutional contexts, a fact welcomed by anyone committed to ensuring equal access to the arts in this country. Many of these are of the highest quality and vision, and offer a unique service to tens of thousands of people. However, the work does not suit everyone. It can be emotionally draining, and it is easy to feel isolated in the hybrid position the artist occupies between staff and resident or client. On the other hand, creative activity can have a major impact on a closed institution, and practitioners often find it easy to see the effect and benefits of their work. If you are thinking of extending your work into this area, it would be good to start by talking it through with some of the specialist agencies, and with other artists who have experience of working in institutions; think about your reasons as well.

Organisations currently or formerly members of the Shape Network are a good starting point for advice in this area. **15.6 Contacts**

The local Shape organisation or RAB will be able to advise further.

For most artists and arts organisations there are two main reasons for taking the arts into institutions:

- because the people concerned cannot get access to the arts unless they are brought inside;

- because the institution offers an opportunity to bring the arts to a group of people who have similar concerns or problems.

141

However, neither of these are of much interest to most institutions which have their own quite different concerns, agendas and problems. Indeed, where the arts appear at all on most institutions' list of concerns is at the very end, under 'any other business'. If you expect a similar value to be placed on your work as you place yourself - even when you have been invited in - you are likely to end up confused and resentful. It is wiser to accept that the priorities are clinical improvement, internal management, therapy, security, self-advocacy etc, depending on the situation, and to see how you can function in that framework. If you can work with, rather than against the grain of the institution, you will be able to get on with your project more effectively. That should not be taken to imply that there is no opportunity for challenging work in this situation - the reverse is true - but unless the work can be accommodated by the institution, it simply will not happen at all.

Remember also that most institutions are under-resourced and short-staffed, and that consequently your reasonable requirements may appear quite unreasonable to members of staff already under pressure. However, you should not get drawn into providing any care functions however apparent the need might be: you are an artist or arts worker, and not qualified, employed or insured to undertake any care responsibilities.

You must also remember that you are there to meet the needs of the people for whose benefit the institution is ostensibly established, not those of the institution itself. If you follow the management agenda, you will yourself become institutionalised and of little benefit to anyone. Instead you have to occupy a sort of limbo where you can gain the trust of both sides. It isn't easy.

A word on art therapy

Any artist or practitioner venturing into an institution will be asked sooner or later if they are an art therapist, so it's important to be clear about your role. An art therapist is part of a clinical team, working to a clinical agenda. In other words, an art therapist is generally aware of the diagnosis made about an individual - knows what is considered to be 'wrong' with them - and is working specifically to bring about improvements in that condition. This is a professional job - for which people have often received extensive training - which has a valuable role to play in a clinical environment. But it is not an artist's job.

An artist working in an institution generally knows little about the people they are working with, other than what they

themselves choose to reveal. The relationship between an artist
and a participant in a workshop should be completely equal.
An artist is not trying to do anything to anyone, except enable
them to have access to artistic skills and develop their own creativity on their own terms. Any health or educational benefits
accrue as a by-product of the creative activity.

You will know from your own experience that all sorts of
good things will emerge from an arts workshop. The important thing is that they do so specifically because no-one is trying to control them, to make them happen. Managers who
have a duty to spend their resources on health care, or education, or rehabilitation will spend them on the arts only if they
believe that benefits will accrue in those areas. You need to
help them understand that those benefits will be gained, but
only if participants have control of their own work.

Checklist for planning work in an institution

- How many people are going to be involved?
- Will everyone be freely able to choose whether or not to participate?
- What space will you work in?
- Will you have exclusive use of the space?
- Will there be a member of staff present?
- Is there a space in which you can store equipment or materials?
- Will the timetable affect your work?
- What have the staff in the unit been told about your presence?
- To whom are you responsible, for what?
- Are there any 'house rules' or regulations which you and the participants will have to observe?
- How will the work be sustained after you have finished?

There are many other issues which you will need to think
about in different situations - security implications, perhaps, or
consent for photographs - which cannot be dealt with adequately here. You are recommended to take advice from relevant organisations and from experienced artists and companies. The following paragraphs briefly describe some of the

types of institutions into which artists have successfully carried their work.

Prisons

There are several different types of prison (though some establishments serve more than one function), holding prisoners in four categories of perceived security risk. The types of prison for men include:

Local prisons, which are generally overcrowded and run down, hold remand prisoners and convicted prisoners serving short sentences or the first part of longer sentences;

Remand centres for unconvicted prisoners held on remand;

Closed training prisons holding prisoners over 21 years old, serving sentences of all lengths and graded according to a security classification where A is high-risk and D is low;

Open prisons which have no physical barriers preventing escape, and hold low-risk prisoners. (Training prisons and YOIs can be run on open conditions but not local prisons);

Dispersal prisons which have high security wings for category A prisoners. (Some training prisons are also dispersal prisons);

Young Offender Institutions, cater for prisoners under 21 years old.

There are, in addition to these, four closed and two open prisons for women, who are not usually categorised. The prison service, which has for some years offered arts classes through the education authority, has become more interested in the arts, and the Home Office commissioned valuable research in this area from the Centre for Research in Social Policy at Loughborough University. Promoting arts activities in prisons, in itself a difficult activity, has not been made easier in recent years by tensions with the service, and the privatisation of prison education services.

For an artist, the particular demands presented by prison work centre on security, since this is the foundation of the prison's role. The first hurdle may be getting clearance to enter the prison at all. In most cases it is necessary to provide some basic information in order that a security check can be made. Some artists working in prison have been required to sign the Official Secrets Act, though this is not usual in the case of short-term workshops. Finally, there are important restrictions on a wide range of objects and materials which can be brought into or used in a prison, and it is essential to be properly informed on these matters.

Hospitals

Most hospitals operate within the national health service (NHS) either as independent NHS Trusts or within the control of district health authorities. There are also a number of private hospitals. There are various types of general and specialist hospitals, and the role played by the arts within them varies. Although all types of hospitals can make suitable venues both for performances and workshops, it is in the longer-stay units that the greatest impact is often made. These include some units - such as children's and orthopaedic wards, or young disabled units - of general hospitals, and specialist hospitals including those catering for people with learning difficulties or mental health problems.

Although the Care in the Community programme has meant the closure of many large psychiatric hospitals, many still remain, often caring for patients less able to live in the community. In the mental health field there are also the three English special hospitals - Ashworth, Broadmoor, Rampton - in each of which substantial arts work has been undertaken. Of more general relevance are the regional secure units in each regional health authority area which accommodate people with mental health problems who need secure conditions. Apart from Shape services which have wide experience in this field, there are two national organisations providing an advisory and consultancy service in this area: Arts for Health in Manchester, and the Health Care Arts in Dundee.

Hospices

The term hospice is generally applied to units - whether in the public or the private sector - which care for people who are terminally ill. The hospice movement is relatively recent, but has achieved much with its vision of providing a caring and dignified environment for people who are dying. Arts projects have run very successfully in hospices, and advice can be sought from various organisations. However, this work, which can be tremendously demanding on an emotional and spiritual level, will not suit all arts workers, and you should take advice. Hospice Arts is a specialist organisation advising on and providing support for arts projects in hospices.

One artist, who had been invited to work in a maximum security prison by the education department and an arts development agency, had the unhappy experience of being refused entry by the prison governor on the grounds of a drug-related offence, although this was ten years old and in legal terms a spent conviction.

Useful contacts include organisations in the Shape Network, Arts for Health, and the Health Care Arts. **15.6 Contacts**

The education department of the Tate Gallery in Liverpool has been involved, with others, in a substantial programme of work at Ashworth, leading to the establishment of a hospital arts council to develop and support the work.

11.3 Creative writing in a hospice

15.6 Contacts

Residential homes

Make initial contact with residential homes through the social services department.

There is a wide range of residential homes operated by local authorities, local and national charities and the private sector. They seek to meet the needs of many different groups of people - including people with mental health problems, people with physical disabilities, people with learning difficulties, older people and others. Some residential homes offer respite care with people staying for relatively short periods. They vary enormously in their aims and services, and it is impossible to generalise about them. Some are well staffed and resourced with imaginative activity programmes, but this is certainly not the case everywhere. Much excellent arts activity has been generated and promoted in residential homes but much more could be achieved with greater resources.

10.2 Dance work with older people

Day services

Make initial contact with day centres through the Social Services department of the local authority.

Most day care services - known variously as day centres, resource centres, adult training centres etc - are run by local authority social services departments or by charities such as Mencap. Day services offer a range of activities, usually between 9.00am and 4.00pm, to a wide range of disabled and/or older people. The activities of individual units range from largely work-orientated programmes to the promotion of independence and self-advocacy through education and related work. The arts have been widely used to support and extend day service programmes, and can make very valuable contributions.

5.11 FEEDBACK

Basic principles

Getting feedback is sometimes perceived as getting people who just want to go home, to tell you things that *you* want to know. In fact it is more useful to look at it from the other side and see it as an access issue: how can participants in a project get access to the people who planned it and carried it out, to say what they think. Their right to comment on their experience is as important as their right to have it in the first place.

3.3 Democratic or accountable?

Seeing it from the participants' or audience's point of view makes thinking through how to get feedback easier. It is no longer a question of how you can get people to tell you what you want to know, but of enabling them to tell you what they have to say. Placing the agenda in the users' hands may make the process of relating your work and concerns to their needs more difficult, but should help you keep an open mind about your practice.

You also need to get feedback from any artists or other people (like teachers) who have been involved. In some ways this is easier to achieve, particularly since you can build it into any agreement. For a project lasting longer than a couple of days, it may be worth getting the artists, teachers, participants to keep a project diary. It could be a private thing, or simply a big piece of paper pinned to a wall on which people can write comments as they go. Sharing discussion of the aims and purposes of the project from the beginning will make feedback easier.

There are various ways to get feedback:

Discussion
A structured discussion between participants, artists and others at the end of the event, or shortly afterwards, may be the simplest way to get feedback. Its advantages are that:

- it is simple and straightforward

- it can happen at the end of the event or later

- people may give each other ideas, spark conversation

- it is easier for participants to control the agenda

- it is accessible to people for whom English is not a first language, and to non-readers

On the other hand:

- not everyone likes to speak out in a group

- people may be reluctant to criticise your work directly

- it can produce rambling, unfocused feedback

- it can be dominated by a few, unrepresentative people

- it may be difficult to take down what is said

Conducting interviews
Conducting interviews, perhaps based around completing a form, may be the best way to get detailed responses from participants; a combination of one-to-one conversations and small group discussions works well. The advantages are that:

- everyone gets a good chance to say what they feel, and you get a good chance to hear and understand it

- people's views are not affected by what they have heard others say

- it is easier to take notes

- it is accessible to people for whom English is not a first language, and to non-readers

- it can be kept confidential

- it can be flexible and respond to people's needs

On the other hand:

- it is time consuming

- people may be reluctant to criticise your work directly

Distributing evaluation forms

Handing out evaluation forms is perhaps the most common way of getting feedback, though its effectiveness is questionable. The advantages are that:

- it is cheap and easy

- it is relatively confidential

- it can be used to gain basically comparable information for statistical purposes

But these are offset by the fact that:

- it is inaccessible to people for whom English is not a first language, and non-readers

- it is hard for participants to change your agenda

- few people like writing much, so you may end up with short, unhelpful replies

- it often produces a poor rate of return

- it is impersonal, and doesn't give scope for impressions

Recording

If you have the resources, setting up a 'video box' can be a good addition to your range of feedback opportunities. Let people know that there's a video camera in a room on its own and that they can use it to record their impressions of the event: you could also try it with just a tape recorder. The advantages are that:

- it is accessible to people for whom English is not a first language, and to non-readers

- it is unpredictable

But on the other hand:

- it demands a degree of self-confidence from people

- it may be expensive and difficult to arrange

- it can produce rambling, unfocused feedback

- it can be dominated by a few, unrepresentative people

Unfortunately the most effective strategy - conducting interviews - proves to be the most time-consuming, so in practice people end up using a combination of approaches depending on the event and their resources. But enabling people to tell you what they think and want should never be an afterthought. Understanding and respecting those things are at the heart of any community-based arts work.

FUNDING 6

151

6 FUNDING

Summary

Following a brief introduction, the first three sections of this chapter describe the structure for arts funding in this country. The next three sections concentrate on how to secure the money you need for the work that you are trying to do. They deal only briefly with revenue funding because getting and keeping such funding is a long-term process which depends on the quality of your work and the particular situation in your area. Instead they concentrate on securing funding on a project-by-project basis, and show how this approach can supplement revenue funding or become a potentially viable way to operate without it. The sections cover planning a strategy and individual applications, and look at how to present your case. The final section covers earned income and fundraising events.

6.1 EFFECTIVE FUNDRAISING

Fundraising can seem the most daunting part of an arts development worker's job, something which only other people know how to do. In practice there is no mystery to fundraising, though the decisions made by funders sometimes remain mysterious. If you understand the system, follow some simple rules, and are trying to fund good work, you should be able to secure most of what you need, if not all you would like. This section covers the structures through which money can be secured for arts work, and ways in which to make an approach effective. It relates specifically to community-based arts work, not to funding the arts generally, a distinction which will become clear in relation to matters such as sponsorship.

14.5 ☞ *The Arts Funding Guide*, provides a good introduction to fundraising for the arts and an overview of the different funding possibilities in all sectors.

Since there is not enough money to fund all the work proposed by artists and arts organisations, fundraising is a competitive business. In trying to get funding for your work you are competing against other worthwhile projects, and you have to present the strongest case possible. The skills you use are akin to those of a salesperson: you are, in effect, selling a product, whether it be your skills in general or a specific project. The funders you are approaching are in the market to buy some community-based arts work: your job is to persuade them to have yours. This will seem an unpleasantly commercial view to many people, but it is none the less true for that.

It follows that effective selling depends on having a good product. It is possible to get funding for indifferent projects with skillful fundraising techniques, but it cannot usually be sustained long-term: conversely, although good projects do not always attract funding at once, they tend to in the end. The point is that unless the subject of the funding proposal is well-planned, cost-effective and worthwhile, it is unlikely to gain support, however well-presented. The starting point of effective fundraising is good arts work.

Like any other trader, you also need to know your market, so research is essential. You need to know who the potential customers are, and what their particular interests are RABs, the Arts Council, local authorities, charitable trusts, the private sector - all make decisions based on certain policy priorities, whether clearly stated or not. Similarly some funders may have specific areas of concern or responsibility - for people with mental health problems perhaps, or young people in care. Knowing the market also means knowing the competition: only by understanding the other sorts of funding proposals being put forward, can you identify and present the uniquely valuable characteristics of your own.

Funding decisions are generally made by people who are accountable to others for the quality of those decisions. Since they want, above all, to be able to demonstrate that they have allocated the money in their care wisely, their decisions tend to be cautious. A dull, but reliable project may get funded because it will clearly be successful in its own terms, whereas an innovative project that looks risky may get turned down. So a key aim of a funding proposal must be to reassure the people that a decision to support the project will reflect well on them and their organisation. For this and other reasons, the better the relationship you can build with a potential or actual funder, the more successful you will be.

Finally, avoid the temptation to make your work follow the funding; like mythical sirens, the offers of potential funders can lead you onto some very sharp rocks. If you start by identifying a funding source, and then trying to twist your planned scheme to fit the criteria, the best outcome you can hope for is to get money to carry out work which you don't really want to do. In time you will become exhausted by trying to keep up with the changing agendas of other bodies, and lose control of your work and identity. In these circumstances your revenue funders will become concerned with the nature and quality of your work, and may question the validity of your base funding. The only responsible way to undertake fundraising is to create proposals for good, valuable work, and then look for a funding partner to work with you. It may take longer to find the resources you need, but when you do, you will be able to carry out work that you believe in, on your own terms.

6.2   FUNDING FROM THE PUBLIC SECTOR

The Arts Council

Since the war, during which the government became involved in funding the arts as a morale-boosting exercise, the state has funded professional arts activity through the Arts Council of Great Britain (ACGB). The Arts Council's role was defined by a Royal Charter as being (broadly) to support artists and extend access to the arts. The Office of Arts and Libraries - a government department - gave an annual grant to the Arts Council to support the arts. This system, which distanced government from direct decision-making about which arts to support and to what extent, became known as the 'arm's length principle'. The Arts Council distributed some grants directly to artists and companies (known as clients) whose work was considered to be of national importance and some to other bodies (including the Scottish, Welsh and Northern Irish Arts Councils and the Regional Arts Associations) who gave it to clients working at regional or local level.

See the latest annual report of the Arts Council for an account of its current structure and work.

This system operated until 1989 when Richard Wilding, former head of the Office of Arts and Libraries, was appointed by the then arts minister, Richard Luce, to review it. The subsequent recommendations passed through many stages before resulting in the replacement of the RAAs by new Regional Arts Boards who have a tighter relationship with the Arts Council itself. The Scottish Arts Council,Welsh Arts Council and Arts Council of Northern Ireland are also to be made independent of the ACGB, which will become the Arts Council of England (ACE) in April 1994. A further element of this revision was the consultation process which produced the Arts and Media Strategy in 1993.

14.1 ☛ Published as *A Creative Future* this gives one picture of current attitudes to the arts in Britain.

But larger changes have also occurred. The Office of Arts and Libraries was replaced in April 1992 by the Department of National Heritage (DNH), and the arts minister by the Secretary of State for National Heritage. The DNH has much wider functions than its predecessor, having responsibility for sport, ancient monuments, the new national lottery and much else besides. It has also been reviewing both the role and the performance of the Arts Council and, at the time of writing, the exact future of any part of the arts funding system remains unclear.

The Arts Council for England will administer that part of the proceeds of the National Lottery which will go to support the arts. This funding should be additional to existing government funding of the arts.

Within the context of these changes, however, the Arts Council continues its functions of grant-aiding arts organisations and companies and supporting the arts through its various specialist departments. These include artform departments responsible for the support of dance, music, literature and so on, and cross-artform departments like education, marketing, and arts and disability. Each department is staffed by specialist officers with decisions being made by a committee of practitioners and other experienced advisers. In addition to this ordinary programme of work, the Arts Council has launched a number of new initiatives including an architecture department, and Arts 2000, a scheme which associates different cities and regions with particular artforms for a year at a time. Birmingham was city of music in 1992, the East Midlands was region of dance in 1993, and Manchester is city of drama in 1994. Swansea is city of literature and writing 1995, and the Northern region is visual arts 1996, Eastern region is the region of opera and musical theatre 1997.

Unless it is already involved in a particular initiative, the Arts Council is likely to be interested in locally-based arts work only where it can be shown for one reason or another to have national relevance. For most people working at community level the RAB will be the appropriate starting place in the search for funds and advice.

Regional Arts Boards (RABs)

The ten Regional Arts Boards replaced the twelve Regional Arts Associations which for many years supported and promoted the arts in the regions of England. RABs are limited companies controlled by boards of directors, the chairs of which are appointed by the Secretary of State for National Heritage. Their structures vary, but each has a chief executive reporting to the board, and a number of departments to manage their work. Artforms and other functions have generally been grouped together in fewer, larger departments than in the past, and the number and functions of advisory committees has been reduced.

Although RABs fund the arts on both a revenue and a project basis, the former is naturally more difficult to secure, simply because the pattern of revenue funding for the arts changes slowly. Even very good new developments may have to wait for resources to be found, either from other revenue clients or from funding increases, and this sort of flexibility tends to be possible only over more than one financial year. Where revenue funding is offered by an RAB it may be three year funding linked to a business plan, though this has become more unusual recently.

The Secretary of State's instruction to the Arts Council to reduce its administrative costs will undoubtedly result in the closure of some departments.

Some of the longer-term benefits of Arts 2000 lie in the community-based elements of each year's programme. These can sometimes seem to have a lower profile during the year itself, but are both in demand and sustainable afterwards. In Birmingham, the Year of Music's community programme, *Sound It Out*, has continued and is now an independent community music organisation.

Get hold of the latest annual report of your RAB for an account of its current structure and work. Some RABs - eg London Arts Board - produce leaflets which describe the various funding schemes they offer.

However, RABs often have excellent project funding schemes through which short-term work can be supported, and you can ask for details and deadlines. It is worth looking not only at the schemes which relate to your own artform, but also to cross-artform schemes and issue-related initiatives. Project funding offered by an RAB will normally be paid in stages, with the final part only being released on submission of a report and project accounts, and this can cause cash-flow difficulties. This is particularly the case if a grant is offered in the form of a guarantee against loss, since you will need to show what loss has been made on an event in order to claim.

Local authorities

Local authorities - county, city, borough and district councils - have become increasingly important funders of the arts over the past 20 years, though their involvement varies from place to place and with different political priorities. It is important to remember that local authority funding of the arts is discretionary, so policies vary. However, the objective of funding will always be to benefit audiences and the local community - not to support artists and companies as such. Generally speaking the larger the authority, the more active its support for the arts is likely to be, so county councils, metropolitan boroughs and city councils can be expected to be more involved than some rural districts with much smaller resources. Nonetheless some small councils have exemplary arts policies and programmes from which others could learn. Approaches also vary, from councils who prefer to employ arts workers directly to those who support independent arts organisations through a small directly-employed staff team and those who do both.

The decision-making process, based on principles of local democracy, is normally straightforward. Decisions are made by elected councillors (members) in relevant committee meetings, on the advice of their officers. In larger authorities there is often a leisure, recreation or even an arts department, though in many cases the arts form a section within a larger department such as education. There will almost always be an arts officer, or at least an officer with responsibility for the arts among other duties. Those councils who regularly fund the arts generally have clear and well-established processes through which it is possible to apply for funds. Larger local authorities also have responsibility for education, social services and other important local services which may be relevant to your work. For instance there are many precedents for obtaining social services or education funding for projects which can be shown to advance the work of those departments.

1.4 A Changing Agenda - Local government reorganisation

In 1989/90 spending on the arts by local authorities was:

County Councils	£11m
Metropolitan districts	£22m
City of London	£26m
London boroughs	£29m
Shire districts	£70m
Total	£158m

Much of the shire districts' expenditure was on venues, while County Council expenditure predominantly takes the form of grants to organisations. **14.1** ☞ *Local Authorities, Entertainment and the Arts*

Contacts for arts officers in local authorities can be found in the British *Performing Arts Yearbook.*

1.4 A Changing Agenda, see sections on education, social services and CCT.

Government departments

The Department of Health provided Section 64 funding towards the cost of an arts programme by people with learning difficulties associated with the 1989 Special Olympics held in Leicester.

Although most government funding of the arts is channelled through the arts funding system, it is occasionally possible to get funding for innovative arts projects through departments other than the DNH, including the Department for Education, Department of Health, the Home Office and others. In most cases funding will come through specific schemes whose titles are not always informative. Thus Section 11 funding, administered through the Home Office, is designed to help local authorities meet the costs of staff working with some ethnic minority groups (a post can be based within and managed by a voluntary organisation). The first hurdle is discovering the possible schemes, since individual departments vary in their handling of them and their responses to voluntary organisations. Some helpful guides are published, but you will need to allow sufficient time to research the possibilities. Moreover, the project for which you are seeking funding will have to meet the scheme's criteria. Ensuring that it does may be simply a case of rethinking - and presenting - your work from the department's point of view, but in other cases you may need to make changes. It's possible that these changes could improve the project, by introducing ideas or possibilities which you had not considered, but you need to be wary of losing sight of your actual objectives.

14.5 ☞ The Central Government Grants Guide

Non-governmental organisations

Public Bodies, published by the Cabinet Office, describes 1,412 non-departmental public bodies currently functioning in Britain. Although the number of these has reduced by 755 since 1979, their powers and expenditure have increased markedly. Expenditure by quangos on local services - excluding health and training - has been estimated at £5.6 billion in 1992/3.

Non-governmental organisations form a significant and growing part of the public sector. They include autonomous organisations, whose funding, functions and senior management are determined by government, and organisations which have a closer relation to government. Their legal status and processes are often unclear to outsiders. They include Development Corporations, Housing Action Trusts, NHS Trusts, the Rural Development Commission, the British Council, the Sports Council, the Commission for Racial Equality and many more. Many of these organisations can make successful partners and funders for arts projects, though their approach and interest will vary widely from health authorities prepared to offer three-year funding agreements to organisations like English Heritage which might be interested in making a historic building available for an arts project.

The European dimension

14.5 ☞ Bread and Circuses 14.4 ☞ Destination Europe; Networking in Europe; Who Does What in Europe?

The European Union succeeded the European Community on 1st January 1994, and the progressive erosion of barriers between member states continues. There is a vast range of programmes and schemes administered by the EU, a number of which potentially represent a source of funding for community-based arts work. As with the funding schemes of British government departments, the hardest task is threading your way through a massive bureaucratic structure and finding out what the options are. Having done so, you may find it difficult to satisfy the criteria: one scheme offering funding for arts work by disabled people requires the involvement of no less than four EU countries. Generally speaking, these schemes are particularly appropriate for international projects linking groups or projects in more than one country. They are also sometimes appropriate for projects working with disadvantaged groups, particularly where it could lead to skills acquisition or employment.

6.3   FUNDING FROM CHARITABLE TRUSTS

Charitable trusts, some of which have been operating since the 19th century or earlier, exist to apply the resources (usually money) which they hold in trust to designated charitable objectives. They donate several hundred million pounds to voluntary organisations and other beneficiaries each year, and they can be a very good source of funding for specific projects. (To put that into perspective, the single largest source of income received by the voluntary sector is from legacies, which provide a quarter of total annual revenue.) There is a huge number - the Directory of Social Change has split its latest directory into two volumes listing 1,000 trusts - ranging from large organisations like the Joseph Rowntree Foundation, Children In Need or the Tudor Trust to those with no permanent staff, though the size of the organisation is not in itself evidence of its wealth or its giving. Many charitable trusts specifically include the arts in their areas of concern while the interests of others - in areas such as education, disability or social welfare - can easily relate to a wide range of community-based arts projects, though you need to learn to think laterally about your work. Some charitable trusts restrict their areas of benefit to particular parts of the country.

Success in fundraising from charitable trusts depends on good research and common sense. Several directories are published annually giving details of charitable trusts and their interests. If this is a potentially important source of income for your work, you may find it worthwhile to subscribe to *Trust Monitor*, which is published three times a year by the Directory of Social Change, and provides information about new trusts as well as background on changes in the trust world. *Funding*

14.5 ☛ *A Guide to the Major Trusts* (Volumes 1 & 2), *Mailout* magazine publishes some information about current funding opportunities, as do the magazines (*Sounding Board, Animated, Total Theatre* etc) of national art-form organisations. *Trust Monitor* and *Funding Digest* are useful to people with significant responsibility for fundraising.

Funder Finder is a registered charity which has developed computer software to assist people seeking grants in identifying appropriate charitable trusts. The software is licenced to the user - at different rates depending on the type of organisation - who installs it on computer and is then able to search a database of some 1,400 charitable trusts for potential funders whose interests match those of the project. The database is updated at six-monthly intervals.
15.8 Contacts

Digest is another regularly produced source of information which covers trusts, as well as other funding opportunities.

6.4 FUNDING FROM THE PRIVATE SECTOR

Private sector companies have become more interested in supporting the arts in recent years. This support comes as sponsorship, as a donation or as help in kind, though the dividing line between sponsorship and donation is often blurred in practice.

Sponsorship

Sponsorship of the arts, properly termed, is a commercial activity akin to advertising. A company which is considering investing in arts sponsorship will be looking for a solid return for its money - enhanced public visibility, association with quality, even glamour, and opportunities to offer hospitality to its guests. Although these can be offered by the RSC at Stratford, or a regional concert hall, they cannot so easily be offered by someone trying to organise a weekend dance event, or support a regular writer's group in a residential home. Pressure on arts organisations to find commercial sponsorship has increased in recent years, and there is kudos to be gained by securing it, but unless you have a serious commercial proposition to offer, you should relegate it to the end of your list of fundraising options. Think about the tangible benefits you could offer a potential sponsor which might encourage them to fund your project.

There is an exception to this general rule. It is possible to persuade a company to sponsor an annual report or other publication, or to place an advertisement in a programme, though even this can take a considerable amount of time in relation to the income generated. In looking for this sort of sponsor, you will probably do best to start with the people you actually do business with.

Donations

14.5 ☞ *A Guide to Company Giving*

For anyone trying to promote community-based arts work, corporate donations offer another realistic route to funding in the commercial sector. The 300 most generous companies give about £115m annually, a figure which has been increasing steadily in real terms for some years: the latest *Guide to Company Giving* lists more than 200 companies which have increased their donations by 100% or more since the previous edition (though others have made reductions). They include many smaller companies and it does not follow that the scale of charitable giving is always related to profits or turnover. Among the reasons which prompt companies to give money to charitable causes is the tax-effectiveness of doing so, but the complexities of the law in this area means that some companies pass their donations through a separate company trust (such as the Laura Ashley Foundation) or through the Charities Aid Foundation.

Other help

Money is not the only help which can be sought from the private sector. Arts and voluntary organisations have successfully negotiated donations of equipment or materials and secondments of staff to help achieve specific goals. Action Employees In The Community is a national charity (with regional offices) which helps act as a link between the private and voluntary sectors to negotiate secondments and placements Some businesses with whom you deal regularly may also be prepared to offer you a discount on goods and services because of your non-profit-making aims. This is also true of some of the professional people whose services you use on an ongoing basis - solicitors, accountants etc. Indeed the generous charging policies of some members of these professions amounts to a hidden form of arts sponsorship and charitable donation.

Action Employees In The Community produces a publication called **14.5** ☛ *Getting the Best from Secondment.* Other organisations in this field include REACH (Retired Executives Action Clearing House) and Emeritus Register.

4.7 Legal matters

Association for Business Sponsorship in the Arts (ABSA)

ABSA was established in 1976 by businesses involved in sponsorship of the arts to support and facilitate their activities. The head office is in London, with branches in Edinburgh, Cardiff, Belfast and Halifax. The organisation set up and runs the Business Sponsorship Incentive Scheme (BSIS), designed to draw in new commercial sponsors, and produces useful publications as well as offering advice and training in the field. It is also involved in secondments of business people to arts organisations. Membership of ABSA is open to arts organisations as well as private sector companies.

6.5 PLANNING A FUNDRAISING STRATEGY

The funding needs of community-based arts projects fall into two categories: ongoing (revenue) funding to establish an organisation, and short-term (project) funding to finance individual pieces of work. For many people working as animateurs or development workers this will often mean linking revenue

14.5 ☛ **Funding**

funding with salary and overheads, and project funding with the programme of work although, as is discussed below, the lines between the two can, and probably should be blurred.

Since it usually represents an ongoing and substantial financial commitment, revenue funding is hard to get. It may take several years of negotiation to put together a two or three funder partnership to fund even a single post. If, in relation to your post, that task was accomplished before your appointment, your concern will be to maintain, prolong or expand the revenue base, something which can be achieved only through the quality of your work and negotiations with the existing funders. It's a long-term process and depends on building good working relationships.

If you do not already have revenue funding, you may be anxious to get it, both for the financial security it offers, and for the recognition of value it confers. But, as mentioned above, public funding systems - and especially the RABs - find it very difficult to take on new revenue funding commitments. Once the annual budget has been set, there often remains only very small amounts of money with which to respond to new initiatives. Flexibility exists only between financial years and then only if the overall budget has grown, or there are good reasons to shift money from existing clients to fund new ones.

But, whether you already have revenue funding and want to increase it, or are simply trying to get some money for your work, your fundraising will be much more effective if you rethink your work in terms of projects.

Fundraising through projects

The reasons why funders can be reluctant to offer revenue funding should be clear from the last section. But it is not just the terms of the funding that make a difference: there are some things whose very nature make them difficult to fundraise for:

- salaries

- administrative support

- office accommodation

- equipment

- travel, insurance and other invisible costs

- publicity and print

At the same time funders *are* prepared to support short-term projects which directly involve people, for understandable reasons:

- they cost less

- they represent a short-term commitment

- their objectives can be simply expressed and easily understood

- they are directly concerned with activity and people

- they are more attractive to be associated with

- their benefits can be identified and assessed

- they produce outcomes quickly

- their costs can be clearly stated

- the consequences of failure are limited

This sort of thinking by funders means that the same body which rejected your request for £2,000 towards your salary and overheads, may happily give you that amount or more in the course of a year towards individual community-based arts projects. Although this position is inconsistent since, without adequate administrative support the projects can't be run, it exists and is not something you can change. But you can change how you respond to it.

Instead of asking for general support for your work or your organisation, tie funding applications to your programme of work. The management process described above shows how to narrow your overall aim down to clear objectives and precise targets. It enables you to draw up a plan of work for the coming 12, 18 or 36 months, listing the projects you plan to run, when and how. Every proposed piece of work should be listed and costed. The work will probably fall into one of the following categories:

3.5 Policy and planning

- **Sessions you will run yourself**
  Although your time may be paid for through your fee or salary, you may have to meet the cost of room or equipment hire, transport for disabled participants, refreshments, publicity, interpreters etc.

- **Sessions you need another artist or practitioner to run**
  If the sessions are in a field or style in which you do not have expertise, you may need to bring in someone else to run them, in which case their fees and expenses will have to be added to the other costs mentioned above.

- **Other projects**
  This would include anything above and beyond regular sessions, including festivals, performances, tours, residencies etc.

- **Capital projects**
  Some projects you have planned will have capital implications: for instance, if you plan to set up a database of local people interested in mime, you will have to buy equipment, software and probably training.

For each of these projects you will need to draw up a budget estimating the cost as well as you can, allowing for the effect of rising prices in projects which are further off. So the cost of a week's residency by a mime company in a community centre might look like this:

Company fees	1,500
Travel and accommodation	500
Room hire and crèche	400
Publicity	250
Total expenditure	£2,650

But this is actually only a part of the real cost of putting on the project. Your time, administrative overheads and related costs are all invisibly supporting the project. So make them visible:

Company fees	1,500
Travel and accommodation	500
Room hire and crèche	400
Publicity	250
Staff time (3 days)	300
Administrative overheads	125
Monitoring and evaluation	100
Contingency	50
Total expenditure	£3,225

Now the actual cost of the week-long residency is clear, you can look at how it is going to be met. If your post is fully-funded and all your overheads are met, you may think it right not to charge any of your costs to the project, but simply to write in as income a contribution from your main organisational budget to balance the costs of your time. On the other hand, you may have no funding, in which case all those costs will have to be met from the project's income. In practice, because few posts or organisations have enough revenue funding to meet all their costs, you may be able to cover only a part of your time and administrative overheads from your existing resources. Having done so, you can then complete your budget:

Expenditure:

Company fees	1,500
Travel and accommodation	500
Room hire and crèche	400
Publicity	250
Staff time (3 days)	300
Administrative overheads	125
Monitoring and evaluation	100
Contingency	50
Total expenditure	**£3,225**

Income:

Regional Arts Board	750
City Council	750
County Council	500
Charitable trusts	1,000
Total income:	**£3,000**
Shortfall (met from reserves):	£225

There are various ways in which the contribution from your revenue funding can be shown, depending on circumstances. If you have a project budget, your fundraising task will also be made easier, not only because you will have to raise less money, but because you can use your own resources both to find matching funding and to underwrite a project.

In the example given above, the costs charged to the project were calculated by deciding how much time the development worker or animateur would need to set up and monitor the project, with an allowance for travel and subsistence. The further costs of actually planning the work and writing the grant applications was deemed to be covered by revenue funding, though these could be included. Another way to determine how much to charge to projects is to apportion the difference between actual revenue funding and projected salaries and overheads to all projects indiscriminately or according to a formula. This approach should be treated with caution since it can produce financial problems if targets are not met. It is much safer to plan to spend on salaries and overheads only as much as is covered by revenue funding. Then income generated by projects over the course of one year can build reserves

If you are building core costs into projects which you will be submitting to your existing revenue funders for project grants, you will need to agree the basis on which this can be done. The simplest answer is probably to tie any additional grants received from them to specific - and clearly additional - items of expenditure, like fees for visiting artists.

with which to expand core functions the following year, or used to safeguard projects which are hard to fundraise for or don't achieve their income generation targets.

Planning a coherent fundraising strategy based on a rolling programme of distinct projects has many advantages:

- You are in control not only of your programme, but of its financing, and can make adjustments to take account of developments.

- You give yourself the best chance of securing the funding you need by putting the real nature of what you do - the creative work - up front, while acknowledging its need for administrative foundations.

- You may be able to negotiate an input into more than one project, or even the whole programme, from the same funding body.

- You can assess the likelihood of achieving your financial targets before you make spending commitments.

- You can plan the timing of your approaches to funders to meet their deadlines and maximise the likelihood of success.

- You have a clear, workable document on the basis of which you can negotiate to bring your needs and those of funders together.

One of the most crucial elements of successful fundraising is working to a long enough timescale, yet another reason for planning your work in advance.

It is not possible to set up a system like this quickly. If you are not familiar with the approach, it may take some time to think it through. In particular the habit of planning months or years in advance can seem to threaten your ability to be spontaneous and responsive. But there are a number of ways in which to build in the capacity to be responsive to a programme plan: you can sketch in two or three projects which could be executed in different ways, or set up a continuous small-scale project with rolling funding, or build up your reserves so that you have the resources to set up things quickly. It is also true to say that most people would prefer to be involved in a properly-planned and funded project, even if that means delaying it for six months.

In deciding where to look for your funding, always balance your time investment against the funds you might raise: it is easy to invest more time securing £500 than £5,000 by misjudging this.

A planned programme and fundraising strategy will take effort to put in place, and you may need to take advice. You will need to gain experience in all aspects of your work and region, and to work with your management and funders to make it possible. It will be necessary to keep careful records of all potential funders and your dealings with them - when you applied, how much for, and the outcome etc - in order to make the best use of your time. Even then it will take some months to begin working for you. But it remains the most effective way to raise money for community-based arts work partly because it stems from and supports good management practice.

Professional support for fundraising

Your fundraising work can be supported by the use of outside consultants in two ways. You can pay someone to fundraise for you, usually on a performance-related scale, or you can pay someone to help you make your own fundraising more effective. The second option is generally preferable for people working in community-based arts promotion, because it can help make the organisation structurally better equipped to fundraise and the people within it more skillful at the task. Therefore if you want support in this area, and can find the resources to pay for it, you should look for someone who is interested in helping develop your skills or those of the organisation in general, rather than someone who proposes to go away and come back with some money. You should also make sure that they have experience of the particular concerns and practice in the arts. Your RAB, or the Arts Council database of consultants, would be a good starting point.

3.9 Using Consultants

3.9 Using consultants
7.3 Types of training -
Tailor-made training

6.6   PLANNING A PROJECT APPLICATION

In the context of solid planning and a coherent fundraising strategy, it is much easier to plan individual project applications. Over time you will develop relationships with a number of key funders, among which the RAB and local authority will probably be paramount. Agreement about levels and methods for project funding your work with these two or three bodies will be invaluable, and will form a foundation onto which you can build funding from other less regular sources like charitable trusts, commercial companies and others.

But before you start looking for funders, or writing applications, you need to think through the project from a funder's point of view. They will consider your application in relation to a number of questions:

- **What need is being addressed by the project?**
  Unless you can identify and express the need for a project, you will find it very difficult to persuade anyone to pay for it. This does not imply that all projects should be an extension of charitable or social work: the need

may be the absence of music opportunities in an area, but if so, it should be stated, and the applications should be made to those bodies with an interest in addressing such a need. Even they are unlikely to be interested in funding more arts work where it already exists.

- **What evidence is there that this need exists?**
  You need evidence to convince people that the need is real - statistics, figures, arguments, quotations - objective facts to support your case. No funder will be impressed by simple assertions, however forcefully put.

- **How will the project address that need?**
  You must show clearly how, for example, weekly dance workshops will address the identified needs of the single parents they are aimed at. This is a tighter way of describing the project's benefits.

- **Is the person or organisation applying the right one to do the work?**
  You must explain why you, rather than anyone else, are best suited to run the project and so bring about the benefits.

- **What track record do they have?**
  You have to inspire confidence in yourself and your work by referring to your successes: facts, figures, press cuttings, comments from participants, quotes from other funders and supporters will all help.

- **Are they well-managed, reliable, efficient and cost-effective?**
  This is similar to the question above, but relates to how the organisation or post is run, rather than what it has achieved. The nature and presentation of your approach to the funder - eg have you followed their guidelines, do you know who to write to? - will be the most obvious evidence of this. The financial information you present such as budget and annual accounts are also essential.

- **What effect will the funders' decisions have on the project ?**
  Funders need to understand the consequences of rejection: does this mean the project will not be able to go ahead, or only in a limited form? Are the other funders committed, and what will happen if some agree but others do not?

- **What are the weaknesses of the applicant's case?**
  You have to consider the possible weaknesses in your case, the reasons why your proposal might be turned down, and build counter-arguments into your application. Look at the project from the point of view of someone who is hostile to your work.

Identifying potential funders

Some potential funders will be obvious (the RAB and local authority for instance) or a body with a clear remit (like the Rural Development Commission) but others will be identified through research. Take the time to look through the various guides published by organisations like the Directory of Social Change, and read the information carefully. Make sure that you understand the funders' priorities and procedures, and, if they seem a likely possibility, try to contact them by phone. Although some funders are reluctant to discuss projects over the phone, others can be very helpful. A preliminary conversation can ensure that you don't waste anyone's time by making unsuitable or untimely applications, and can help you get a better understanding of the body you are dealing with. Checking simple facts, like who to address the application to and when it may be dealt with, can also save time. If you have spoken to someone on the phone they will recognise your application when it arrives, and be able to picture the person who sent it. You will have laid the foundations of interest and eventually of trust.

Finally, in thinking about potential funders, try to look at your project from different angles than the one you are used to: there may be benefits you have not considered which would be of interest to funders you have not thought of.

6.7   WRITING AN APPLICATION

To run a successful project, you have to think through each part of it beforehand. Writing an application is only a matter of putting that thinking onto paper in a clear and straightforward way. The journalist's instruction to include who, what, when, where, how and why is useful here, so long as you remember to add how much.

There are different formats which can be adopted according to taste and circumstance, and in some cases you will need to complete an application form, but the following structure may provide a starting point.

1. Summary

Summarise the project on one side of double-spaced, typed A4: this may be as much as anyone reads, so make it clear, strong, and simple. An alternative is to summarise the project in a covering letter, but this may get detached from the application in some organisations. Making a good summary is not easy, particularly when a project is complicated, but it is a skill worth acquiring.

2. Background

Explain who you are and how and why the project came about. In most cases this can be kept to a paragraph or two, with reference to an appendix or an annual report for further information on your history, track record, funding and legal status. Don't hold up the flow of the application with routine information here.

3. Aim and objectives

3.5 Policy and planning

State the aim and objectives of the project.

4. The project

This is the heart of your application, so give yourself space to describe the project clearly, explaining what will happen, where, when and who with. There will be more space here to develop the reasons for its importance which will have been touched on in part 2.

5. Project management

Explain how you are going to manage and administer the project and how it will be monitored and evaluated.

6. Follow up

Explain how you will develop the project after completion, or why it is not appropriate to do so. (You may need to reassure the funder subtly that you will not be asking them for long-term funding.)

7. Budget

Include a budget, with any notes required to make it clear.

Although the form of project applications will vary, there are some common ground rules which are worth following:

Do

- State clearly why the project is important

- State clearly why the funder should support it

- Support your case with evidence

- Follow any guidelines for applications which are given
- Type your application neatly on A4 paper (one side of the sheet)
- Use good English, avoid jargon, and write positively
- Number your paragraphs for ease of reference
- Be brief - you can provide more details if you are asked
- Enclose a good annual report, if possible
- Carry out the work you are funded to do in accordance with the commitments you have made, or negotiate changes if these become unavoidable
- Keep in touch with funders at all points
- Be persistent, and apply for another project if you are turned down

Don't

- Address a letter Dear Sir/Madam unless it is unavoidable
- Send general, circular appeals
- Try to impress with the bulk of your application or the complexity of your language
- Assume that the funder understands and supports the arts unless you have good reason to think so
- Make unsupported claims, use extravagant adjectives, or offer promises which are vague or undeliverable
- Forget to thank your funders and credit them as appropriate

The secretary of at least one company trust discards all letters addressed Dear Sir/Madam without reading them, simply as a way of beginning the weeding out process.

6.8   EARNED INCOME AND FUNDRAISING EVENTS

You can supplement funding and grant aid by generating income from various aspects of your work, including ticket sales, workshop fees, sales of publications, tapes etc. Charging fees for training events, or to make presentations on your field of expertise may also be a viable alternative. However, raising income in this way demands a very sensitive pricing policy to ensure that access objectives are not undermined by cost factors. In practice the income generated by most community-

Check with the funder before crediting them: some charitable trusts and companies carefully avoid being mentioned by recipients, others have clear instructions as to how and when acknowledgement should be made.

based arts work is probably best seen as a bonus rather than something which can be relied upon, though it may make a significant contribution to an individual project.

The exceptions to this are promotions with substantial audience reach - performances or outdoor events - and specific fundraising events. These last can include anything from sponsored cycle rides to charity auctions, or raffles to benefit gigs, and can be very successful. In this context, they probably work best when they are closely linked to your central activity - eg a benefit concert for a music development agency, or a sponsored read to support literature development work. Their impact in raising the profile of your work may actually be greater than their financial benefit. These events can also be, in terms of the ratio between time invested and money raised, far less efficient ways of generating income than old-fashioned applications and negotiations. Finally, you should consider the implications of seeking charitable donations of this sort. Does the organisation want to be identified in the public mind as a charity seeking money in competition with other worthwhile causes? Is it equipped to make itself accountable to individual donors? The Charities Act now regulates such fundraising quite closely, and the issues should be carefully thought through before venturing into this area.

TRAINING AND PERSONAL DEVELOPMENT

7

7 TRAINING AND PERSONAL DEVELOPMENT

Summary
This chapter looks at training and personal development. The importance of these things to animateurs and practitioners, and how to prepare a personal training plan. Section 7.3 describes types of training from short courses to mentoring, and 7.4 looks at who provides training. The last section gives an indication of where to get financial support.

7.1 THE VALUE OF TRAINING

The amount of information which has been packed into this book so far should give a fair idea of the range of skills and knowledge any animateur or arts development worker needs to do their job, (and no mention has been made of creative practice). Different college courses can provide a good grounding in specific artforms or in arts management, but few offer the combination of these skills which is so fundamental to developing professional arts work in the community. In any case, nobody stops learning when they leave full-time education. The working environment is constantly changing as social policy and business practice develop: the demands made upon practitioners and arts organisations develop equally quickly. Since these changes are inevitable, so is the need for continuing learning, the rate of which should be at least equal to the pace of change. In-service training is one of the crucial ways in which workers continue to develop. Among the benefits of investment in training which most employers recognise are that it:

- improves individual and group performance;
- helps the organisation keep up-to-date with developments in practice, and current issues and brings in new ideas;
- enables personal and career development and is good for morale and job satisfaction;
- helps retain effective employees;

- offers, in the context of managerial appraisal, opportunities to support and improve the work of individuals where necessary;

- repays the time and resources committed to it.

All arts development workers, whether employed or freelance, should have access to training in the course of their work. Although this implies time off work and a financial commitment on the part of the post's funders, it should be seen as fundamental to ensuring the success of such an initiative. An investment of 2-5% of the total budget can, in providing training support and development, not only improve performance by much larger margins, but in some cases prevent the failure of a post because an individual worker has inadequate support.

The arts world has invested increasingly in training in recent years, with a wide range of initiatives, most of which are described below. Potentially of considerable significance is the work of the Arts and Entertainments Training Council (AETC) which has been working on draft standards for National Vocational Qualifications (NVQ) in the arts. NVQs have been developed in recent years by industry groups, with the involvement of the education sector, as a way of working towards a recognised consistency of standards, and many college courses are now linked to an NVQ offering, alongside workplace assessment, a structured path to recognised qualifications. The application of NVQs to training in the arts has provoked different responses, from those who see them as a way of professionalising the work and enhancing the recognition and status of practitioners, to those who see the codification of creative achievements as at best irrelevant and at worst potentially restrictive. The AETC publishes a free quarterly newsletter, *Training Matters*, which offers an insight into these debates.

It is easy, given the pressure of work under which arts development workers operate, to neglect training, but its importance both to your present job and to your overall career development should not be underestimated. Whether or not you expect to stay in your present job for the foreseeable future, you need to give proper value to yourself as a professional worker, and that means maintaining and developing your skills in the context of your long-term career objectives.

15.7 Contacts

In Scotland parallel work is being undertaken to develop Scottish Vocational Qualifications (SVQs).

14.6 ☛ *A Bluffer's Guide to NVQs*

7.2 PREPARING A TRAINING PLAN

Some training needs will probably become obvious fairly soon after you take up a new post, and it will be natural to deal with these first However, once things have settled down a little, you can review your skills and knowledge in the context of the demands made upon you by the job, and then draw up a training plan. It would be helpful to do this in consultation with your line manager, a member of your management committee or a colleague. The training plan can be a simple document, identifying and prioritising your needs and the best training solutions for them. It will need to take account of how much time you can spend away from the the primary task of doing your job, and the cost implications of different options.

4.3 Employment - Induction for new employees

Assessing your training needs

Everyone will have different training needs, but the following checklist may help you identify your own in relation to the particular job you do:

- **Artform practice** - to improve your own skills as a practitioner

- **Teaching** - running workshops, classes and residencies

- **Communication** - speaking and writing skills, presentation, negotiation, assertiveness training

- **Financial** - bookkeeping, keeping records, budgeting and understanding accounts, cash flow, management accounts, auditing

- **Fundraising** - developing better applications, working with the private sector, presenting your projects

- **Management** - legal structures and obligations, working with management committees, planning work, business planning, time management

- **Employment** - management of staff, use of freelance workers, use of volunteers, the legal framework

- **Computers** - word-processing, financial management, databases, DTP

- **Equal opportunities** - developing understanding of current issues and thinking in gender, race, sexuality, disability

- **Marketing** - producing publicity material, working with the media, writing copy, DTP

Reviewing the plan

A training plan should be reviewed annually, normally as part of an employee's appraisal, to see how training targets have been met, and whether changes should be made. It is important to remember that the changes do not only affect the worker, since the environment in which they operate is also continually changing.

1.4 A changing agenda

Making training work

Investment in training is sometimes undermined by the worker's inability to apply what they have learnt to their work in practice. This is partly because most training is general, rather than focused on the particular situation in which the person operates. It is also partly because when you return to work the day-by-day demands don't leave enough space to think about how to put in place the things that you have learned. There are a number of things you can do to facilitate the integration of your training experiences into your work:

- keep an action list while you are attending a training course, noting good ideas, who you need to discuss them with, and when you plan to start to put them into effect

- set aside some time a week or ten days after the training course, to go through your notes, type up a short report on what you have learned, and review its application

- set aside time to share your newly-acquired experience with colleagues or members of your management committee as appropriate

It is important that the new ideas which are bought by investing in training do not remain with the person who benefited from the training if they are to have lasting value for the organisation as a whole. People who are working on their own may find it difficult to share these things in practice, though networking provides a good opportunity. If you are meeting, formally or informally, with colleagues in your field, a discussion of training needs and experiences can be very valuable.

2.4 Partnerships and networking

7.3   TYPES OF TRAINING

Training opportunities have grown substantially over the past decade and there is a good choice of short courses aimed directly at arts workers and the voluntary sector generally. At the same time, the way people think about training has changed with increasing use being made of work placements, traineeships and mentoring. The way in which you use different approaches to training will depend on your needs, what is available and your own preferences.

Short courses
Probably the most easily-accessible form of training, short courses are provided by a large number of voluntary-sector and education organisations. They typically address a clearly defined area - time management, assertiveness training, basic bookkeeping etc - and follow various formats from a single day to residential blocks of three or five days. They can be a good way of building skills and understanding quickly, though it is essential to plan how the new ideas will be applied back at work. Colleges and adult education services also offer evening classes and part-time courses; Day release courses and distance learning may also be useful possibilities.

Placements
Placements with other organisations can be an excellent way of learning from the experiences of people who have been doing similar work to you. They offer a chance to learn about how other people have managed the problems that you face, and provide not only practical solutions, but a wide range of less tangible benefits in terms of personal development. They should always be carefully managed, so that everyone involved understands clearly their role and the aims of the placement

A less experienced practitioner worked alongside the consultant employed on the South East Arts Mime Development Project.

Mentoring
Mentoring is a training model which has been receiving increasing attention in recent years. Schemes vary, but each links a new, or less-experienced worker, with a 'mentor' who is well-established in their field, so they can play a particularly useful role in the induction process. The link may operate formally for a year or more, with the trainee spending time shadowing the mentor, or discussing problems and ideas. In successful schemes - which depend partly on making the right match between individuals - the resultant friendship will often mean that links continue informally thereafter. Although mentoring can represent a significant investment in training, having access to a very experienced guide can transform the effectiveness of a newly-appointed worker.

A relatively inexperienced community arts worker was chosen by a tenants' association for a new project in the Midlands. The funders, whilst happy with the choice of candidate, made available an additional £2,000 to pay for support and guidance from a more experienced worker to offer support from a distance. The training worked very well, and proved to be an excellent investment.

Merseyside Youth Dance Forum, a consortium of youth dance groups, commissioned a fundraising course to meet their joint fundraising needs. During 1993 Yorkshire Dance Centre bought CDMF's fundraising course for its regional practitioners.

3.9 Using consultants

Tailor-made training

In addition to drawing on the available training opportunities, it is sometimes worth creating new ones to address particular needs. This will usually mean contracting a freelance trainer or consultant to work with you on a particular project. For instance, instead of going on a short course in three-year planning, much of which will be theoretical and general, you could employ a consultant to work with you on your own plan. To be cost-effective, such an approach needs good preparation, but a couple of days with the right consultant could leave you with your plan largely completed, and the skills to do it yourself next time. Apart from the benefit of focusing the training on your specific needs, such an approach enables you to involve management and colleagues in the process. It should leave you well-equipped to manage the task independently from then on. Alternatively, a group of animateurs or practitioners could co-operate to buy such a training course, with similar benefits.

Conferences

A skills-centred training plan will need to be supplemented by knowledge-centred training - usually in the form of attending conferences, seminars and similar events addressing particular issues. There are many such events in the course of a year covering a vast range of subjects, and your choice will depend on your job. The conferences and seminars of the specialist art-form organisations will be a priority for most animateurs and practitioners, but others looking at particular social issues or practice will provide further scope for development. Conferences are particularly good at informing you of changes in the legal climate - eg the Charities Act 1992 - and steeping you in the atmosphere and pre-occupations of a particular group such as charitable trusts.

During 1993 CDMF offered traineeships to four people to develop their careers as freelance or employed community dance practitioners. One traineeship was offered on a job-share basis to a South Asian dancer and a Raqs Sharqi dance, both of whom wanted to develop skills in this area.

Traineeships

Traineeships usually offer a basic salary or bursary and run for anything from 3 to 24 months. They offer training through work placements supported by individual guidance and short courses. The Arts Council, RABs and some arts organisations have supported a number over the years, to provide a solid foundation from which individuals can move into arts employment. In this context, they may be most relevant to people seeking to extend their work by setting up new traineeships.

7.4 TRAINING PROVIDERS

You can get access to training courses from a number of public and independent providers. If you want to set up tailor-made training, start by talking with other people working in the field, the specialist artform organisation or your RAB to draw on other people's experiences and identify potential consultants. The Arts Council training unit is very knowledgeable about all aspects of training in the arts.

Regional arts training centres
The Arts Council and RABs have for a number of years been investing in regional arts training centres to offer short courses in arts training. The five centres operating to date are in Leicester, Liverpool, Sussex, Newcastle and the South West. The first three are attached to universities; the Newcastle centre has been re-established with the Management Centre, while the most recent, the Regional Training Unit South West operates through the RAB. Each centre runs an ongoing programme of courses, mostly orientated to management and administration skills, but with some practice-orientated courses. Through the National RTC Network they encourage training provision throughout the industry through advisory and consultancy support. Get yourself added to the mailing list to keep informed of courses and other opportunities.

15.7 Contacts

Voluntary sector trainers
There are a number of organisations - mostly operating on a non-profit-making basis - which offer training courses geared to the specific needs of the arts and voluntary sector. Many of these courses are not only excellent in their content, but provide valuable opportunities to meet other people and share experiences. Among these organisations are The Directory of Social Change, the National Council of Voluntary Organisations, InterChange Training, and The Management Centre. Some of these organisations are also major publishers in the field, so being on their mailing lists will keep you in touch with a wide range of useful opportunities.

15.7 Contacts

Mime Action Group and Dance UK have set up Training Action Group to develop training opportunities in dance, mime and physical theatre.

TECs and other providers
Training and Enterprise Councils (Local Enterprise Companies in Scotland) are independent local training providers which have taken over the work of the Training Agency. TECs support a wide range of courses, often delivered by local voluntary organisations; check the phone book for contacts, or use the Training Access Points in central libraries. Other providers

181

include local colleges and adult education institutes, the Workers Educational Association (WEA), university extra-mural departments, local voluntary organisations and the private sector. The training opportunities offered by these providers may be more academically-orientated, and will not necessarily relate closely to the daily needs of people working in community-based arts development.

7.5 PAYING FOR TRAINING

If you have access to a generous training budget you may be able to meet your training costs without needing to raise additional funds. Even so you may find it worthwhile to seek support for training costs from other sources, if only to make your existing budgets go further. There are a number of potential sources to whom you can apply, but the first step should perhaps be to discuss your plans with the relevant officer of your RAB - some have designated training officers, but there will always be someone whose brief includes training.

Arts sector funding

Both the Arts Council and the RABs have a strong commitment to training, expressed through funding providers, encouraging clients to develop good practice and giving discretionary bursaries and grants to help meet the costs of training. Most training grants to individuals cover 50% of the fees and related costs (such as travel). Contact the relevant officer of your RAB in the first instance to find out more about schemes and opportunities. The Arts Council and some RABs also fund traineeships to address particular areas of concern.

LEAs and other sources

14.5 ☞ *The Educational Grants Directory*

Career Development Loans, Freepost Newcastle-upon-Tyne X, NE85 1BR
☎ 0800 585505

Local education authorities generally provide grants only for full-time students, and grants to study in the arts are mostly discretionary. Some charitable trusts provide grants to support individuals in training, though you will have to target applications carefully, and work on a long timescale. The Department of Employment also offers Career Development Loans through Barclays, Clydesdale and Co-operative banks. Loans for personal training are available to cover 80% of course fees and the full cost of other expenses.

EQUAL OPPORTUNITIES 8

8   EQUAL OPPORTUNITIES

Summary
This chapter provides further background information on the equal opportunities issues which have been touched on elsewhere in the book. It explains the basic principles and the legal framework which exists to support them, before going on, in section 8.2, to give some basic guidance on how to address equal opportunities issues in an organisational context.

8.1   BASIC PRINCIPLES

Equal opportunities

The term equal opportunities is given to a wide and developing range of issues relating to the way different people in society are treated. The starting point is a recognition that although citizens have the same basic rights, their treatment by society's structures and institutions is not, in practice, the same. Unfair discrimination exists in society. Those who are not convinced of its reality from their own experience, or from media reporting, may consult the growing body of case law for evidence. Discrimination against individuals on the grounds of gender, race, disability, sexuality, age and other equally unfair reasons is commonplace. Although it may result from strong personal prejudice, it is arguable that the real problem is the institutional nature of discrimination. In other words our social institutions, laws and organisational structures can discriminate unthinkingly because they were established in the framework of different social attitudes, by people in positions of power who formed an unrepresentative section of the community, and had little awareness of the needs, interests, cultures and aspirations of other people.

1.1 Coherent and workable

The development of equal opportunities practice through policy formulation, training and monitoring is an effective response to institutionalised discrimination. It is important to see organisational cultures, rather than individual attitudes, as the primary target for this work: individual prejudice and behaviour should be addressed in an organisational context. However those prejudices can create difficulties at the stage of preliminary discussion of the issues, because they can provoke a negative reaction to the whole question of equal opportunities. The matter may be seen variously as absurd, threatening, irrelevant, discriminatory, intrusive, or tediously worthy by people who are trying to get on with their jobs and lives. Knowing that it is none of these things is not enough - it is essential to communicate to everyone involved the value of creating fair social structures which offer everyone equal opportunities. The principal reasons are that:

- it is just to do so

- extending the range of people involved in your work offers scope for bringing in new ideas and contributions

- not to do so places artificial limits on the quality and range of your work

- failure to recruit and retain the most suitable people, of whatever culture, race, gender or physical characteristics, to your management and workforce reduces your effectiveness and value

- it will enhance your reputation as an employer and enable you to attract people of the highest calibre to the organisation

- it will strengthen the relationship between you and the diverse community you are there to serve

- you have to operate within the law

The importance of good equal opportunities practice

The right of equal access to the arts has been placed at the heart of this book in the belief that it should be at the heart of any community-based arts activity, and that any practitioner or development worker in the field will subscribe to it. But while such a belief forms an essential foundation, it is not in itself adequate to ensure that your work actually meets your objectives. You need the skeleton of an organisational structure to support it, and avoid its dependence on individual commitment. You also need to ensure that you, and the organisation within which you work, are able to meet your legal obligations in this area.

The main anti-discriminatory legislation in Britain is:
Race Relations Act 1976
Sex Discrimination Acts 1975 and 1986
Equal Pay Act 1970 and Amendment Regulations 1983
Disabled Persons (Employment) Acts 1944, 1958 and 1986

The legislative framework

Discrimination on certain grounds - principally race and gender - is unlawful in Britain. The legislation is complex in some areas and you should refer to a specialist publication for full details. None the less all employers should be aware that they are liable for discriminatory acts, as set out in the legislation, which they commit. The principal forms of discrimination are:

- **harassment** - unwarranted personal attention or contact amounting to harassment can amount to unlawful discrimination

- **direct discrimination** - unfair treatment of employees or potential employees on the grounds of race or gender

- **indirect discrimination** - the creation of artificial barriers which result in unfair treatment of employees or potential employees

4.3 Employment

Employers should also appreciate that they can be held liable for some discriminatory acts committed by their employees, whether or not with their knowledge or approval. In the latter case it may be a defence to show that all reasonable steps were taken to prevent the commission by employees of such acts. For this reason if for no other, it is necessary for any employer to put in place structures to prevent unlawful discrimination, and to train employees in their operation. It will probably be necessary to bring in specialist advice or trainers to help establish these.

However, it would be inadequate to structure your equal opportunities practice simply to satisfy the demands of the law. There is no legal protection against discrimination on grounds of age, disability, religion, sexuality, HIV status, or class but a good equal opportunities policy will address all these issues.

In the same way that it is illegal to discriminate against an individual on some grounds, it is not lawful, in Britain, to discriminate *in favour* of anyone on the same grounds. This practice is often termed 'positive discrimination' and can have no place in an equal opportunities policy. On the other hand, it is lawful to take steps to facilitate the training of targeted sectors of the community as long as the training carries no guarantee of subsequent employment. It is also lawful for employers to encourage applications from under-represented groups in the advertising and public relations. Such positive action might be linked to the achievement of a stated target - for instance a number of women in senior management positions - since a proposed figure can be supported by legitimate management action. It is not lawful - except in the case of registered disabled people - to establish a quota of positions or places expressly reserved for particular sectors of the community.

The only exception to this last point is where it is a Genuine Occupational Qualification (GOQ) as defined in law, that a post should be filled by a person of a particular gender or race

There is no protection in law against discrimination on grounds of disability, but the workforces of more than 20 must include 3% of registered disabled people. This is the only lawful employment quota in Britain, and it can be avoided by applying for an exemption certificate.

(eg it is possible to audition only men to play a male role in a play).

8.2   DEVELOPING GOOD PRACTICE

Creating a strategy

Since an organisation trying to address its equal opportunities practice for the first time may encounter a negative response among staff or management committee members who don't yet understand the issues, or the way in which they will be addressed, it is necessary to proceed carefully, ensuring good communication with everyone involved. In many cases it will be sensible to draw on the advice, expertise and organisational neutrality of an outside trainer or consultant. Whether or not you use external help, make sure that everyone in the organisation is involved in the process, and understands that its value lies not in conforming to externally-imposed standards, but in improving the quality of the organisation's performance, relationships and internal culture.

3.5 Policy and planning
3.6 Monitoring and evaluation
5.3 Commissioning other practitioners

Look at all aspects of the work - management, employment, programming and marketing - and consider existing practice in an equal opportunities context. Identify changes or improvements which need to be made, agree priorities, and plan how to integrate the required training and other work into your annual programme. This should be thought of as an ongoing management process, not a once-for-all task to produce a policy. As society develops, expectations change: maintaining good practice in equal opportunities requires continuous monitoring of aims and achievements.

Policy development

There are two approaches to policy in the area of equal opportunities. The first sees the establishment of a discrete equal opportunities policy as a way of emphasising its importance, and ensuring that it is properly considered and reviewed. The second approach is to integrate a commitment to equal opportunities into all other policies - artistic, employment, training etc - on the grounds that a separate document is easily ignored and the best way to ensure change in organisational practice is to build it into the policies which people use on a daily basis. Each has its benefits and drawbacks, and your choice will be determined by your own thinking and organisational culture. But as with any policy statement, it is essential that a management process is established to review how the organisation meets its commitments.

Training

Training, for staff and management, will be an important element both of policy development and of improving practice itself. There is a wide range of training available from general courses which aim to introduce the principles of equal opportunities to courses which seek to develop understanding of particular issues. Some trainers address attitudes, believing that unless people's underlying feelings are challenged, any change is likely to be superficial. Other trainers see this approach as confrontational, arguing that far from producing lasting change, it can leave people resentful and unable to translate what they have learned into their working environment. Their alternative is to address behaviour by looking at the actual conduct of people in their work, in the belief that only changes in behaviour can be clearly implemented and measured. The debate between approaches continues, and in seeking training you will have to choose a trainer and an approach which meets your needs.

15.7 Contacts Talk to the training organisations listed for information on training providers or courses. Some local authorities have equal opportunities units which provide advice, information and training.

Terminology

The 'correct' use of language can often be a source of worry to people, and tales of the absurdities perpetrated in the name of equal opportunities both reflect and feed that worry. People are sometimes afraid that, if they use the wrong word, they will be condemned, or assumed to have attitudes which, in fact, they don't have, There is no infallible checklist of 'right' or 'wrong' terms but, as our communities and attitudes change, so the language we use to express our thoughts changes. Looking at the use of language, and the ideas which underlie it, can be a useful way of thinking about our social and personal relationships, and often forms part of equal opportunities training courses. But the use of language is not always a reliable indicator of people's attitudes. Whether someone uses the term *mentally handicapped, people with learning difficulties* or *people with learning disabilities* may indicate that they are aware of current debates in this area, or simply that they have been told that one is the 'right' term to use. It does not necessarily say anything about how they behave towards members of the group they are characterising. Most people's primary concern is not to give offence, and being aware of the terms people prefer and understanding the reasons for that preference is important.

But everybody is more affected by someone's underlying attitudes than by the precise words they use. The question of terminology is best addressed within the context of overall

189

training so that the reasons behind people's use of language, rather than simply the words themselves, can be understood.

Monitoring

As with any other management initiative, setting up structures to deliver good equal opportunities practice is only half the job. You need to monitor their operation in each area of your work - management, employment, programming, and marketing. You should have access to statistical information about who makes up your audience, who seeks and gains employment or freelance work with the organisation, and who is involved in your management. None of this is very difficult to get, though its accuracy will vary from one situation to another. Everyone seeking work, or working for an organisation should be asked to complete an equal opportunities monitoring form. These should be kept simple, anonymous and operate on the basis of self-definition. Whilst is not always possible or appropriate to seek similar information from your audience, you can combine approximate statistics with the role of targeted projects to inform your practice. Whatever solutions you find, the information is essential since without it you cannot assess whether the steps you have taken are actually achieving the policy objectives that you set.

Further information

You can get advice and information on equal opportunities issues and training possibilities from the Arts Council training unit or your RAB. The organisations mentioned in chapter 7 are a good starting point for finding out about training **7.4 Training providers** courses. You can also get booklets and information from the Commission for Racial Equality and the Equal Opportunities Commission.

NATIONAL ARTFORM ORGANISATIONS

9 NATIONAL ARTFORM ORGANISATIONS

9.1 COMMUNITY DANCE & MIME FOUNDATION

The Community Dance & Mime Foundation (CDMF) was established in 1989 as the umbrella organisation for community dance and mime. It grew out of the National Association of Dance & Mime Animateurs (NADMA) which had been in existence since 1986. CDMF's remit is to raise the profile of community dance and to support practitioners in their work. From April 1994 CDMF relinquished responsibility for community mime (taken on by Mime Action Group) and now focuses on community dance. CDMF works primarily in England, though it has strong links with Scotland, Wales and increasingly with practitioners in Europe and beyond.

CDMF's current programme falls into five main areas: research and policy development; publications and services; training; events and commissions; and advice and support. Lobbying to make the case for community dance, and helping practitioners to raise the profile of their own work are important themes running throughout CDMF's overall programme. Individuals and organisations involved in community dance activity are represented by CDMF at national level. It is actively involved in many dance and arts initiatives, ensuring that community dance is recognised, understood and supported. This has included policy debates on issues such as dance in education, national arts strategies and the development of N/SVQs (National and Scottish Vocational Qualifications). Furthering the debate around community dance work is also a high priority for CDMF, and it strives to achieve this through its main areas of work listed above.

CDMF runs a membership system which practitioners and organisations can join on an annual basis. Members receive regular information about CDMF and community dance including access to advice and support and a range of publications including *Animated*, the quarterly national community dance magazine. Other publications include the *Network Brochure* (the UK listing of community dance practitioners), *Contract Guidelines & Payscales*, the *Fundraising Handbook* and a series of briefing papers and information pamphlets.

The organisation is based in Leicester and is run by a small staff team. As a limited company with charitable status, CDMF has a voluntary Executive Committee of practitioners and specialists, and their task is to oversee the organisation's affairs.

CDMF is not only the staff and Executive Committee, but the practitioners who set it up and the many hundreds of others now working in the field. Their support and involvement is essential to the organisation and the movement's future. A constant dialogue will mean that practitioners and their professional body, CDMF, are kept informed of developments and there are many ways of doing this. CDMF is always keen to hear from practitioners and to offer them support wherever possible.

13-15 Belvoir Street, Leicester LE1 6SL
☎ 0533 418517 (due to change)

9.2 MIME ACTION GROUP

Mime Action Group (MAG), founded in 1984, is the only UK-wide umbrella organisation for mime and physical theatre. In addition to providing support for those working in and with the fields of mime, physical theatre and visual performance, it also lobbies for increased profile and funding, and produces a quarterly magazine, *Total Theatre*.

MAG has also produced various publications (including the *Blueprint for Regional Mime Development*, and the first *UK Mime and Physical Theatre Training Directory*) in addition to organising national conferences and training seminars.

Central to the organisation are advocacy and brokerage, and this is the level at which many practitioners and arts workers first encounter Mime Action Group. MAG's current objectives are:

- Advocacy for development of mime and physical theatre, through regional, national and international partnerships, links and contacts.

- Raising the public profile of mime and physical theatre.

- Support for community mime and mime in education.

- Developing training opportunities.

- Developing critical debate and analysis.

- Increasing access to mime and physical theatre.

MAG is a membership organisation and welcomes all those working in or associated with mime and physical theatre into its membership.

Sadlers Wells, 179 Rosebery Avenue, London EC1R 4TN
☎ 071 713 7944

9.3 NATIONAL ASSOCIATION FOR LITERATURE DEVELOPMENT

The National Association for Literature Development (NALD) grew out of a series of informal gatherings of literature development workers between 1986 and 1992. It was recognised that there was a need for an umbrella organisation to provide a voice for community literature workers at a regional and national level, to:

- Facilitate the promotion of the Association and of the members' work to the media, in order to increase public, book trade and the arts world's awareness of posts.

- Improve pay levels and terms and conditions for all workers and to build new posts into forward plans. It will also advocate coherent and comprehensive training and induction programmes in all initiatives.

- Build formal links with other national organisations including CDMF, Sound Sense, Mime Action Group and so on.

- Be involved in and influence literature policy discussions at all levels.

- Promote good codes of practice from within the Association and co-ordinate information about literature activity across the country.

- Produce and administer a national literature database of writers, storytellers and literature performers.

The Association will be producing a quarterly newsletter, organising national meetings and a training programme, and providing an advice and referral service for all community literature workers.

c/o Literature Department, Arts Council, 14 Great Peter Street, London SW1P 3NQ
☎ 071 333 0100

9.4 SOUND SENSE
The National Community Music Association

Community music can trace its roots back to punk and community arts in the 1970s. Another development occurred in the early 1980s as orchestras began outreach programmes, music animateur posts were established and new music co-operatives or collectives appeared. Community music embraces many musical styles and, like community dance, a rich range of projects including participatory work in day centres, prisons, hospitals, schools and youth clubs.

By the late '80s many of the animateur posts and co-operatives had disappeared, but freelance opportunities were expanding and, in April 1989, the first community music conference to be held in Britain attracted some 130 delegates. Out of this conference Sound Sense emerged, an umbrella organisation which since 1990 has been the national voice of community musicians.

Sound Sense aims to support the needs of freelance musicians and animateurs, arts workers, music and recording studios and co-operatives. It also works with individuals and organisations in related fields (such as the formal music education sector and music therapy), and with the funding infrastructure. Sound Sense offers its members support, advice and training and acts as an information exchange network to other arts organisations. In 1993 Sound Sense published the first ever national directory of community projects and musicians. It publishes a quarterly journal, *Sounding Board*, and is in the process of setting up regional networks with the aim of reflecting both the broad constituency of its members and of community music users themselves. Sound Sense has also set up training initiatives in association with members around the country, and actively seeks collaborations with other partners such as CDMF. Sound Sense is a registered charity, and is run by a voluntary committee with two part-time members of staff. It is supported by the Arts Council, and its patrons are Sir Claus Moser, Evelyn Glennie and Ken Livingstone.

19b Albert Road, Teddington, Middlesex TW11 0BD
☎ 081 977 2961

COMMUNITY DANCE PROJECTS

10

Richard Ings

10 COMMUNITY DANCE PROJECTS

Richard Ings

Richard Ings has worked in arts administration and journalism since 1984. He currently edits *Ninety-Five Per Cent*, the national youth arts magazine, and *Animated*, the community dance journal.

Summary

This chapter describes four recent community dance projects: work in Suffolk which has led to the creation of a new National Dance Agency, a project with older people in Gateshead, inner-city dance work in Lancashire and a community dance company which combines sight-impaired and sighted performers. They have been described here to give a glimpse of the range and richness of community dance work in Britain today, and to bring concrete examples to balance the preceding, more theoretical chapters.

10.1 FROM ANIMATEUR TO NATIONAL DANCE AGENCY

Whether your involvement in dance is in working for a dance company, running a dance and fitness studio or filling an animateur post, popular support is essential. If audiences fall away, if people cancel classes, if no-one responds to your efforts to involve them in dance, you will soon be out of a job. Suffolk Dance's development into a National Dance Agency is a good example of how a modest animateur post can build a groundswell of support and loyalty in a rural county with few of the resources or economies of scale available to many urban projects.

The need for an animateur was first identified in discussions held between the county PE adviser and the drama and dance officer of Eastern Arts Association. Both agreed that dance needed to be encouraged throughout the county, with activity balanced between schools and the community. Scilla Dyke was appointed as the animateur in 1982 and soon established links with schools, community groups, dance teachers, existing and potential promoters and local authorities. Contact was also made with nationally-touring dance companies and freelance practitioners.

A Laban leaders training scheme was set up to train a team of freelance dance workers, youth groups were launched, venues opened their doors to a more adventurous programme of dance and companies were encouraged to run workshops. As well as developing the dance curriculum in schools, Suffolk Dance was instrumental in introducing dance to particular sections of the community, including disabled people and prison inmates.

Suffolk Dance's work at HMP Blundeston was a major step forward in this area and gained national recognition. Unusually, the project brought prisoners together with children with learning difficulties. Before sessions with the youngsters began, the men were given training in disability awareness as well as aspects of dance and choreography.

One inmate recalled the first session: 'When the children came in, it worked brilliantly. All the training we'd had just fell into place. Within five minutes our inhibitions had all gone out of the window and it was just a matter of getting down to what we'd been taught. I'd like to have another course and advance myself in some way, whether in dance or with disabled children. It could be done in other prisons. It should be.'

The enthusiasm and commitment evident in his words is echoed in communities large and small which have been affected by Suffolk Dance's programme of dance classes, workshops, residencies and guest performances.

The apparent gap between the grassroots and the arguably more glamorous side of the dance world - the side that gets coverage in the national press - is not so wide that a dance animateur or project like Suffolk Dance cannot bridge it, or demonstrate their interdependence. Motionhouse is a well-known national contemporary dance company with a choreographer, Kevin Finnan, who is pushing out the boundaries of his art. At Suffolk Dance's invitation, Kevin came to work with community groups and local dance artists, and his company was commissioned to produce a new work which saw its première in Bury St Edmunds rather than London.

This initiative, coupled with the decision by the Arts Council to award Suffolk Dance development funds as a National Dance Agency, underlines that community-based arts work is not the marginal activity some would have it, but a sound and healthy basis for arts development as a whole.

HMP Blundeston and community venues throughout Suffolk Suffolk Dance

10.2 DANCE WORK WITH OLDER PEOPLE

Setting up a dance project can be a challenging experience anywhere, but there are particular challenges in working within an
institution. Not only do you have to win the confidence and
trust of the residents: you also need to earn the support of the
staff, who have their own professional role to play. The
Gateshead Elderly Arts Project offers an encouraging example
of how those challenges can be successfully met. Set up by
Equal Arts (formerly Northern Shape) as a long-term model
project, its aim was to engage older people and their carers in a
professional arts programme. Residential units for older people were identified as primary locations for this experiment
and, after careful research, three homes were chosen:
Alderwood, Cedarwood and Fernwood.

Dance was by no means the only artform offered to the
older people: literature, storytelling, music and theatre were
also included in a programme which took place at venues outside the home as well as inside. The emphasis was on active
participation rather than passive entertainment. Some might
find it a strange proposal to promote dance and movement
among older people, who are often perceived as inactive (especially in a residential environment), but dance they did.

Heidi Wilson worked on the Gateshead project for two
years, in her first post on leaving college. She had to establish
the project in three homes, and prove her credentials with residents and staff who were almost all older than her. Setting up
a programme of movement sessions and training opportunities
was difficult in the face of rigid routines, staff rotas and occasional incomprehension or hostility. Once these had been sorted out, often with the help of the participants, sympathetic
staff or Equal Arts, Heidi could start to deal with the familiar
cry: 'I can't dance'.

Beginning modestly with four or five people, and with a lot
of conversation and music, Heidi introduced movement at a
gentle pace: 'As my confidence grew and numbers increased,
we moved out of the private lounges into a more public and
larger space. The work became more visible and more people
joined.' The size of each group and the duration of each session were determined by the abilities and preferences of the
participants. 'The role of the dance worker,' says Heidi, 'is to
encourage and enable, not to instruct or teach. There is no right
or wrong way of doing something and each individual contribution needs to be recognised, however small.'

What Heidi found personally rewarding was witnessing
people not simply discovering a new range of movement but -

in rediscovering their bodies - becoming more confident in expressing themselves and forming new relationships with other residents. 'Movement work,' Heidi feels, 'went some way towards creating a sense of community in a communal living environment.'

The staff were drawn in too, as training was seen as an integral part of the project. Artists and arts workers like Heidi carried out training for care staff and other health care professionals, while opportunities existed for arts workers to undertake Social Services training or short courses in subjects like counselling and reminiscence work. This sharing of knowledge and experience between arts and other professionals is crucial, and can only happen where the dance worker, as in this case, demonstrates her or his commitment to the community.

Alderwood, Cedarwood and Fernwood residential homes,
  Gateshead
Heidi Wilson
Equal Arts

10.3   INNER CITY SOUTH ASIAN DANCE WORK

One of the paradoxes of community-based arts work is that the most desperate conditions often give rise to the most exciting results. The poverty, violence and despair encountered in some urban areas offer a formidable challenge to arts workers. This project took place on a large Lancashire estate which faces its share of difficulties, with relatively high levels of crime, violence and drug-related problems. Christina Spencer, the worker at the local youth centre, sees that this has had a 'knock-on' effect on many of the young people who live there.

Christina works with a group of girls who meet at her centre which is called The Refuge. To help develop stronger relationships with the older girls who attended, it was decided to invite a dance worker to run a project just for them. She specifically wanted to employ a South Asian dancer, to counter the pervasive atmosphere of racism of what is an all-white estate in a largely Asian area. The resulting project was initiated and managed by Lancashire Youth and Community Service and the South Asian Dance Education Forum.

One of the most experienced South Asian community dance practitioners, Bisakha Sarker, was chosen to lead the project. For unavoidable reasons the vital planning meeting never took place, so Bisakha had the daunting task of starting the project 'cold'. Going to The Refuge that first night, Bisakha was understandably nervous, but she was reassured by the warm welcome that the group of lively 12 to 16 year old girls gave her.

After a cup of tea, the first session began: 'They were unsure but enthusiastic. They wanted to know how I danced and how they were going to dance. I was still observing them, trying to work out what I could do that might appeal to these young girls. In the end I decided I must simply offer what I could. They had come there of their own free will, hoping to have an enjoyable time, and shouldn't be pushed into anything to suit my plans.'

What Bisakha offered that first night was a simple greeting sequence which the girls proved eager to learn. As the sessions developed, Bisakha dropped her original plan to focus on the social difficulties faced by the participants in favour of a more imaginative theme: what they were looking for was scope for dreaming.

A hint of the latent violence of the estate came one day when Bisakha arrived at The Refuge to find a group of boys trying to force open the shutter over the front door, banging on the windows and trying to jam the lock with matchsticks. Frustration at being excluded from the activity was bubbling over and at risk of getting out of hand. When they had gone, Bisakha slipped in through the back door and the dancing resumed.

At the end of six weeks, the girls took their dance, which was now based on ideas about nature with one segment featuring umbrellas and rain, to a local Asian girls group. To Bisakha's surprise two new faces appeared at this point: when two regular members had been unable to come, the rest of the group had taught the dance to two more friends.

Bisakha came away impressed by their achievement: 'These were all highly-sensitive, strong-willed young people. One had to be very careful not to hurt their feelings. It was not easy to get them to do the same thing at the same time, yet when they actually did their dance, it went like a dream.' Christina Spencer felt that Bisakha had done more than simply pass on dance skills: 'By using Asian dance and drama with Bisakha, the girls had the opportunity to break down some of the racist myths caused by lack of knowledge and contact with a different culture.'

The Refuge, Lancashire
Bisakha Sarker
**Lancashire Youth and Community Service & the South
  Asian Dance Education Forum**

10.4 A PERSONAL JOURNEY TO COMMUNITY DANCE

The personal experience is an essential ingredient in community-based arts work: what each person brings to a project is vital. The formation of Eye Contact dance company, which is composed of sighted, blind and sight-impaired dancers, is largely due to the personal vision of its director, Isabel Jones. Her journey from ballet school to running this company is unique in its details, but representative of the journey that all practitioners make from learning a skill to sharing it with others, each in their own way a catalyst in the community.

Isabel's own experience of dance began in storybook fashion with a scholarship to study as a child with the Royal Ballet. Although she fitted the rigid requirements for a ballet dancer, being the right height and shape, she later rejected that path in favour of an area of dance where such restrictive requirements were not important. To understand the significance of this choice one needs to know it was powerfully affected by her father, who is both deaf and blind.

Communication and movement had become the two broad themes in Isabel's life. Talking with her father via tapes while she was at Bretton Hall, she learnt of his memories of movement as a child, the longed-for sense of rushing downhill on a bike. She began to explore the censored world of 'blindisms' - those movements, such as rocking or spinning on the spot, that blind people are discouraged from making for fear of being stigmatised. She wanted to know: when your vocabulary is crossed out, where does the energy behind self-expression go, if not into stress-related illness?

Around this time Isabel was also learning about contact improvisation, taught her by a pupil of Mary Fulkerson's. For several tortuous months, Isabel struggled to break free of what had been imposed on her body during her ballet training, in order to establish her own authentic movement - to be herself. A chance sighting of Wolfgang Stange on television led indirectly to Isabel working with him and with mentally-ill patients at Charing Cross hospital, then joining Amici, Stange's company of disabled dancers. That in turn led to attending workshops run by Steve Paxton with blind people at Dartington, and returning there in subsequent years with a growing number of blind and visually-impaired dancers, including her own father, Lewis Jones.

This then was the germ of Eye Contact. What turned this very personal odyssey into a company that has now performed to mainstream audiences at festivals and in theatres is that other element of community dance - the community. Isabel began by setting up a Saturday afternoon workshop at the WEA offices in Nottingham. A core of four people soon swelled to a dozen, then nearly twenty blind and sighted students and dancers. Inspired by New York's Judson Church dance space, Isabel borrowed a school hall and soon had forty people coming to two classes. This created a pool on which Eye Contact could draw. Nottinghamshire County Council has now set up a new centre for adult education in the arts, and Eye Contact has been invited to move in. Future classes and workshops, and the continued development of Eye Contact as both a performing company and a group that offers professional training and residencies seems assured.

Because such a strong local presence has been established, Eye Contact has survived members leaving. People have learnt that this opportunity exists for them, so there has been no shortage of new sighted or sight-impaired recruits. Where one-off projects may face real difficulties in reaching the particular groups they want to involve, deep roots in the community have paid off.

Isabel rejected ballet training in part because it was based on enforcing an ideal physique. In working so closely with people who do not feel the need to match themselves to a supposed norm, she is continuing to liberate herself, as well as encouraging them to explore a new world of expressive movement. She and her company are now setting out to achieve an equal transformation in the audience's expectations of where beauty is to be found in dance.

Eye Contact, Nottingham
Isabel Jones

COMMUNITY LITERATURE PROJECTS

11

Mark Homer

11 COMMUNITY LITERATURE PROJECTS

Mark Homer

Mark Homer has been involved in literature development since 1990, and he has also been the programmer of the Birmingham Readers and Writers Festival. He is currently the Literature Development Worker for Surrey, and the Treasurer of NALD.

Summary
This chapter describes four recent community literature projects: work through the library service in Northamptonshire, a site-specific project for Garden Festival Wales, a South Asian literary journal, and work by a writer with people in a hospice in Surrey. They have been described here to give a glimpse of the range and richness of community literature work in Britain today, and to bring concrete examples to balance the preceding, more theoretical chapters.

11.1 LITERATURE DEVELOPMENT AND LIBRARIES

The relationship between the library service and literature development is an obvious one, and this is certainly reflected in the high percentage of literature development funding partnerships which involve the relevant library service. This in itself is a recognition by local authorities that libraries have a very influential role in the promotion and development of a literature programme, as well as being prominent participants in it.

The creation of the Literature Development Initiative in Northamptonshire came about through changes in the outlook of the library service in that county. It was one of many developments which demonstrated an increased commitment to the promotion of literature, and the provision of 'value-added' services by the new management team. Central to this new approach was a willingness to identify gaps in literary provision - both within and outside the service itself - and to strive to fill them. Certainly the enthusiastic support given to *Wordworks* stems from the service's commitment to enhancing the accessibility of literature in the county.

4.8 Marketing

In its simplest form *Wordworks* is a county-wide literature listings publication, featuring contributions from community groups and individuals committed to an improved provision in the area. As its subtitle proclaims, it aspires to provide 'all the news that matters to Readers and Writers in Northamptonshire'. The need for the publication arose from a sense that literature had traditionally been neglected because of the editorial enthusiasm for other art forms in the general listing diaries. Where literature activities did feature in other publications, it was considered that they tended to get lost in a world of alternative choices. The library service saw the production and support of a high-quality dedicated publication as central to its aim of raising the profile of literature, and the development of *Wordworks* as a prominent element of the Literature Development Initiative has been the result.

But *Wordworks* was seen as a means to an end, rather than an end in itself. The library service had further ambitions to promote an extensive literature development programme through the publication. In fact it has helped to establish four county libraries as centres of literary activity, regularly programming events and featuring new touring book promotions in areas like poetry, biography and humourous novels to compliment visits from writers, all with the support of the Literature Development Officer. Particularly notable among these have been an innovative writers' exchange between Jamaica and the East Midlands to explore the cultural diversity of Standard English and Caribbean Creole, and the John Clare Poetry Competition, to celebrate the bicentenary of the Northamptonshire poet. Each event continues to attract new people who have not previously attended, and where names are added to the fast-growing *Wordworks* mailing list. The newsletter provides an accessible central focus for all this activity and the success of these promotions has been directly linked with its effectiveness. It was recognised early in the project's development that its long-term success depended upon it being embraced by local writers and promoters. Gradually individuals and organisations are using *Wordworks* to promote meetings, events or workshops, and beginning to realise their potential through the publication.

The reputation of *Wordworks* is now well-established across Northamptonshire. It has achieved its objective of raising the profile of literature in the county, and is becoming a key mechanism for developing increased opportunities for activity. *Wordworks* is providing an important and individual voice for literature in the county and with the continued commitment to

Literature Development in Northamptonshire, will do so for the foreseeable future.

Wordworks
Adrian Johnson, Northamptonshire Literature Development Officer

11.2 SOUTH ASIAN LITERATURE PROJECT

One of the demands which continually confronts the community literature worker is the question of how people can get their work published. The answer manifests itself in many different forms but perhaps the most familiar example is the publication of a local writers' group anthology. But it can be doubly difficult to help specific ethnic communities to find opportunities to celebrate their language, creativity and heritage in print. *Wasafiri*, the black literature journal supported and distributed by the Arts Council, represents one successful response to this problem, though its range, which encompasses African, Caribbean and Asian readerships, is huge. Demand for a publication with a specifically South Asian perspective has led to the creation of *Daskhat* by the South Asian Literature Project in Luton.

The Project had been involved in the programming of a comprehensive series of readings, workshops and bookfairs for the local Asian community in Bedfordshire. The popularity of the programme had given rise to the creation of a literary society full of talented writers looking for opportunities to profile their work. As a result the original aim was to produce a small-scale, A5, twenty-page journal for local and regional distribution. While the practicalities of this were being investigated, a number of established South Asian writers resident in Britain suggested that such a project not only had national potential, but could also be targeted at an international readership and provide a link between homelands and expatriate writers around the world. Given their limited knowledge of international publishing and distribution, the South Asian Literature Project approached the idea with caution, but secured funding from Eastern Arts for two issues.

The next task was to attract sufficient subscriptions to justify the idea, and this was tackled in two ways. The first issue was designed as an introduction to things to come, and therefore the editorial guidelines were generally broadly-based. The first issue had to reflect the central aim of the journal, namely to provide a platform for both established and new writers, by publishing work in the original language and in translation. Crucially, as a way of ensuring high-quality and committed work, each of the commissioned writers was to be paid for their contributions.

Then, on publication, the first issue was distributed free of charge to public libraries, bookshops, and literature organisations in addition to the many individuals on the South Asian Literature Project's mailing list. In retrospect this has proved to be a very successful, albeit risky, form of speculation, since it has helped *Daskhat* build an impressive, world-wide subscription list. It is envisaged that future issues will tighten guidelines to contributors, and focus on new writing about specific issues such as 'Expatriate writers' or 'South Asian theatre'.

In addition to providing a forum for creative writing, *Daskhat* is also realising its potential for reviews, diaries and the promotion of specialist events such as bookfairs, residencies and festivals. The potential for the continued development of the journal is great and its value is already being recognised through the interest of the Arts Council and the publishing world. Thanks to the groundwork of the South Asian Literature Project, *Daskhat* has got off to an excellent start, and it is hoped that it will be possible to sustain this unique publication.

Daskhat
Seema Jena, South Asian Literature Project, Luton

11.3 CREATIVE WRITING IN A HOSPICE

Work with institutions such as hospitals, prisons and schools provides some of the greatest opportunities for both the writer and literature worker. However, it must also be stressed that they harbour many challenges which can potentially undermine the whole experience of the project. The first of these is access. These organisations tend to be closed to the public, and can seem like a maze of management procedures and protocol. Unravelling this and identifying the right people can be difficult and time-consuming, but the rewards for participant and practitioner alike are unrivalled: perseverance, good humour and enthusiasm are the order of the day.

5.10 Working in institutions

Colin Archer was able to put these qualities to good effect in the Princess Alice Hospice creative writing project. Although the idea for the project came from a general manager who had since moved on, the hospice still wished to proceed and employ a writer. But, perhaps inevitably given the absence of the originator, there was scope for different members of the support group to have different aspirations for the project. It is crucial that the motive for work like this is resolved at the outset of the project: the environment of creative work is very sensitive and to achieve the best results objectives must be clear from the start.

Following his appointment Colin met with the support group and agreed that the work should focus on the patients' needs and interests. Similar projects in other parts of the country have involved staff and families, but in this case, and without questioning the validity of alternative approaches, it was felt best to ensure that the patients had sole ownership of the project. It was originally planned that the writer would provide two sessions a week over a six-month period. Although this pattern worked reasonably well for day patients, a different approach was required for those staying on the wards. The lifestyle of a hospice ward is such that a regimented approach is not practical, and it quickly became apparent that the writer needed to be 'loitering with intent'. Colin spent much of the early part of the project working flexibly, gaining the trust of staff and volunteers as well as patients. The time taken to get onto the wards cannot be overestimated, nor the demands it places on the charm and diplomacy of the writer.

The original practical session was adapted to be much more personal, becoming a recorded conversation between writer and patient. It is important to recognise that this activity was never seen as being of therapeutic value to the patient, who remained in control of the situation throughout, deciding when to start and finish each session. Freedom of choice and individual expression lay at the heart of the project. After each session Colin would take away the recording and transcribe the conversation. The experience was completed by reading the text back to the author. This final part proved influential in gaining acceptance of the project, since it often provoked great discussion amongst other patients and staff on the ward. The enthusiastic atmosphere convinced more patients to trust the project and to become involved.

Understandably, this project has proved to be physically and emotionally draining. The planning of such work should always place great importance on the provision of support for the writer. This goes beyond the traditional concept of the support group, which often becomes preoccupied with managerial and administrative detail, and involves the creation of opportunities for the writer to discuss the constant loss that they encounter. Their enthusiasm and energy is an integral part of the success of this work, and every assistance should be

13.3 Community music and disability describes a very different project involving disabled people. **12.3 Community mime in a prison** describes another type of institution.

extended to maintain it. A successful project where people who are terminally-ill are given the opportunity to affirm the value and worth of their life brings great rewards for all concerned.

Princess Alice Hospice, Esher, Surrey
Colin Archer

11.4 USING LITERATURE IN SITE-SPECIFIC WORK

The simple idea of bringing together the work of writers and artists in the creation of a piece of artwork is not in itself either new or original, but it offers scope for marvellous work. The motivation behind the *Earthwords* project was to extend and explore the collaborative possibilities between creative writers and the Public Art Programme of Garden Festival Wales.

Professional artists and creative writers working in pairs were invited to submit proposals for new pieces of work. They were asked to visit the Festival site together and to respond directly to the environment - like other contributors to the Public Art Programme - but to do so in a way which integrated their work. It was stressed that projects should go beyond illustrating each other's ideas, or merely embellishing the landscape. The visual arts and literature co-ordinators were looking for imaginative ideas which enhanced the emotional qualities of the environment, not simply a gallery without walls. The diversity of the successful projects was wide, with each pair finding a unique response to the demands of the project. They ranged from the poetic to the mythical to the metaphysical; from the use of wood to perspex to industrial crusher cone; from the exploration of the past to the present to the future.

13.2 Community music in rural areas describes another site-specific project.

It is important to recognise that the six completed pieces of work had no single author. Through regular meetings between the artists and those living in the valley, a project was able to reflect its unique character - fertile farmland, the blackness of smoke-filled sky and the re-awakening of valley life. These were pieces inspired by local history and created to serve as long-lasting reminders of the area's regeneration.

The educational benefits of the project were notable. The practitioners had a unique opportunity to work with an experienced professional in another field, learning and teaching about their respective approaches to creative work. They also provided an excellent base for introductory sessions with schools and local community centres, giving students an opportunity to experience the interaction between practitioners and art forms. This encouraged a number of cross-artform projects to take place away from the Festival site, including a mural created by a group of school children at a nearby day centre, and featuring an extract from the *Mabinogion*.

Ebbw Vale Valley and Garden Festival Wales provided an exceptional opportunity for both creative writer and visual artist. However, such work does not depend on the existence of vast regeneration schemes, only on the imagination of a literature development worker. Similarly there is wide scope for collaboration between literature and other artforms such as dance or music. In the end the success of such work lies in the quality of the integration between the artforms and with the underlying purposes of the project. Seeing literature interacting with other artforms is to see it in its most enlightening form, and it represents a very special way of creating and learning which should be wholeheartedly encouraged.

Earthwords
The Public Art Programme, Garden Festival Wales,
  Ebbw Vale, Gwent

COMMUNITY MIME PROJECTS

12

Jac Wilkinson

12 COMMUNITY MIME PROJECTS

Jac Wilkinson

Jac Wilkinson is the Education Officer at the Arts Centre, University of Warwick, creating an active programme of events and nationally-available resources across the spectrum of the artforms. Jac has previously been a physical theatre performer, director, animateur and author in the United Kingdom, Europe and Scandinavia.

Summary
This chapter describes five recent community mime projects: work with students in Wolverhampton, a festival project in Luton, a school residency in Sussex, work in a Scottish prison, and a number of schools projects in West Yorkshire. They have been described here to give a glimpse of the range and richness of community mime work in Britain today, and to bring concrete examples to balance the preceding, more theoretical chapters.

COMMUNITY MIME

As I hope the following projects will begin to demonstrate, mime and physical theatre have a flexibility and resourcefulness that engages people in many ways. Its playfulness and equality of access ensure a broad range of experiences applicable to any situation. This is further supported by an openness and a simplicity of objective which nurture the creativity and human relationships that lie at the heart of artistic value. This vast potential is directly linked to the methods and means that practitioners explore in their own training, resulting in a symbiotic relationship with the artist's own work.

The practitioners included in this chapter have very varied backgrounds, and work in very different contexts. However, they all value and enjoy being able to share their work and encouraging others to explore the magical, trusting and surprising arena of mime and physical theatre. Through its openness, journeys and risks are constantly taken, drawing on practical skills and the imagination. Having been involved in the field for many years, I have always been amazed at the level of prowess and artistic vision displayed by community and education groups involved in creative projects. They are part of the cutting edge of performance work, not simplistic and tentative forays into the unknown. There is something so basic about the work - about communication, play and social behaviour - that it lights a spark in all of us.

Mime and physical theatre have so much to offer community and education clients, although perhaps it has not always managed to blow its own trumpet loudly enough. There are also too few facilitators and arts officers who have had sufficient access to the work, either in performance or in participatory projects. I hope that this chapter will whet some appetites and encourage people to delve further.

12.1 A COLLEGE RESIDENCY BY A PERFORMANCE COMPANY

The impetus for this project came from two lecturers who had seen Volcano perform at the Arena Theatre in Wolverhampton. They presented a simple challenge to the company: 'What can you do in ten days with a group of 30-40 first-year Humanities students?' Rather than leading a series of workshops, Volcano decided to use the allotted time to make a show with the group. They took *Savages* by Christopher Hampton as their starting point, although this was a play which the company themselves would not have considered doing at that time. Their tactic was to deconstruct the text and create a fresh interpretation and approach with the students. The group decided on its division of labour in terms of performance, scenography and design, in order to examine the text more thoroughly, and to fit in with the course since theatre constitutes only one element of a wide-ranging course.

Volcano were given great freedom in their methods, and the students worked basically in the same way as the company does - ie from 9am to 9pm with no quarter given to slackers. As visitors the company could be forthright about breaking down students' resistance to learning, and cavalier about ways of tackling the work. The experience was consequently very demanding for everyone. Because the whole project was compressed into ten days and also had the pressure of producing a performance fit for a paying audience, lead-in and rehearsal time was somewhat restricted. The philosophy had to be 'get swept up in the whole thing or get left behind'. There were considerable risks in making a show with people that the company did not know at all, and Volcano were suitably nervous about the task in hand. Unlike individual workshops, the residency had to be sustained over time, so the whole period was carefully and clearly structured.

Although the resulting piece was very different from Volcano's work, it has subsequently influenced the company - indeed, they are planning to present an Ibsen play. It also formed a turning-point for Volcano, for although they had previously collaborated with another theatre company, and had worked with students in Swansea, they had not before worked towards a performance with participants. The project gave the company confidence, reinforced their working methods and established a model which could be repeated with other groups.

The feedback from the group was also very positive. The main benefit, beyond total immersion in creating theatre, was that the group had been through the process together, and the students had bonded through the collective experience. Although it might be assumed that students spend their entire undergraduate lives in dynamic groupings, learning and growing together, this is often not the case.

Such projects stimulate practitioners to articulate the thinking behind their work and practice, something which Volcano feel is an essential part of the work. They also encourage a reassessment of assumptions on all sides, and help those working in academic and theoretical structures to acknowledge and accommodate the practical, creative work of professional artists as a valid means of development and understanding.

A further outcome of the residency was that a separate group of students from Swansea reworked *Savages* under Volcano's guidance and took it to the Edinburgh Fringe Festival, where it played to packed houses and was much lauded. These students are now setting up as a professional company. Thus the in-depth and intense physical theatre experience sends out its ripples far and wide, increasing familiarity with the work and the desire to extend its creative boundaries.

Wolverhampton University
Volcano Theatre Company

12.2 DIFFERENT APPROACHES BY THE SAME COMPANY

Community mime is so flexible that the same company - in this case Inside Out Theatre - can undertake projects which differ widely in their intentions, content and scale, as the following examples illustrate.

The idea behind the first project was to use the arts to encourage one of Luton's newest community centres to participate in the annual carnival. Two months beforehand the company performed a street theatre show to the junior youth club at the centre. This offered everyone a chance to meet, and to drum up anticipatory interest. Despite the very informal and somewhat unmanageable audience response, the attenders had very positive and detailed memories of the occasion and the . company.

The company's basic task was to create a float and procession with the centre's users, drawing on the carnival theme of the four elements. With rudimentary structural constraints and basic materials, all participants had the freedom to create their own vision of the theme. Working mainly with the junior youth club and the after school club (along with centre staff and parents), the company embarked on carefully-designed making processes that enabled participants to create their own masks and to contribute to larger structures. In this way four large ambulatory puppets, four totem poles and numerous face masks were created from papier maché and other basic materials.

The day before the carnival, everyone came together to explore techniques for marching, mask-wearing, drumming and puppet-parading. Carnival day itself saw everyone mucking in to get the float ready and then walking the three mile parade route. Afterwards everyone agreed that they had done something wonderful, and a great sense of satisfaction prevailed.

The second project was undertaken as part of the South East Arts Mime Development Project in collaboration with Face Pack a regionally-based theatre company. The aims of the project were to introduce the pupils to physical theatre through an exercise in creativity, and to enable Inside Out to work with Face Pack, creating the chance to share experience and techniques. The two companies were in residence at the school for five days, beginning and ending with performances. They worked with 150 eleven-year old pupils, spending four hours with each class group of 30 which was split into smaller groups for the devising process.

Although a large community event was first envisaged, discussions between the companies and project steering group led to a decision to focus on more personalised workshops with each class. The main vehicle for achieving this was the use of a brief ambiguous phrase. This acted as a springboard for questioning and imagination that resulted in each group of five children devising its own story. Thus everyone felt secure with the process from the start: the framework was clear, and the individual vision was not quashed or channelled.

Each session started with a warm-up and games for the whole class of 30, followed by exploration of techniques and skills that could be fed into their devising work. Inside Out concentrated on focus, staging, telling a story, characterisation and audience clarity, while Face Pack worked in illusion, visuals, props and costumes. The work was physically-based, so the pupils could not use words, only noises. The response to the instruction was very positive and levelling, especially for pupils not confident about speaking out. The use of the short phrase as a starting point helped participants accept the challenge and minimised any defensive reactions. The company noticed how each group used very different areas of imagination, absorbing very different individual approaches into their group work. The final stages of each session prepared each group for performance with direction from the practitioners.

What emerged was a diverse range of pieces that were performed to at least one other class group. Each was also discussed and analysed in terms of presentation and content, to clarify the process and instill greater confidence in the students' subsequent efforts. Perhaps one of the strongest things to emerge for both the companies and participants was the awareness of just how simple, easy and organic it *can* be to create theatre, especially when there is a problem to solve. The structure of the project ensured that the whole school year had the same positive experience and solid grounding in physical theatre. The companies valued the opportunity to collaborate with each other and to exchange and challenge ideas, a process which was facilitated by their being accommodated in the school's youth centre during the week.

Some children were inevitably shy at first, but inhibitions were quickly dispelled through physical play and the focus of playing characters and objects. The result was a high degree of self-expression, something which we all to rarely have the opportunity to celebrate. The practical exploration of physical theatre (which is not necessarily as rational as text-based theatre) gave them a rapport and insight impossible to gain by simply watching performances.

(1) Bushmede Community Centre, Luton and (2) Wadhurst Community School
Inside Out Theatre Company with (2) Face Pack

12.3 COMMUNITY MIME IN A PRISON

This project is an ongoing process, having initially come into being from the vision of the prison education officer, Frances O'Boyle, and subsequently been nurtured by the council's drama worker and dance-artist-in-residence. The weekly sessions with the voluntary group of 'vulnerable' prisoners tend to focus on blocks of skill input such as neutral mask. When this has been absorbed by the group, they can shift to the production of performance work. Shows are performed to invited guests and fellow-inmates (a tough test for the steadiest nerves) and the group enjoys a high reputation inside the prison. The work serves as something of a flagship for the education unit and has featured on national television.

Sue Mitchell sees the sustained weekly input as one of the few outlets available to the men. On first meeting the group she was struck by their slightness of build and debilitated physical presence and energy, presumably due in part to their situation. However, the lack of stimulus offered by that situation results in a remarkable level of commitment. For instance, in exploring neutral mask, they entered a totally new area where they explored stillness, focus, isolation and economy of movement. Their considered and patient approach enabled them to retain the skills explored and extend their theatrical vocabulary.

Trust and group work are also highlighted in the sessions, something which has been rewarded by a phenomenal willingness to take physical and emotional risks, in the context of a strong sense of support and community within the group. The participants respond well to the acute demands made upon them, and this challenge has resulted in increased confidence and sense of self-worth.

The use of varied music has proved to be a rewarding stimulus, serving also as a means of access to other cultures. In their next production the group are incorporating their morning prison rituals into choreographed choral work and scenic construction, fuelled by their immense imaginative capacity.

Sue enjoys a professional relationship with the group, despite attendant prison officers and security cameras. One of the main values of the project is being able to sustain an activity which has nothing to do with institutional routine, and as such it is obviously a useful model for other organisations and institutions. Mime and physical theatre, in its play, has the ability to generate energy and concentration, and to release creativity through tightly-structured tasks. In turn Sue has learnt a great deal from working in the prison, particularly about not compromising one's material but having confidence that it will stand up in its own right, and to be fearless in making demands on participants.

Although the response made by community groups to the work is often unexpected, it is always rooted and possesses its own special quality. Perhaps the last word should come from one of the group members: 'a neutral mask gave me the feelings of a normal person.'

Peterhead Prison
Sue Mitchell, Dance-Artist-in-Residence, Banff and Buchan
   District Council

12.4   COMMUNITY MIME INPUT OVER THE COURSE
         OF A YEAR

For a year Rowan Tolley worked with pupils at 32 different schools in Kirklees, Bradford and Calderdale. The approach - residency or series of workshops - varied from school to school, and it is only possible to give a flavour of the year's work here. The project culminated in stunning performances by some 250 pupils at the Halifax Civic Theatre for a total audience of 1,400 people.

The overall aims were to develop the pupils' ability to communicate through mime, encouraging clarity in the expression of ideas; and, by using mime as an artform and as a learning device, to stimulate interest in mime as an educational tool. It was intended that all the work should build on classroom activity, use the pupils' own ideas and work, and introduce the young people to theatre by producing it in their own schools, with them as performers and stage crew.

In Calderdale, the project focused on its base in the Industrial Museum, which schools visited to work with Rowan and use its collection as a stimulus. It offered opportunities for other groups - including some local retired people - to become involved, and scope for the introduction of other artforms, notably photography. Pre-residency activities with some of the other schools included creative writing and poetry, film study and visits to industrial sites.

Some older pupils were involved as assistant directors and workshop leaders on projects involving younger students. This was an extremely valuable experience for them which fed directly into their course work. These students became the core stage crew for the final performance. Some idea of the value of the projects can be gained by looking more closely at the experiences of two schools.

At Carlton Bolling College in Bradford the group began by exploring concerns and themes through discussion, writing poetry and creating short mime pieces. The emphasis gradually shifted to more intensive rehearsals which brought increased commitment and bound the group more closely together. Social skills, especially the giving and receiving of constructive criticism, improved noticeably. Together with students on an A-level communication studies course, Rowan explored marketing and promotion skills. These were ultimately used to promote the final performance. Teachers and pupils alike drew a range of skills and ideas from the project, which left them with inspirational building blocks for the future.

At Fartown High School in Kirklees, the school particularly valued having an artist-in-residence because it provided the students with specialist expertise, and helped set the work done in the classroom in the context of the wider community and their own everyday lives. They felt that the participating group (which had little previous experience of the expressive arts) came to realise their own abilities and worth, and so gained confidence in expressing their feelings and emotions.

The participants' comments on their experiences are telling: 'For once I was able to speak out in a language where I was understood.' 'I learnt that there are so many ways of expressing a point with the body.' 'Physical and demanding, it made me realise that drama is much wider than words and improvisations.'

And, from a teacher: 'In an age of central control of education, such activities stand out as a beacon against mediocrity and conformity. What was achieved by each child was unique to them and hopefully something they will never forget. Can this be said of last week's history, RE, maths or English?'

Schools in Kirklees, Bradford and Calderdale
Rowan Tolley, United Images of Mime

COMMUNITY MUSIC PROJECTS

Sibyl Burgess

13 COMMUNITY MUSIC PROJECTS

Sibyl Burgess

Sibyl Burgess is director of the Firebird Trust, a developmental music agency which works in the East of England. She has had wide experience as an arts administrator with a Regional Arts Association, as co-ordinator of Artlink, and as a freelance administrator and researcher.

Summary
This chapter describes four recent community music projects: work with older people in Nottingham, a project on a nature reserve in Norfolk, another involving disabled people throughout Wales, and an orchestral percussion project in Manchester. They have been described here to give a glimpse of the range and richness of community music work in Britain today, and to bring concrete examples to balance the preceding, more theoretical chapters.

13.1 MUSIC, ANIMATION AND OLDER PEOPLE

The idea that people over the age of 65 can enjoy innovative arts projects using the latest technological equipment is beginning to interest community musicians. For too long practitioners and administrators decided that arts + old age = reminiscence work, with a resulting plethora of plays about the First World War, elderly people packing up their troubles in their old kit bags and music sessions based around tambourine and maracas.

This project sought to devise a way of working with older people which was relevant to their own experiences while being modern and based in the present rather than the past. Two experienced musicians and composers were commissioned to work with two groups of active older people to write the film score for an animated film from the Arts Council's archive collection. The film, *Joie de Vivre*, dates from the 1930s and is a collaboration between the film-maker Hector Hoppin and the engraver Anthony Gross.

The musicians' role in the project was to encourage the older people to realise their potential as creators and performers. It was a partnership between artists and participants, with an emphasis on experimentation, which would broaden everyone's perception of what constitutes music, using voices, bodies and a broad range of instruments. The older people liked the film; it gave them plenty of ideas and the link with early Disney and Felix the Cat cartoons was something they knew and had opinions about.

Preliminary visits were made to the two groups and a structure worked out for the first workshop session: rhythm building, call/response, passing sounds around and name familiarisation games set the scene for what was to follow. The musicians demonstrated the multi-track recording capabilities of the portastudio and the effects from the sound processing unit. The groups quickly understood the principles of multi-track recording and were keen to debate the ideas behind the film soundtrack.

Four more workshops followed, with one group working in the theatre in the mornings, and the other in the afternoons. Work on the soundtrack itself was preceded by rhythm work and playing sessions. 'What has this got to do with the work we did on the film?' asked one of the participants. The musicians explained how relaxation, co-ordination and listening were the building blocks of composition which could then be applied to the film.

Workshop Four: the musicians note in their diary 'Having completed the first part of the film, we moved onto the later episode, the water scene. It was agreed that there should be a background rippling effect throughout, over which other sounds could be laid at the various points of action. Delicate, sparkling music was devised by the group using glockenspiels, chime bars and keyboards, and by the end of the workshop this was successfully recorded.' The musicians spent three days in the recording studio, dubbing the sequences of workshop music onto the corresponding parts of the film. The Arts Council had prepared a U-matic copy of the film and the studio's editing equipment enabled the musicians to synchronise sound and images precisely. When completed the film and soundtrack was copied onto VHS videos for distribution to participants, artists and funding bodies. A sharing and viewing session was held for each of the two groups later in the year so that families and friends could join participants and musicians to see and discuss the film.

The musicians summed up the sessions in their notes: 'the groups seemed keen to experiment, rather than gravitate towards familiar types of music... We were exhausted by their energy...'

Clifton Day Centre, Beeston Mind Alert
Sean Gregory, Stuart Bruce
The Firebird Trust, Nottingham Playhouse

13.2 COMMUNITY MUSIC IN RURAL AREAS

By definition a community music project is restricted to a particular geographic area or group of participants. This project took place in a rural location, drawing together people with different backgrounds who, because of where they lived, all had limited access to participation in high quality, innovative arts work.

The project was a broad collaboration: it involved two dance practitioners, two musicians/composers and a theatre designer working closely with the education officer of a large nature reserve in East Anglia. The project had two principal objectives: to offer participants of all ages and abilities the opportunity to meet, build friendships, create and perform together; and to create a piece of site-specific work which would encourage participants and audience alike to consider ways in which the arts are inspired by landscape. The rehearsal period culminated in three public performances in which the audience followed performers along a trail studded with set-pieces reflecting the habits of the local bird population, and the parallels in human behaviour.

Schools, colleges, a community dance group, day centres for people with learning difficulties and numerous individuals were involved in the project. The hundred human participants were supported by the bird life of the nature reserve whose sense of timing was immaculate, and whose nesting calls reinforced the singers' voices, set against the reeds and marshes of the sanctuary. Flight patterns, pecking orders, issues of territory and courtship rituals formed the inspiration of the work, threading together *The Magic Flute*, *Little Red Rooster* and *A Nightingale Sang in Berkeley Square*. All of this was reflected in the still waters of the reserve, with a spectacular East Anglian sunset making its appearance on cue.

During the rehearsal period, the confidence of the groups developed noticeably. Communication increased both at an individual and a group level, and the new skills learned led to a deeper understanding of the style and quality of the material created. The members of the music group worked enthusiastically on the music to be learnt, offering their own suggestions on both the content and its interpretation. Some music was written specially for the project, some was traditional, some was created by the performing groups, and some commissioned from local musicians.

5.4 Commissions

The use of the nature reserve was a happy choice, despite early worries from the staff, nervous at the disturbance the project might cause the nesting birds. The music, dance and design contributed to an increased awareness of the environment and of the behaviour of the birds and their human visitors. It raised questions about the connections between bird and human behaviour, relationships and patterns of existence. The sense of place was important: what might have seemed obscure and difficult to an audience in a theatre seemed understandable and fitting in the natural environment.

The links and relationships created by people working together creatively for the first time form one of the important benefits of a community project such as this. It was summed up by one of the participants: 'I liked it all. Made new friends, liked going to the Tech, the warm-up dances, eating in the marquee, the journey on the minibus. Mum and dad really enjoyed the performance and this made me feel happy. I liked the music in the circle at the end.'

Schools, colleges and day centres in North Norfolk
Jane Wells and Brian Eade (Norfolk Music Works),
Rosemary Lee, Thomas Kempe, Louise Belson
Pensthorpe Nature Reserve; Education Officer, David North

13.3 COMMUNITY MUSIC AND DISABILITY

Community music organisations which have a very large geographic remit - in this case, the whole of Wales - must devise ways of working which capitalise on good networking and strategic planning, or sink in the attempt to be all things to all people. A similar approach to the problem is to act as a facilitator and training agency, devising high-quality 'taster' projects, and then assisting local practitioners and groups to carry the work further with support and training as necessary.

This strategy is being deployed by Community Music Wales over a two-year period, and involves a planned series of projects with people with physical disabilities, beginning with one-day taster sessions and leading to the establishment of local, autonomous music groups. The organisation has a special interest in new music technologies which enable people with physical disabilities to create and play music. Principles of self-advocacy and user control underlie and complement the planning of the project and the organisation's own equal opportunities policy.

The project began with the Music Box, a series of workshops in day centres and individual homes in South Glamorgan led by two musicians, one of whom was physically disabled. The equipment included the Soundbeam, which enables the user to create music by moving around in an invisible beam of ultrasonic sound, and a range of music software allowing participants to build up music patterns using Cubase.

This led to a week-long residency in collaboration with an organisation which specialises in devising ways of working with people with physical disabilities using music technology. The two organisations pooled their resources which meant that some one-to-one playing and some group work could be included. At the end of each day a DAT recording was made of the day's work; by the end of the week an impressive repertoire of work had been collected. This led to a live performance at a local community arts centre with workshop participants - none of whom had previous experience - surrounded by banks of keyboards and computers.

Enter, Stage Left, a community arts project from the Rhondda Valley which was devising integrated dance projects with people with disabilities. They performed a new piece to music composed by the two musicians who had been involved in the planning of the music technology residency. The demand for more work was growing. The Foundation for Sport and the Arts came up with funds which enabled the community music organisation to buy more specialist equipment and then take the project on the road in an ambitious scheme to involve disabled people in North and West Wales. There was practical hands-on work, but also discussion and planning sessions with others working in the field - day centre staff, social services managers, carers - some of whom were potential future funders.

Community Music Wales had previously provided a training course to meet the growing needs of locally-based community musicians. Six musicians completed the course, which was run in association with Community Music (London), and a Tutor's Certificate in Community Music was subsequently initiated in association with the Welsh College of Music and Drama. The organisation is now set to play a leading role in the development of the National Vocational Qualifications in community music currently being devised by the Arts and Entertainment Training Council and it will ensure that special emphasis is given to providing the opportunity for people with disabilities to take part in the training.

The final element of the strategy is in place with the creation of a new group of disabled and non-disabled musicians. This, with a little help from the parent organisation, will be seeking charitable status and funding for its work. The whole project is a good example of how a legacy of self-advocacy, choice and empowerment can have far-reaching results for a community hitherto largely excluded from innovative music-making.

Community Music Wales/Cerddoriaeth Gymunedol Cymru
Dave Levett and Andy Pidcock
The Drake Research Project, Rhondda Community Arts

13.4 ORCHESTRAL MUSIC IN THE COMMUNITY

There is a continuing debate about how the education and out-reach work of an orchestra should be defined and named. While some people refer to it as community music, others argue that it is orchestral outreach and that the two things are fundamentally very different. But whatever we call it, there is some exciting work being devised by orchestras, most of whom now employ their own education staff for this kind of specialised work.

The Hallé orchestra in particular is building up an impressive body of knowledge and experience in an area which has hitherto been outside the range of orchestral work. The peace and power of percussion is a central element of almost all the world's musical language. This simple fact encouraged the orchestra to bring together musicians from widely varied traditions to work in schools in Manchester in what was to be the first of a series of major, multi-cultural percussion projects. The idea grew from discussions between the Schools' Music Service, the orchestra and a local centre for African and Afro-Caribbean arts, and aimed to illustrate the city's rich cultural diversity. Four secondary schools were involved in the scheme and a composer was commissioned to write a piece for the musicians. The orchestra's percussion players were joined by percussionists from four other bands making a total of fifteen performers and workshop leaders. The whole project finished **5.4 Commissions** with a sizzling drumming performance at the arts centre.

This was too good not to explore again elsewhere. For the second project, in Leicester, there were twelve percussionists; the participants included three groups of people with learning difficulties, and one group of people with physical disabilities. Four more secondary schools were involved, and advice was taken from the LEA's music inspectorate and the local authority arts officer. The musicians separated into four groups which each visited a day centre and a school on three consecutive weeks.

Week four saw a rehearsal and performance at a city arts centre, with seven excited groups of people brought in by coach and minibus. The participants, including one group of 'very difficult' boys, rose to the challenge, worked hard and had a whale of a time. The workshops demanded self-discipline and concentration. The musicians were particularly impressed by the day centre sessions which revealed some serious talent. Following an evaluation meeting, more work was requested by two day centres, while the orchestra's education officer visited each school to work with the young percussionists and discuss further ideas with the music teacher.

By now the professional musicians were working together as a team and it was decided to embark on the final stage of what had become a musical trilogy. The final and most ambitious element - called Powerful Percussion - won a Sainsbury's Arts Education Award. It involved sixteen musicians working in African, Brazilian, Indian, Javanese and Western traditions, leading students from thirteen mainstream and special schools throughout Manchester in a series of workshops to explore each tradition and the links between them. Four of the schools catered for children with special educational needs, with a particular focus on children with hearing impairments.

The workshop programme was preceded by a preparation day for all the musicians involved, and INSET work for participating teachers. The project culminated in a three-day Drumming Festival at the centre for African and Afro-Caribbean Arts, during which all the schools performed the work they had prepared alongside performances by the professional musicians. The Festival was shadowed by students from the Royal Northern College of Music as an integral part of their training.

The aim of all three projects was to break down some of the cultural barriers which exist in any large city, to provide a stimulus for new long-term, curriculum-based work in schools and to enable young people to work alongside professional musicians in a creative and stimulating environment.

Schools and day centres in Greater Manchester and Leicester
Hallé Orchestra, Kantamanto, Inner Sense Percussion,
Sangeet Academy of Indian Music, Star Quality Steel Band
Sean Gregory (composer)
Nia Centre, Manchester, Phoenix Arts, Leicester

FURTHER READING 14

14 FURTHER READING

There are many useful books which could help you, some of which are referred to in the main text, while others are listed here. The books below are a small selection from a large field in which Bedford Square Press (the NCVO imprint), the Arts Council and the Directory of Social Change are particularly important publishers. Get the catalogues, and check the information resources of your RAB, library and artform organisation before making purchases.

14.1 BACKGROUND

Amateur Arts in the UK, Robert Hutchison & Andrew Feist (Policy Studies Institute 1991)
Arts and Communities, the Report of the National Inquiry into Arts and the Community, ed. Peter Brinson (Community Development Foundation 1992)
The Charter for the Arts in Scotland (Scottish Arts Council 1993)
Community, Art and the State, Owen Kelly (Comedia 1984)
Community Development and the Arts, Lola Clinton (Community Development Foundation 1993)
Contracts in Practice, Ken Edwards (Directory of Social Change and NCVO 1992)
A Creative Future (Arts Council of Great Britain 1993)
From Grants to Contracts, Keith Hawley (Directory of Social Change and NCVO 1992)
Getting Ready for Contracts, Sandy Adirondack & Richard MacFarlane (Directory of Social Change 1993)
The Guardian Arts Guide 1994 (4th Estate 1993)
Guidance Notes: 1 The Legal Context, 2 The Contract Culture 3 The Impact on Management and Organisation, R Gutch & R MacFarlane (NCVO 1989-90)
The Intellectuals and the Masses, John Carey (Faber 1992)
Local Authorities, Entertainment and the Arts, Audit Commission (HMSO 1991)
Making Ways, the Visual Artist's Guide to Surviving and Thriving, ed. David Butler (AN Publications 1993)
Writers & Artists Yearbook (A & C Black published annually)

14.2 MANAGEMENT

Board Member Manual (ACGB 1993)
Care, Diligence & Skill, a Handbook for the Governing Bodies of Arts Organisations (Scottish Arts Council 1987)
Getting Organised, a Handbook for Non-Statutory Organisations, Christine Holloway & Shirley Otto (Bedford Square Press 1989)
Getting to Yes - Negotiating Agreement Without Giving In, Roger Fry and William Ury (Hutchinson 1982)
Managing Consultancy, Rick Rogers (Bedford Square Press/Arts Council 1990)

14.3 ADMINISTRATION

A Basic PR Guide for Charities, Dorothy & Alastair McIntosh (Directory of Social
  Change 1987)
Charities, the New Law, F Middleton & S Lloyd (Jordans 1992)
Charitable Status: A Practical Handbook, Andrew Phillips (Directory of Social Change
  1993)
Charity Annual Reports, K Burnett (Directory of Social Change 1987)
The Data Protection Act (CDMF information pamphlet 1993)
The Effective Trustee (Parts 1, 2 and 3), Kevin Ford (Directory of Social Change 1993-4)
Employed or Self-Employed? (Inland Revenue IR56/NI39)
The Employer's Guide to Childcare, L Daniels & R Shooter (Working Mothers
  Association 1992)
Employing People (ACAS 1987)
Employing People in Voluntary Organisations, Sheila Kurowska (NCVO 1985)
Executive Survival, Martin Edwards (Kogan Page 1988)
Guidelines for Contracts, Working Conditions & Payscales (CDMF 1991)
The Marketing Manual, Heather Maitland & Judith Meddick, (ACGB 1990)
Management of Voluntary Organisations (Croner Publications 1993 updated regularly)
On Trust: Increasing the Effectiveness of Charity Trustees and Management Committees
  (NCVO 1992)
Organising Your Finances, Maggi Sikking (NCVO 1987)
*Protecting the Public Purse, Probity in the Public Sector: Combating Fraud and Corruption
  in Local Government* (HMSO 1993)
Trustee Training and Support Needs, Kevin Ford (NCVO 1992)
Working Parents Handbook (Working Mothers Association 1994)

14.4 PROGRAMMING

Arts Activities in Prisons Directory 1990-1993, Anne Peaker & Jill Vincent (CRSP,
  Loughborough University of Technology 1993)
Arts Education Agencies (ACGB/Paul Hamlyn Foundation nd)
Arts in Prisons: towards a sense of achievement, Anne Peaker & Jill Vincent (CRSP,
  Loughborough University of Technology 1990)
Artists in Schools - a handbook for teachers and artists, Caroline Sharp & Karen Dust
  (Bedford Square Press 1990)
The Arts in Schools, ed. Ken Robinson (Calouste Gulbenkian Foundation 1989)
Arts Promoters' Pack, Jo Hilton (East Midlands Arts 1991)
British Performing Arts Yearbook, ed. S Barbour (Rhinegold, published annually)
The Creative Tree, ed. Gina Levete (Michael Russell 1987)
Destination Europe, An Information Pack, Susanne Burns (Merseyside Youth Dance
  Forum 1992)
Europe, A Manual (The Prince's Trust 1992)
Intention to Reality, Developing Youth Arts Policy, Dick Chamberlain (Youth Clubs UK,
  1991)
Irish Performing Arts Yearbook (Rhinegold, published annually)
Marketing to Disabled Audiences, Elspeth Morrison & Annie Delin (ACGB 1993)

Networking in Europe, Rod Fisher (ACGB 1992)
Partners: Arts Council Education Unit Resource Packs (ACGB 1991-2)
Performing Arts Yearbook for Europe, Rod Fisher and Martin Huber (Arts Publishing
    International, published annually)
Pride of Place, The Arts in Rural Areas, Diana Johnson (ADA 1991 - available from the
    Directory of Social Change)
Theatre and Disability Conference Report, ed. Elspeth Morrison (ACGB 1993)
Who Does What in Europe?, Rod Fisher (ACGB 1992)
Working with Prisons: a Guide for Community Agencies (NACRO 1987)

14.5 FUNDING

Bread and Circuses, EC Programmes and Schemes Open to the Performing Arts, ed. M L
    Scott (IETM 1992)
Directory of Social Change publications (new editions appear regularly):
    A Guide to the Major Trusts Volumes 1 & 2 (1993)
    A Guide to Company Giving (1991)
    Major Companies Guide (1993)
    The Educational Grants Directory (1992)
    The Central Government Grants Guide (1991)
    The Arts Funding Guide (1992)
    The Complete Fundraising Handbook (1992)
    The Arts Sponsorship Handbook (1993)
Funding Digest, published monthly by RTI, 4 The Terrace, Ovingham,
    Northumberland NE42 6AJ
Getting the Best from Secondment (Action Employees In The Community 1988)
How to Raise Funds for the Work You Want to Do, Susanne Burns (CDMF 1993)
The Regional Arts Funding Handbook, Angus Broadbent (Boundtech 1993)
Trust Monitor, published three times a year by the Directory of Social Change

14.6 TRAINING AND PERSONAL DEVELOPMENT

A Bluffer's Guide to NVQs, Huw Champion (West Midlands Arts 1993)
*Getting into Training, Guidelines for People Organising Training for Local Voluntary
    Groups* (NCVO 1993)
Help! Guidelines on International Youth Exchanges, Hilary Jarman (Youth Exchange
    Centre)
On Course, training listing published by West Midlands Arts
Training in Arts Management: Where to Find Help (CDMF 1993)
Training Matters, published quarterly by AETC
Training Needs Analysis: A Resource Pack for Arts Organisations, Larry Reynolds (Arts
    Management Centre 1993)

14.7 EQUAL OPPORTUNITIES

After Attenborough, Arts and Disabled People, (Carnegie UK Trust, Bedford Square
    Press 1988)

Arts and Disabled People, The Attenborough Report (Carnegie UK Trust, Bedford Square
Press 1985)
Arts and Equality: an action pack, Christine Jackson (ADA 1989 - available from the
Directory of Social Change)
The Creatures Time Forgot, David Heavey (Routledge, 1992)
Equal Rights for Disabled People, Ian Bynoe, Mike Oliver and Colin Barnes (Institute
for Public Policy Research 1991)
How to Design and Deliver Equal Opportunities Training, H Garrett & J Taylor (Kogan
Page 1993)
Report on the Initiative to Increase the Employment of Disabled People in the Arts (ACGB
1993)

14.8 DANCE

A Booker's Guide to British Dance, Chris de Marigny & Fiona Burnside (ACGB 1994)
Community Dance, A Progress Report, Anthony Peppiatt & Katie Venner (ACGB 1993)
Dance in Schools, Arts Council Guidance on Dance Education (ACGB 1993)
Dance as Education, Peter Brinson (The Falmer Press 1991)
In Touch with Dance, Marion Gough (Whitehorn Books 1993)
Network Brochure: A Directory of Community Dance Practitioners (CDMF)
On the Move, Dance and Movement Activities for Young People, Sue Davies
(ACGB/Sports Council 1992)
No Handicap to Dance, Gina Levete (Souvenir Press 1987)

14.9 LITERATURE

Literature Belongs to Everyone: A Report on Widening Access to Literature, Violet Hughes
(ACGB)
Report on the Literature Development Worker Movement in England, Richard Ings (ACGB
1992)
Under the Rainbow: Writers and Artists in Schools, David Morley (Bloodaxe)
Writers on Tour Bulletin, published regularly by the Arts Council
Writers in Prisons and Writers-in-Residence (ACGB)

14.10 MIME

Blueprint for Regional Mime Development, Jac Wilkinson (MAG 1992)
Drama in Schools - National Curriculum Guidance (ACGB 1992)
Marketing Mime, Anne Millman (ACGB 1991)
Marketing Mime, Judith Meddick (MAG 1988)
Mime Over Matter, Pat Keysell (John Clare Books 1990)
Mime Bibliography, Simon Henderson (MAG 1990)
UK Mime and Physical Theatre Training Directory, Neil Blunt (MAG 1993)
UK Mime Audience Qualitative Research, Findings and Report, Anne Millman (ACGB
1989)
UK Mime Audience Quantitative Research, Findings and Report, Anne Millman (ACGB
1991-2)

14.11 MUSIC

Music of the Common Tongue, Christopher Small (John Calder 1987)
Music, Society, Education, Christopher Small (John Calder 1977)
Musicians Go To School (London Arts Board 1993)
Search and Reflect, John Stevens (Community Music London 1985)
Sounds Fun: A Book of Musical Games, Trevor Wishart, (Universal Edition 1990)
Sounds Fun 2, Trevor Wishart (Universal Edition 1977)
The First National Directory of Community Music, Tim Joss & Dave Price (Sound
    Sense/The Arts Business Ltd 1993)
The From Scratch Rhythm Workbook, Phil Dadson & Don McGlashan (O/p - new
    edition expected 1994)
The Community Musician: Training a New Professional, Report of the Oslo Seminar of
    the ISME Commission on Community Music Activity, ed. John Drummond
    (Norwegian Affiliation of ISME 1991 - available from Sound Sense)

14.12 MAGAZINES

Animated (published quarterly by CDMF) De Montfort University, Scraptoft,
    Leicester LE7 9SU
    ☎ 0533 418517
Disability Arts in London (DAIL)
    34 Osnaburgh Street, London NW1 3ND
    ☎ 071 916 6351
Disability Arts Magazine (DAM)
    10 Woad Lane, Great Coates, Grimsby DN37 9NH
    ☎ 0472 280031
Mailout (Arts work with people)
    9 Chapel Street, Holywell Green, Halifax HX4 9AY
    ☎ 0422 310161
Ninety-Five Per Cent (A Voice for Youth Arts)
    241 Clarendon Park Road, Leicester LE2 3AN
    ☎ (0533) 705132
Sounding Board (published quarterly by Sound Sense)
    19b Albert Road, Teddington, Middlesex TW11 0BD
    ☎ 081 977 2961
Total Theatre (published quarterly by Mime Action Group)
    Sadlers Wells, 179 Rosebery Avenue, London EC1R 4TN
    ☎ 071 713 7944

CONTACTS 15

15 CONTACTS

15.1 THE ARTS FUNDING SYSTEM

Arts Council of England
  14 Great Peter Street, London SW1P 3NQ
  ☎ 071 333 0100

Scottish Arts Council
  12 Manor Place, Edinburgh EH3 7DD
  ☎ 031 226 6051

Welsh Arts Council
  Holst House, 9 Museum Place, Cardiff CF1 3NX
  ☎ 0222 394711

Arts Council of Northern Ireland
  185 Stranmillis Road, Belfast BT9 5DU
  ☎ 0232 381591

The British Council
  10 Spring Gardens, London SW1A 2BN
  ☎ 071 930 8466

The British Film Institute (BFI)
  21 Stephen Street, London W1P 1PL
  ☎ 071 255 1444

The Crafts Council
  44a Pentonville Road, London N1 9BY
  ☎ 071 278 7700

Eastern Arts Board
  Cherry Hinton Hall, Cherry Hinton Road, Cambridge CB1 4DW
  ☎ 0223 215355

East Midlands Arts Board
  Mountfields House, Forest Road, Loughborough LE11 3HU
  ☎ 0509 218292

London Arts Board
  Elme House, 133 Long Acre, London WC2E 9AF
  ☎ 071 240 1313

Northern Arts Board
  9-10 Osborne Terrace, Newcastle-Upon-Tyne NE2 1NZ
  ☎ 091 281 6334

North West Arts Board
12 Harter Street, Manchester M1 6HY
☎ 061 228 3062

South East Arts Board
10 Mount Ephraim, Tunbridge Wells TN4 8AS
☎ 0892 515210

Southern Arts Board
13 St Clement Street, Winchester SO23 9DQ
☎ 0962 855099

South West Arts Board
Bradninch Place, Gandy Street, Exeter EX4 3LS
☎ 0392 218188

West Midlands Arts Board
82 Granville Street, Birmingham B1 2LH
☎ 021 631 3121

Yorkshire and Humberside Arts Board
21 Bond Street, Dewsbury, West Yorkshire WF13 1AX
☎ 0924 455555

15.2 DANCE

ADiTi
Willowfield Street, Bradford, BD7 2AH
☎ 0274 522059

Association of Dance Movement Therapy (ADMT)
c/o Art Therapies Department, Springfield Hospital, Glenburnie Road, Tooting Bec, London SW17 7DJ

Community Dance & Mime Foundation (CDMF)
13-15 Belvoir Street, Leicester LE1 6SL
☎ 0533 418517 (due to change)

Community Dance Scotland
c/o Dance Base, Assembly Rooms, 54 George Street, Edinburgh EH2 2LR
☎ 031 225 5525

Community Dance Wales
c/o Powys Dance, The Dance Centre, Arlais Road, Llandrindod Wells, Powys LD1 5HE
☎ 0597 824370

Council for Dance Education and Training (CDET)
Riverside Studios, Crisp Road, Hammersmith, London W6 9RL
☎ 081 741 5084

Dance Books (bookshop)
9 Cecil Court, London WC2N 4EZ
☎ 071 836 2314

Dance UK
23 Crisp Road, London W6 9RL
☎ 081 741 1932

National Dance Teachers' Association (NDTA)
c/o 47 Grove Hill Road, Camberwell, London SE5 8DF
☎ 071 274 0526

National Resource Centre for Dance (NRCD)
University of Surrey, Guildford, Surrey GU2 5XH
☎ 0483 509316

15.3 LITERATURE

Arvon Foundation
Lumb Bank, Heptonstall, Hebden Bridge, West Yorkshire HX7 6DF
☎ 0422 843714
Totleigh Barton, Sheepwash, Beaworthy, Devon EX21 5NS
☎ 0409 23338

The Book Trust
Book House, 45 East Hill, London SW18 2QZ
☎ 081 870 9055

Federation of Worker Writers and Community Publishers (FWWCP)
23 Victoria Park Road, Tunstall, Stoke-on-Trent ST6 6DX
☎ 0782 822327

National Association for Literature Development (NALD)
c/o Literature Department, Arts Council, 14 Great Peter St., London SW1P 3NQ
☎ 071 333 0100

The Poetry Book Society
10 Barley Mow Passage, London W4 4PH
☎ 081 994 6477

The Poetry Library
Royal Festival Hall, South Bank Centre, London SE1 8XX
☎ 071 921 0940

The Poetry Society
22 Betterton Street, London WC2H 9BU
☎ 071 240 4810

The Society for Storytelling
  c/o Joan Barr, 8 Bert Allen Drive, Old Leake, Boston, Lincolnshire PE22 9LG
  ☎ 0205 871359

15.4 MIME

Bodily Functions
  (SE Mime and Physical Theatre Practitioners Forum)
  67 Coleman Street, Brighton BN2 2SQ
  ☎ 0273 699147

Children's Theatre Association (CTA)
  Unicorn Theatre, 6/7 Great Newport Street, London WC2H 7JB
  ☎ 071 836 3623

London International Mime Festival
  35 Little Russell Street, London WC1A 2HH
  ☎ 071 637 5661

Mime Action Group (MAG)
  Sadlers Wells, 179 Rosebery Avenue, London EC1R 4TN
  ☎ 071 713 7944

Northern Festival of Mime
  The Brewery Arts Centre, Highgate, Kendal, Cumbria LA9 4HE
  ☎ 0539 725133

Physical State International
  60 Charles Street, Manchester M1 7DF
  ☎ 061 272 7273

The Puppet Centre
  BAC, Lavender Hill, London SW11 5TN
  ☎ 071 228 5335

Scottish Mime Forum
  Stepping Stones, 112 West Bow, Edinburgh EH1 2HH
  ☎ 031 225 3145

South East Mime Forum
  c/o 10 Mount Ephraim, Tunbridge Wells TN4 8AS
  ☎ 0892 515210

West Midlands Mime Forum
  Coventry Centre for the Performing Arts, Leasowes Avenue, Coventry CV3 6BH
  ☎ 0203 418868

Yorkshire & Humberside Live Arts Forum
  c/o 21 Bond Street, Dewsbury, West Yorkshire WF13 1AX
  ☎ 0924 455555

15.5 MUSIC

Community Music
  Community Music House, 60 Farringdon Road, London EC1R 3BP
  ☎ 071 490 2577

Community Music Wales
  5 Llandaf Road, Canton, Cardiff CF1 9NF
  ☎ 0222 387620

Community Music East
  Hi Tec House, 10 Blackfriars Street, Norwich NR3 1SF
  ☎ 0603 628367

The Firebird Trust
  27 Newport, Lincoln LN1 3DN
  ☎ 0522 522995

International Society for Music Education (ISME)
  ISME International Office, Community Music Activity Commission, Music
  Education Centre, University of Reading, Bulmershe Court, Reading RG6 1HY
  ☎ 0734 318846

Sound Sense
  19b Albert Road, Teddington, Middx TW11 0BD
  ☎ 081 977 2961

Music Education Council
  c/o Prof. Keith Swanwick, Institute of Education, University of London,
  20 Bedford Way, London WC1H 0AL
  ☎ 071 612 6740

Musicians' Union
  60/62 Clapham Road, London SW9 0JJ
  ☎ 071 582 5566

The National Music & Disability Information Service (NMDIS)
  Foxhole, Dartington, Totnes, Devon TQ9 6EB
  ☎ 0803 866701

15.6 OTHER ARTS ORGANISATIONS

Age Exchange
  Reminiscence Centre, 11 Blackheath Village, London SE3 9LA
  ☎ 081 318 9105

Artists Agency
  18 Norfolk Street, Sunderland SR1 1EA
  ☎ 091 510 9318

Arts Education in a Multicultural Society (AEMS)
c/o 14 Great Peter Street, London SW1P 3NQ
☎ 071 333 0100

Arts for Health
The Manchester Metropolitan University, All Saints, Oxford Road, Manchester M15 6BY
☎ 061 236 8916

Association for Business Sponsorship of the Arts (ABSA)
Nutmeg House, 60 Gainsford Street, Butlers Wharf, London SE1 2NY
☎ 071 378 8143

Health Care Arts
23 Springfield, Dundee DD1 4JE
☎ 0382 203099

Hospice Arts
Farleigh, Mid-Essex Hospice, 212 New London Rd., Chelmsford, Essex CM2 9AE
☎ 0245 358130

Independent Theatre Council
4 Baden Place, Crosby Row, London SE1 1YW
☎ 071 403 1727

Minorities Arts Advisory Service (MAAS)
4th Floor, 28 Shacklewell Lane, London E8 2EZ
☎ 071 249 5031

National Association of Youth Theatres (NAYT)
Unit 1304, Custard Factory, Gibb Street, Digbeth, Birmingham B9 4AA
☎ 021 608 2111

The National Campaign for the Arts (NCA)
Francis House, Francis Street, London SW1P 1DE
☎ 071 828 4448

National Foundation for Arts Education (NFAE)
Spendlove Centre, Enstone Road, Charlbury, Oxon OX7 3PQ
☎ 0608 811488

SALVO (Scottish Arts Lobby)
Royal Lyceum, Grindley Street, Edinburgh EH3 9AY
☎ 031 228 3885

Shape London
London Voluntary Sector Resource Centre, 356 Holloway Road, London N7 6PA
☎ 071 700 0100

There are similar specialist organisations working with disabled people and other groups in each RAB area. Some are called Shape or Artlink, some have altogether different names; some are members of the Shape Network, others not. Their addresses can be obtained through Shape London or your Regional Arts Board.

Voluntary Arts Network (VAN)
    PO Box 1LE, Newcastle-upon-Tyne NE99 1LE
    ☎ 091 281 2245

15.7 TRAINING

Arts & Entertainment Training Council (AETC)
    3 St Peter's Buildings, York Street, Leeds, West Yorkshire LS9 8AJ
    ☎ 0532 448845

The Management Centre
    9-15 Blackett Street, Newcastle-upon-Tyne NE1 5BS
    ☎ 091 222 1632

Arts Training Programme
    De Montfort University, Scraptoft Campus, Leicester LE7 9SU
    ☎ 0533 577804

Arts Training South
    CCE, Education Department, University of Sussex, Falmer, Brighton BN1 9RG
    ☎ 0273 606755

Centre for Arts Management
    Institute of Public Administration and Management, PO Box 147,
    Liverpool University, Liverpool L69 3BX
    ☎ 051 794 2918

Regional Training Unit South West
    23 Trenchard Street, Bristol BS1 5AN
    ☎ 0272 254011

15.8 VOLUNTARY SECTOR SUPPORT, TRAINING AND FUNDING

Action Employees In The Community
    8 Stratton Street, London W1X 5FD
    ☎ 071 629 2209

Charities Aid Foundation (CAF)
    48 Pembury Road, Tonbridge, Kent TN9 2JD
    ☎ 0732 771333

Commonwealth Youth Exchange Council
    7 Lion Yard, Tremadoc Road, London SW4 7NQ
    ☎ 071 498 6151

Community Development Foundation (CDF)
    60 Highbury Grove, London N5 2AG
    ☎ 071 226 5375

Directory of Social Change
  Radius Works, Back Lane, London NW3 1HL
  ☎ 071 435 8171

Foundation for Sport and the Arts
  PO Box 20, Liverpool L9 6EA
  ☎ 051 524 0235

Funder Finder
  11 Upper York Street, Wakefield WF1 3LQ

InterChange Trust/Interchange Training/InterChange Legal Advisory Service
  InterChange Studios, Dalby Street, London NW5 3NQ
  ☎ 071 267 9421

National Council for Voluntary Organisations (NCVO)
  Regent's Wharf, 8 All Saints Street, London N1 9RL
  ☎ 071 713 6161

National Youth Agency
  17-23 Albion Street, Leicester LE1 6GD
  ☎ 0533 471200

Retired Executives Action Clearing House (REACH)
  89 Southwark Street, London SE1 0HD
  ☎ 071 928 0452

Scottish Council for Voluntary Organisations (SCVO)
  18-19 Claremont Crescent, Edinburgh EH7 4QD
  ☎ 031 556 3882

The Volunteer Centre UK
  29 Lower Kings Road, Berkhamsted, Herts HP4 2AB
  ☎ 0442 873311

Youth Clubs UK
  11 St Bride Street, London EC4A 4AS
  ☎ 071 353 2366

Youth Exchange Centre
  c/o The British Council, 10 Spring Gardens, London SW1A 2BN
  ☎ 071 389 4030

15.9 GOVERNMENT

The House of Commons
  London SW1A 0AA
  ☎ Public information 071 219 4272

The Cabinet Office
    70 Whitehall, London SW1A 2AS
    ☎ 071 270 3000

Department of the Environment
    2 Marsham Street, London SW1P 3EB
    ☎ 071 276 3000

Department for Education
    Sanctuary Buildings, Great Smith Street, London SW1P 3BT
    ☎ 071 925 5000

Department of Health
    Skipton House, 80 London Road, London SE1 6LW
    ☎ 071 972 2000

Department of National Heritage (DNH)
    2-4 Cockspur Street, London SW1Y 5DH
    ☎ 071 211 6200

The Scottish Office
    St Andrew's House, Regent Road, Edinburgh EH1 3DE
    ☎ 031 556 8400

The Welsh Office
    Crown Buildings, Cathays Park, Cardiff CF1 3NQ
    ☎ 0222 825111

15.10 OFFICIAL BODIES AND MISCELLANEOUS ADDRESSES

Advisory Conciliation & Arbitration Service (ACAS)
    Head Office, 27 Wilton Street, London SW1X 7AZ
    ☎ 071 210 3613

British Tourist Authority
    Thames Tower, Black's Road, London W6 9EL
    ☎ 081 846 9000

Charity Commission
    St Albans House, 57-60 Haymarket, London SW1Y 4QX
    ☎ 071 210 3000

Commission for Racial Equality (CRE)
    Elliot House, 10/12 Allington Street, London SW1E 5EH
    ☎ 071 828 7022

Companies House
    55/71 City Road, London EC1Y 1BB
    ☎ 071 253 9393

Countryside Commission
   John Dower House, Crescent Place, Cheltenham GL50 3RA
   ☎ 0242 521381

Customs and Excise
   New King's Beam House, 22 Upper Ground, London SE1 9PJ
   ☎ 071 620 1313

Data Protection Registrar
   Wycliffe House, Water Lane, Wilmslow, Cheshire SK9 5AF
   ☎ 0625 535777

Development Commission
   11 Cowley Street, London SW1P 3NA
   ☎ 071 276 6969

Equal Opportunities Commission
   Overseas House, Quay Street, Manchester M3 3HN
   ☎ 061 833 9244

Health and Safety Executive (HSE)
   The Public Enquiry Point, Broad Lane, Sheffield S3 7HQ
   ☎ 0742 892345

Performing Right Society Ltd (PRS)
British Copyright Council (BCC)
   29-33 Berners Street, London W1P 4AA
   ☎ 071 580 5544 (PRS)
   ☎ 071 580 5544 (BCC)

Phonographic Performance Ltd
   Ganton House, 14-22 Ganton Street, London W1V 1LB
   ☎ 071 437 0311

Registrar of Companies
   Companies House, Crown Way, Maindy, Cardiff CF4 3UZ
   ☎ 0222 388588

Registry of Friendly Societies
   15/17 Great Marlborough Street, London W1V 2AX
   ☎ 071 437 9992

Rural Development Commission
   141 Castle Street, Salisbury, SP1 3TP
   ☎ 0722 336255

The Sports Council
   16 Upper Woburn Place, London WC1H 0QP
   ☎ 071 388 1277

GLOSSARY

Audience	The term can apply not just to people who watch a performance, but to people who are users of an arts service as participants in workshops etc.
Audit	The process of vetting accounts and financial procedures by a properly-qualified independent person.
Corporate	A term applied to an organisation which is legally entitled to act as a single body (eg a company).
Creditor	Someone who is owed money by you.
Debtor	Someone who owes you money.
Fee	A payment for services without deductions for PAYE.
Governing instrument	A general term applied to the constitution, articles, deed of trust by which an organisation is controlled.
Gross pay	The salary due for a particular post.
Limited liability	In certain types of legal organisational structure the personal liability of individual members for the organisation's debts is limited to a specific sum (commonly £1).
Minicom	Text-phone used to communicate by and with deaf people.
Net pay	Pay received by an employee after deductions for PAYE.
Person specification	A statement of the skills and attributes required to do a particular job.
Unitary authority	A local authority which combines the functions of the present two tiers of authority (eg County Councils and District Councils).

ABBREVIATIONS

ACE	Arts Council of England
ACGB	Arts Council of Great Britain
ACNI	Arts Council of Northern Ireland
BSL	British Sign Language
CDMF	Community Dance & Mime Foundation
CVS	Council for Voluntary Service
DAF	Disability Arts Forum
DAT	Digital Audio Tape
DTP	Desktop Publishing
EU	European Union
GMS	Grant Maintained Status
GOQ	Genuine Occupational Qualification
ITC	Independent Theatre Council
LA	Local Authority
LEA	Local Education Authority
LMS	Local Management of Schools
MAG	Mime Action Group
NADMA	National Association of Dance and Mime Animateurs
NALD	National Association for Literature Development
NDA	National Dance Agency
NDAF	National Disability Arts Forum
NHS	National Health Service
NCVO	National Council of Voluntary Organisations
PAYE	Pay As You Earn
RAA	Regional Arts Association
RAB	Regional Arts Board
RSU	Regional Secure Unit
SAC	Scottish Arts Council
SSE	Sign Supported English
VDU	Visual Display Unit
WAC	Welsh Arts Council
YDU	Young Disabled Unit

O chestnut-tree, great-rooted blossomer,
Are you the leaf, the blossom or the bole?
O body swayed to music, O brightening glance,
How can we know the dancer from the dance?

W.B.Yeats